Theism, Atheism and the
Doctrine of the Trinity

American Academy of Religion
Academy Series

edited by
Carl A. Raschke

Number 53
Theism, Atheism and the
Doctrine of the Trinity
by
W. Waite Willis, Jr.

W. Waite Willis, Jr.

THEISM, ATHEISM AND THE DOCTRINE OF THE TRINITY
The Trinitarian Theologies of Karl Barth and Jürgen Moltmann in Response to Protest Atheism

Scholars Press
Atlanta, Georgia

THEISM, ATHEISM AND THE DOCTRINE OF THE TRINITY

The Trinitarian Theologies of
Karl Barth and Jürgen Moltmann
in Response to Protest Atheism

by
W. Waite Willis, Jr.

© 1987
American Academy of Religion

Library of Congress Cataloging in Publication Data

Willis, W. Waite.
  Theism,atheism, and the doctrine of the Trinity.

  (AAR academy series ; no. 53)
  Thesis (Ph.D.) — Emory University, 1983.
  Bibliography: p.
  1. Trinity—History of doctrines—20th century.
2. Barth, Karl, 1886-1968—Contributions in the
doctrine of the Trinity. 3. Moltmann, Jürgen —
Contributions in the doctrine of the Trinity.
4. Theism. 5. Atheism. I. Title. II. Series:
American Academy of Religion academy series ; no. 53.
BT109.W58 1987   231'.044   86-6640
ISBN 1-55540-020-5 (alk. paper)
ISBN 1-55540-021-3 (pbk. : alk. paper)

Printed in the United States of America
on acid free paper

TO MY WIFE SUSAN

CONTENTS

viii

ACKNOWLEDGMENTS

Many persons contributed to the completion of this project. Since this essay represents the culmination of many years of education, appreciation is due the teachers of Candler School of Theology and the Graduate Division of Religion of Emory University. Beyond those who served on the examining committee for my dissertation, special recognition must be given to Dr. Manfred Hoffmann, Dr. Leander E. Keck and Dr. Charles V. Gerkin. All the members of my examining committee made significant contributions to my theological education. They are Dr. William Mallard, Dr. Don E. Saliers, Dr. Theodore R. Weber and Dr. Theodore H. Runyon, Jr. The final two in particular read this essay carefully and offered criticisms and suggestions which were incisive and helpful. A special word of gratitude must be given to my teacher and friend, Dr. Theodore W. Jennings, Jr., who served as director of my dissertation. His crucial guidance exceeded by far normal expectations and is reflected throughout this book.

I also wish to thank President Robert A. Davis and former Dean David G. Mobberley of Florida Southern College for their support during the completion of this project. They made available the Dean's administrative assistant, Mrs. Pat Klein, to help in the preparation of the document. With skill she put the text through several revisions and produced its final form.

I could not close without indicating the importance of my family. My parents, Dr. and Mrs. Warren W. Willis, and my mother-in-law, Mrs. Virginia Marsh, encouraged me in every way. Most of all, appreciation is due my wife, Susan, who not only aided by typing early drafts and in the technical preparation of the notes and bibliography, but also with love and strength supported me at every point, even in the midst of our parenting our three children. It is to Susan that I dedicate this work.

INTRODUCTION

To suggest the usefulness of the doctrine of the Trinity for contemporary faith must appear odd. On the one hand we are citizens of the "age of suspicion."[1] From the great critiques that have arisen from the time of the Enlightenment, we have learned to question every area of human experience. Critical analyses have challenged the ideals of Western culture, the presuppositions about psychological and sociological motivation and the very foundation of knowledge itself. Perhaps more than any other area, however, suspicion has arisen about faith and theology, resulting in and from a variety of critiques which have in common the claim that belief in God is no longer tenable. Because in this context the doctrine of the Trinity appears to be an irrelevant esoteric arcanum, to introduce trinitarian theology as a response to atheism might at first only heighten the suspicion about the viability of the Christian faith.

On the other hand it is not only the outsider or atheist who finds no use for the trinitarian conception of God. Contemporary Christians also have little understanding of or desire to learn about what many consider to be a speculative and unintelligible way of speaking about God. One must, I believe, agree with Karl Rahner when he declares that "despite their orthodox confession of the Trinity, Christians are, in their practical life, almost mere 'monotheists.'"[2] In fact, the situation is such that other major Christian doctrines would be little affected for most believers if the doctrine of the Trinity were forgotten completely. "One has the feeling," Rahner concludes, "that, for the catechism of the head and heart (as contrasted with the printed catechism), the Christian idea of incarnation would not have to change at all if there were no Trinity."[3] If it is the case that Christians themselves often do not take this doctrine seriously, is it not futile to offer it as important for understanding Christian life in the modern world?

And yet Rahner's insight must be taken even further. For not only has the doctrine of the Trinity aroused little interest in the general population of Christians, it also has found few champions among the theologians. In his book, *In This Name*, Claude Welch finds that even those theologians who accept a trinitarian formulation frequently view it as a secondary doctrine, as an "indirect consequence of the revelation in Christ and therefore as subsequent to and an intellectual *synthesis* of other primary and relatively independent affirmations."[4] It is no wonder therefore that the doctrine of the Trinity has been absent from Christian apologetics. In the enormous amount of theological energy that, from Schleiermacher to the present, has been consumed in responding to the many atheistic critiques, the doctrine of the Trinity is noticeably missing.[5] The theologian might argue toward the doctrine of the Trinity, offering it at the end of theology as a dispensable summary. But certainly the theologian would not argue from this doctrine, establishing it in a primary position in theology and forming responses on a trinitarian basis. The normal course of apologetics underscores the distinctiveness (and even 'oddity') of the trinitarian perspective presented in this essay.

The usual manner of responding to atheism assumes that only theism can provide an answer and therefore reasserts theism in one form or another. The typical apologetic strategy is to find a common ground acceptable to the atheist and from this point demonstrate the existence of God or the necessity of god-language and, consequently, the unintelligibility of the atheistic position. For example, if the atheist stands for moral activity, the apologetic response might be that some concept of God is ultimately needed to ground any call for morality. It is important to note that the response given here is a general notion of God. The claim is that *some* God, *some* ultimate reality, must be presupposed. It must also be pointed out that this theistic response generally fails. Continuing our example, in response to the claim that some ultimate reality must exist or at least must be presupposed to make moral action intelligible, the atheist can advance arguments explaining why this is not the case, why moral practices "can be justified independently of theistic beliefs."[6] The atheist can go beyond this and assert that moral activity is comprehensible only when one postulates atheism.[7]   Not only is God destructive of the freedom which is a condition of ethical decision, but God's own goodness is called into question by the evil found in the world. This exemplifies the course that the debate between theism and atheism regularly follows. To the theist's justification for the claim that a God exists or that god-language is intelligible, the atheist responds with reasons for why he does not exist and for why god-language is unintelligible. In fact, it will become clear in this essay that atheism presupposes traditional theism, that it is traditional theism's method of argumentation which generates atheism. But if traditional theism has failed in its response to atheistic critiques perhaps trinitarian theology might prove useful after all. The purpose of this study is to examine this question.

I will suggest that a more fruitful theological response to atheism finds its basis not in theism but in the doctrine of the triune God. More specifically, in this essay I will argue that the doctrine of the Trinity as formulated by Karl Barth and Jürgen Moltmann provides the basis for a cogent response to the charges brought against faith by contemporary atheism. This claim needs clarification in several respects.

First, the trinitarian response differs from and signifies a reversal of the typical theistic response in that it does not argue for the acceptability of a general concept of God. Instead the doctrine of the Trinity as developed in Barth and Moltmann functions to remove the question of the existence of God from a central position in the discussion. Simply believing that God exists does not bring one close to the Christian faith in any case. Rather, the doctrine of the Trinity is employed to articulate the specifically Christian concept of God. But the claim is that it is precisely this concept of God comprehended in the doctrine of the Trinity which offers the basis of an apologetic, that demonstrates that it is not guilty of what the atheists charge against belief. This position does not claim, therefore, that the doctrine of the Trinity functions only apologetically. Both Barth and Moltmann assert that the trinitarian formulation is necessary for a proper identification of the Christian God. Nevertheless, I will argue that Barth, in developing his theology, never forgets Ludwig Feuerbach's critique of religion and finds in the doctrine of the Trinity the resources which prevent his dogmatics from falling victim to it. Likewise, Moltmann, even more explicitly, develops the doctrine of the Trinity in dialogue with and in response to the critiques of Karl Marx and the form of atheism found in Albert Camus and the Critical Theory of Theodor Adorno and Max Horkheimer.

A second point that needs to be made in clarification of my thesis is that this work cannot include an attempt to demonstrate a trinitarian response to all forms of atheism. Rather, showing how the doctrine of the Trinity provides the basis for a response to a particular type of atheism might be suggestive for apologetics in other cases. In this essay we will examine and respond to "protest atheism." Atheism of this type is not interested in speculative arguments which demonstrate the weaknesses of cosmological or ontological arguments for God's existence, for instance. Rather, this form of atheism represents a protest against God grounded in the misery of the concrete human situation. God is rejected because the divine is responsible for and does nothing to transform the human condition.

We will examine four major, inter-related issues which protest atheism raises and to which it finds no answers in traditional theism. In the service of its protest, this atheism (1) focuses on an epistemological question (Feuerbach) in which it asks whether in light of the human condition God does not represent a projected image of alienated humanity. It therefore (2) rejects God because the divine is constituted only at the expense of humanity (Feuerbach). More profoundly, protest atheism (3) is rooted in the theodicy question (Camus, Adorno, Horkheimer) and negates God because of human suffering. Also, this atheism (4) takes the form of a protest against the praxis (Marx) related to belief in God, a praxis which atheism claims serves unjust social structures. Although each of these issues is introduced in discrete chapters in the order given here, the four are really interdependent. While it is true that the trinitarian response to Feuerbach develops the concrete basis necessary to respond to the other issues, it is equally true that the epistemological question receives its fuller answer only in the discussion on praxis. Likewise, the trinitarian response to the question of suffering is incomplete until praxis is taken into account. Nevertheless, in the organization of this work it seemed appropriate to first deal with the theological method associated with the doctrine of the Trinity in response to the epistemological critique, then in the two succeeding chapters with the trinitarian conception of the action and nature of God in response to the critiques based on human alienation and suffering and, finally, (in two chapters) with what this trinitarian position means for praxis. In each case the trinitarian response will be given by drawing material out of the theologies of Barth and Moltmann.

This brings us to a third point: clarification of the use of the doctrine of the Trinity in this essay. Our concern in this essay is not to develop a complete systematic treatment of the doctrine of the Trinity. Rather, it is only to analyze those elements of trinitarian theology that enable a response to protest atheism. Furthermore, we are not interested here with just any trinitarian doctrine. One explanation for the general disregard for the doctrine of the Trinity is that it has been formulated in ways which are speculative and esoteric and, therefore, meaningless for human beings in their concrete existence. The trinitarian formulation with which this discussion is concerned is distinctive in several ways. First, it arises directly from reflection on the claim that God was at work in Jesus of Nazareth. Second, this doctrine of the Trinity is central to faith and theology and is not merely a peripheral concern. Third, this trinitarian thought is developed in distinction to, and as explicitly critical of, other conceptions of God. In other words, we are concerned with the doctrine of the Trinity as it is formulated in the theologies of Barth and Moltmann.

Karl Barth was the greatest theological proponent of the doctrine of the Trinity in several centuries. Many theologians simply ignore this

doctrine. Others who accept a trinitarian formulation give it no significant place in their dogmatics. For Barth, on the other hand, the trinitarian doctrine is "an analysis, an immediate implication and
therefore . . . essentially identical with the content of revelation."[8]
Therefore, Barth views this doctrine as absolutely indispensable and
makes it the central key in his dogmatics.[9] He not only claims that it
"fundamentally distinguishes the Christian doctrine of God as Christian,"[10] but also attempts to articulate its centrality in the "external and
above all in the internal position of the doctrine of the Trinity in
dogmatics."[11] Therefore, Barth locates the discussion of the Trinity at
the beginning of his dogmatics, in the prolegomena, even before the
doctrine of God as such. It is not, however, only its position as the
theological starting point that demonstrates its prominence. Rather, by
beginning with it, Barth hopes that "its contents may be made decisive
and dominant for the whole dogmatics."[12] For Barth, the doctrine of the
Trinity is not an isolated affirmation about God's being, but is fundamental to all of the other aspects of the Christian faith.[13] In short, for
Barth, a "church dogmatics derives from a doctrine of the Trinity."[14]

It is now apparent that the contemporary inheritor of Barth's
trinitarian concentration is Jürgen Moltmann. He has introduced the
doctrine of the Trinity as central to his theology and, in significant ways,
develops the doctrine employing a methodology similar to Barth's. Like
Barth, Moltmann sees the doctrine of the Trinity as an immediate
implication of revelation and therefore as inextricably bound to the
concrete history of Jesus. Moltmann, like Barth, believes the doctrine of
the Trinity to be the characteristic distinguishing feature of the Christian
doctrine of God: "Christian theology is hence, inescapably and of inner
necessity, trinitarian theology; and only trinitarian theology is Christian
theology."[15] Moltmann believes that "in the ancient world of religion,
the doctrine of the Trinity in the concept of God was the doctrine which
marked off Christianity from polytheism, pantheism and monotheism."[16] Likewise, we will see in this essay that for both Barth and
Moltmann the doctrine of the Trinity serves to identify a proper theology
and show its distinction from both the method, the conception of God
and the praxis associated with traditional theism.

Finally, because the trinitarian thinking of Barth and Moltmann
functions in this way, a two-fold response is available to each issue raised
by protest atheism. Trinitarian thinking does not mean the simple
rejection of the atheistic critiques. On the one hand it says "yes" to them.
It learns something from them. Trinitarian thinking understands that
atheism in this form has indicated serious problems with traditional
theism. In fact, we will see that trinitarian theology is able to appropriate

these atheistic critiques and direct them against theistic theologies. On this side the response is that trinitarian theology transcends the atheistic critiques, precisely because it speaks of the God who takes up the protest of atheism. However, this means, on the other hand, that an apologetic based on the doctrine of the Trinity must also say "no" to protest atheism. For it is able to demonstrate that this atheism has formed its critique only in the context of traditional theism and therefore rejects a conception of God which trinitarian theology also rejects. The doctrine of the Trinity then identifies the Christian God whom atheism has misidentified as the God of theism. If the doctrine of the Trinity enables theology to incorporate the atheistic protest and to reject the God atheism negates, then trinitarian theology provides the basis for a response to atheism.

After examining protest atheism and these responses to it, in a final chapter we will then evaluate the trinitarian apologetic in relation both to other contemporary apologetic strategies and to the trinitarian formulations of the Church Fathers. We will conclude by arguing for the relative strength of Barth's and Moltmann's trinitarian position and by suggesting how the apologetic basis found there is in continuity with early, patristic trinitarian thinking.

In order to understand the response of trinitarian thought to protest atheism, it will also be helpful to understand the theistic context in which protest atheism has arisen. In a preliminary chapter, therefore, we will first examine the elements in traditional theism that have generated atheistic critique. To this task we now turn.

NOTES

[1] For an analysis of our era as an "age of suspicion," see Jacques Ellul in *Hope in Time of Abandonment,* trans. C. Edward Hopkin (New York, 1973), pp. 48-54.

[2] Karl Rahner, *The Trinity* (New York, 1970), p. iv.

[3] *Ibid.*, p. 11.

[4] Claude Welch, *In This Name* (New York, 1952), p. 161. Welch suggests Norman Pittenger (p. 128), Leonard Hodgson (p. 131) and Charles Lowry (p. 132) as examples of this position.

[5] We will discuss Schleiermacher in Chapter I and in Chapter VII will review various other contemporary responses.

[6] Alasdair MacIntyre develops this argument in Alasdair MacIntyre and Paul Ricoeur, *The Religious Significance of Atheism* (New York, 1969), pp. 31-55.

[7] Nicolai Hartmann makes this assertion. On this see S. Paul Schilling, *God in an Age of Atheism* (Nashville, 1969), p. 126.

[8] Welch, *In This Name*, p. 161.

[9] See Eberhard Jüngel, *The Doctrine of the Trinity: God's Being is in Becoming*, trans. Scottish Academic Press Ltd. (Grand Rapids, 1976) pp. 4, 49, for a discussion of the way in which the Trinity "basically determines his whole thinking." Colin Gunton in *Becoming and Being: The Doctrine of God in Charles Hartshorne and Karl Barth* (Oxford, 1978), p. 149, agrees with this assessment.

In light of this, one must question von Balthasar's assessment of the relationship between Thomas Aquinas and Karl Barth:

> "It is most evident in the fact that the doctrine of the Trinity and the Church do not play a central role in the shaping of their theologies. Both theologians choose to stress the tracts on the one God, creation and elevation, divine conservation and providence, and perhaps ethics and eschatology. At the center is the overall relationship between God and the world . . . ." [Hans Urs von Balthasar, *The Theology of Karl Barth* (New York, 1971), p. 211.] Certainly there can be no argument that the "relationship between God and the world" stands at the center of both theologies. The different ways of viewing that relationship, however, is the critical distinction between them. This is precisely why Thomas separates the tract on the Triune God from the tract on the One God and puts the former in a secondary position, while Barth begins with the triune God and only on this basis can speak of God's unity.

[10] Karl Barth, *Church Dogmatics,* trans. G. T. Thomson (Edinburgh, 1936), I/1, 346. The remaining volumes, *Church Dogmatics* I/2-IV/4, were translated by G. W. Bromiley and edited by G. W. Bromiley and T. F. Torrance (1956-69). Throughout this essay all these volumes will be cited as *CD.*

[11] *CD* I/1, 347.

[12] *Ibid.*, p. 348.

[13] See Welch, *In This Name*, p. 162.

[14] *CD* II/1, 261.

[15] Jürgen Moltmann, *The Future of Creation*, trans. Margaret Kohl (Philadelphia, 1979), p. 81. (Hereafter cited as *FC*.)

[16] Jürgen Moltmann, *The Crucified God,* trans. R. A. Wilson and John Bowden (New York, 1974) p. 235. (Hereafter cited as *CG*.)

CHAPTER I

THE STRUCTURE OF TRADITIONAL THEISM

In contemporary theology the terms "traditional theism," "classical theism," "metaphysical theism," "cosmological theism" or simply "theism" have come to stand for the form of theology, dominant in recent centuries, which has combined biblical themes of divine sovereignty, power, justice, etc., with philosophical world views producing conceptions of God as Supreme Being which have in turn given rise to atheistic attacks.[1] A preliminary discussion of this traditional theism is necessary for two reasons.

First, the atheism discussed in this essay, while claiming to be a negation of all forms of belief in God, arises in the context of and in response to traditional theism. Second, the doctrine of the Trinity of Barth and Moltmann is developed in the course of their rejections of traditional theism. For both theologians the doctrine of the Trinity re-emerges from theological obscurity and serves to clarify the proper Christian notion of God. In so doing, it indicates a break with theism. Since atheism is the antithesis of traditional theism and since the doctrine of the Trinity as developed by Barth and Moltmann offers, as this essay claims, the basis for a theological response to atheism not available to theism, it is important to clarify the nature of traditional theism which stands as the presupposition of atheism and from which trinitarian thinking attempts to distinguish itself. The purpose of this chapter then is not to present an exhaustive analysis of the details or the variety of forms of traditional theism. That has been done elsewhere.[2] Rather, this chapter will delineate certain features of traditional theism which have become the focus of atheistic protests to which the trinitarian theologies of Barth and Moltmann serve as response and alternative. We will examine two distinct representatives of the theistic tradition — Thomas Aquinas, the fountainhead of traditional theism, and Friedrich Schleiermacher, a modern champion of theistic theology — and the tradition which links them. In spite of the important differences among the representatives of theism, our analysis will suggest that the structure of traditional theism regularly consists of two basic elements — its theological method and the doctrine of God consequent upon this method.

The methodology of traditional theism is usually governed by an apologetic concern and strategy. Traditional theism attempts to establish itself epistemologically by arguing for the acceptability of Christianity on the basis of the acceptability of belief in God's existence or the truth of religion based on generally available human capacities. In other words, traditional theism argues first for the truth or plausibility of faith or religion in general, on the basis of something like reason, moral necessity or human self-consciousness, and only then for the legitimacy of the Christian faith as a specific — and usually the highest — form of this previously established general truth. There are several consequences of this strategy for theological method.

First, this method leads traditional theism to separate faith in the specifically Christian revelation from the human faculties used to establish its general basis. Prior to the call for faith in the Christian revelation, human reason, moral conscience or feeling provide the epistemological means for the proof of the existence of God or the truth of religion in general. Consequently — and this is the center of the theological method of theism — one speaks about God and religion first on the basis of one of these human faculties by a process of abstracting from the experiences of human existence, from nature, the moral order or human feeling.

It matters little in terms of the general methodological principle which human faculty is employed or from which sphere of human experience the terms for speech about God are extracted. The common result is the eclipse of (and at best secondary location of) the distinctly Christian doctrine of the triune God, a doctrine which arises out of identifying speech about God with the appearance of Jesus. Instead, a concentration on the doctrine of the one God prevails, beginning with and focusing on the question of the existence of God who is defined through this theological process of abstraction from the world. In this way the one God is generally conceived of as a supreme being or reality with a primary emphasis upon its relationship to the world as creator or cause. While the conception of this supreme being is developed in divergent ways, a typical result of this method is that God is conceived of in absolutist terms as the omnipotent, immutable, impassible, infinite, simple one. Only after having established the legitimacy of belief in God and the truth of religion on these grounds, does theism move on, if at all, to speak of the specifically Christian doctrine of the triune God. Thus, while theism may speak of God as loving, merciful and related, these attributes are often placed in a secondary position and rendered problematic by what has already been said. By the time one arrives at them, a one-sided conception of God is already operative.

Because Thomas Aquinas stands as the fountainhead of traditional theism, we will begin with an analysis of the theological revolution set in motion by him.

Thomas Aquinas

Theism has not always been the dominant theology. For close to a thousand years, from Athanasius to Aquinas, the doctrine of the Trinity provided the context for Christian speech about God. To be sure, the affirmation of the triune God entailed difficulties arising from the church's borrowing from the Greek philosophical tradition a notion of the divine conceived of in static, substantialist and simple terms. If God is defined *a priori* in this manner, how can Jesus, a changing, suffering man, reveal and be God? How can there be a second and third person in God? Nevertheless, in spite of these problems and without the complete resolution of inevitable paradoxes, by the fourth century the "Trinity became truly a Christian *arche*, a fundamental point of conflict with classical culture" and the "prime distinction" between Christianity and other monotheistic religions.[3] The doctrine of the Trinity functioned in the tradition as a rule of Christian thinking that defended the Christian experience of God's revelation and salvation in Jesus Christ from unwarranted and destructive theological conclusions. It kept, for instance, the Greek philosophical conception of the divine from becoming the controlling metaphor of theology. So it stood over against the Arian position which, on the basis of an *a prior* notion of God's absolute unity and simplicity, refused the Son's equal divinity with the Father, thereby risking the Christian conception of God's revelation and salvation in Jesus.[4] The role of the doctrine of the Trinity, not as one doctrine among the others but as the "grammar of faith" (Augustine), is attested by the fact that throughout the Middle Ages it was vigorously debated[5] and that only within its framework did the discussion of the doctrine of God take place.

However, with the theology of Thomas Aquinas a reversal was effected that led to a loss in the significance of the doctrine of the Trinity and the correlative rise of traditional theism. According to Karl Rahner, Thomas introduced a new and questionable distinction into the doctrine of God.[6] In contrast to the antecedent millennium of Christian theological tradition (Rahner refers especially to Peter Lombard[7]), Thomas separated the doctrine of God into two distinct treatises, On the One God and On the Triune God. He began his discussion with the former, in which the existence and attributes of the one God were elaborated, and only then moved on to speak of the triune nature of God. For Thomas this move was made for the apologetic purpose of appropriating Aristotelean philosophy, which had been introduced to the West by Islamic thinkers.[8] For Thomas the treatise on the one God did not replace the treatise on the Trinity since the knowledge of the one God was not saving. Salvation was attained only through the revealed knowledge of the triune God.[9]

Nevertheless, this pattern had the far reaching consequence of leading to the eclipse of the doctrine of the Trinity, not only in its position in the structure of theology but also as the rule controlling the logic of Christian speech about God. In this manner the way was opened for the emergence of theism. Thomas' split in the doctrine of God allows for a discussion of God abstracted from the trinitarian context of human salvation in Jesus. Here the speculative question of the existence of God becomes of central concern and is placed first. "For," as Aquinas says, "the first thing that is understood about anything is its existence."[10] Moreover, "the question of what a thing is must follow the question of its existence."[11] The concentration on the proof of the existence of God which becomes typical of theism serves as a supposed point of contact between God and humanity, since it is based upon the common ground of rationality. Paralleling Aquinas' partition in the doctrine of God, one finds a partition between faith and reason. Thomas indicates this when he says,

> The existence of God, and similar things which can be known by natural reason . . . are not articles of faith, but preambles to the articles of faith. Faith presupposes natural knowledge as grace presupposes nature . . . .[12]

Reason is capable of attaining the non-salvific knowledge of the existence of the one God and certain qualities attributable to him. But only faith in the revealed truth gives knowledge of God in himself, his essence, his triune nature. For Thomas, however, the knowledge of the one God obtained through reason is no less true than that which comes from revelation. In fact, whatever Thomas' intentions, the effect of the split between the one God, who is discussed first, and the triune God, and the corresponding division between reason and revelation, is to render the salvific, revealed truth of the triune God, known in faith, less significant. The doctrine of the triune God is, as Rahner points out, locked in "splendid isolation, with the ensuing danger that the religious mind finds it devoid of interest." For as Rahner concludes, "It looks as if everything which matters for us in God has already been said in the treatise On the One God."[13] Indeed it is in his discussion of the one God that we find the epistemology and the conception of God that come to control the theism that dominates the subsequent theological tradition.

Epistemologically, Thomas' discussion of the one God is based on reason's ability to draw conclusions about God based on the sensible natural world, that is, to argue from an effect to its cause. In this way God's existence can be proved. Thomas reasons,

> Even though the effect should be better known to us, we can demonstrate from any effect that its cause exists, because effects always depend on some cause, and a cause must exist if its effect exists. We can demonstrate God's existence in this way, from his effects which are known to us . . . .[14]

In Part I, Question 2, Article 3 of the *Summa Theologica* Thomas, following this method, then gives his famous "five ways" of proving God's existence.[15]

However, in addition to discussing the existence of God, Thomas goes on to define the attributes of God as well. Once again this discussion is based on the relation of effects to cause, of the creation to God. We know God from his effects. But because he is the cause of everything and therefore transcends all creation, God cannot be classified directly with the classes of things in the natural world.[16] God "differs from his creatures, since he is none of the things caused by him." Therefore, "his creatures are separated from God" but not because God lacks what his creatures have, "not because of any defect in God," but "because he transcends them."[17] The problem in speaking about God on the basis of creation, then, is that the effects of God are incommensurate with their cause. And, as Thomas points out, "effects which are not proportionate to their cause do not give us perfect knowledge of their cause."[18] Therefore, one cannot achieve knowledge of God's essence, his whole power, on the basis of creation. Nevertheless, this does not mean that nothing can be said of God by examining his effects. As we will see, Aquinas says a great deal. He summarizes his position as follows:

> Sensible things are indeed effects of God, but they are not proportionate to the power of their cause, and for this reason the whole power of God cannot be known from them. Neither, consequently, can his essence be seen. But since effects depend on their cause, sensible things can lead us to know that God exists, and to know what is bound to be attributable to him as the first cause of all things, and as transcending all his effects.[19]

The speech about what is "attributable" to God is made possible, according to Thomas, through the analogy of being. In spite of their incommensurability, the cause and the effects, God and creation, are still related because they both participate in being, "since existence itself is common to all things."

> The things which God has made are like him in this way. In
> so far as they are beings, they are like the first and universal
> principle of all being.[20]

The conclusion of this line of thought is this: Because of their incommensurability, one cannot speak about God and creation univocally. However, because of their relationship neither does one speak about them merely equivocally. Rather, in light of the analogy of being, what is "attributable" to God "as the first cause of all things" can be spoken of analogously.[21] The attributes of God are abstracted from the world and applied to God analogically, according to the appropriate proportion.

A further element in this theological method that has significant consequences for the doctrine of God is that this process of analogy, in order to attain the proper proportionality for God, often works in a *via negativa*. Again, because God is not to be equated with creation, because God's effects are incommensurate with him, because God, in transcending creation is everything the creation is not, "we cannot know of God what he is, but only what he is not."[22] Therefore, the conception of God is defined through a *via negativa*, by denying God the negative characteristics of the natural world.[23]

In this way Thomas can affirm the relation of God to the world and human ability to speak about God, while assuring that the analogous language speaks of God with the eminence due him. By this epistemological method of abstracting the attributes of God from the world in a negative way, Aquinas draws the picture of God that comes to dominate traditional theism. The present state of creation is characterized by composition, imperfection, finitude, transience, temporality, suffering, division. Drawing analogies from creation by means of negation, in the *Summa* God is conceived of as simple, perfect, infinite, omnipotent, omnipresent, immutable, eternal, impassible, one.[24] He is the one supreme being who, as immutable, omnipotent and eternal, is the "unmoved mover," the first cause who possesses the power to create all things without being subject to change and time himself. As impassible, this God can be related to the world only as its cause, for no movement from the world can affect him. In his infinitude he is beyond all limitations and can contain all things. And yet in his simplicity all things in him are one. This theistic God, therefore, is defined as both the antithesis to as well as the perfection of the world. On the one hand what God has creatures do not.[25] The divine is conceived of as containing all the attributes which humans and the rest of creation are lacking or have only partially, but are seeking. On the other hand this concept of God is drawn as the answer to the present state of creation and as the goal and highest perfection for which humans and the rest of creation are longing. As Aquinas puts it, "All things, in seeking the perfections proper to themselves, seek God himself."[26]

We see in Thomas Aquinas both the method of developing and the content of theism's view of God. Based upon a human faculty (in this case reason) one finds language in which to speak of God by a process of abstracting from an area of human experience (in this case the sensible world of nature). By this method a particular conception of God is developed without reference to what had served as a rule of faith, the doctrine of the Trinity; that is, without reference to the revelatory, salvific event of Jesus. One must join Rahner in asking whether much of importance remains to be said about God. We must agree that for Thomas this method "determined once and for all the shape of his concept of God."[27]

From Thomas through the Enlightenment

It is this theism, characterized by this method and conception of God (with various emphases and modifications), which has continued to dominate the theological tradition since Thomas. It is not the intention here to give a history of this tradition. Nevertheless, it is necessary to refer to it to make two further points in regard to traditional theism. First, we can demonstrate that the theism found in Thomas becomes "traditional theism." And second, we can see that traditional theism responds to atheism by reconstituting itself on another basis.

Theology in the later Medieval period followed the method and doctrine of Thomas, although theologians debated which statements about God belonged to the province of reason and which to the province of faith.[28] Even Duns Scotus, who disagrees with Thomism at many points, concentrates his attention on the one God, whose existence is proved by arguing from contingent being to necessary being and who is given the attributes of simplicity, omnipresence, omnipotence, immutability, unity.[29]

The Protestant theology of the Reformation and Orthodox periods also did not accomplish a permanent reversal of theism. Luther did break with Thomism and its methodology by insisting that all of theology must be based on revelation in Jesus, especially at the cross.[30] By his use of the *communicatio idiomatum*, he also made progress in overcoming the dilemma which theistic notions of divinity had created for Christology.[31] Nevertheless, on account of his concentration upon other theological loci (justification by grace, for instance) Luther did not succeed in reworking the doctrine of God. This is signaled by the fact that even though he clearly expounded a rather traditional doctrine of the Trinity,[32] he never developed it in a way that was decisive for his theology. In fact, he was able to say that, together with the doctrine of the two natures of Christ, the doctrine of the Trinity is "incomprehensible to the understanding" and that "the more we speculate about them the darker and less intelligible do they become."[33]

Likewise, Melanchthon made no break with theism's doctrine of God. Following Luther's lead his focus of attention is elsewhere. Primarily he wants to emphasize the *beneficia Christi*. Therefore, in the *Loci communes* of 1521, Melanchthon distinguishes between "exalted" doctrines, like "God," "The Unity and Trinity of God" and "The Manner of the Incarnation," that are incomprehensible and as such should simply be adored and those which are fundamental and need full discussion.[34] Nevertheless, in apparent contradiction to his emphasis on God for us, in the 1555 edition of *Loci*, Melanchthon begins not with how God is known in his revelation to us, but follows the Thomistic pattern of speaking first of the general idea of God, defined in the traditional manner, and only then of the Trinity.[35]

A similar pattern is found in Calvin. In the doctrine of God, the focus of attention is on the one God and his nature. This is again signaled by the fact that the first edition of the *Institutes* merely "mentioned and affirmed the Trinity."[36] Even in the face of Calvin's complicity in the Servetus affair, we may conclude with Barth that his "interest in this matter is not exactly burning."[37] It was in fact the encounter with anti-trinitarians like Servetus that prompted Calvin to deal more with the Trinity, until in the last edition of the *Institutes* it occupied a full chapter.[38] Even so he still places it in a secondary position well after the discussion of the natural knowledge of God, his existence, wisdom, power and goodness.[39] Without claiming that Calvin was a theist, it is clear that in methodology and in the doctrine of God he did not eliminate the influence of theism.

Following the well-established pattern which had not been altered significantly by the reformers and the growing re-emergence of Aristotle in theology begun already in Melanchthon, Protestant Orthodoxy divided the doctrine of God into the two sections established by Thomas. It began with a general doctrine of God, *de deo*, conceiving

God with the attributes of theism, and only subsequently dealt with the *mysterium de sancta trinitate*.[40] Even the doctrine of the Trinity did not emerge in orthodoxy from reflection on revelation, but was deduced through formal logic.[41]

What happens to the doctrine of God in the Enlightenment is well known. If the theistic conception of God dominated orthodox theology of the seventeenth and eighteenth centuries, it did so even more in philosophy where, almost completely isolated from other Christian beliefs, it became the sole doctrine of importance. The doctrine of the one God, which Thomas and the theological tradition had developed for apologetic purposes in order subsequently to introduce the saving knowledge, becomes the only acceptable doctrine. Descartes, carrying further what had begun in Thomas,[42] separates reason and faith in such a way that they become completely independent realms.[43] Reason is given autonomy to investigate and authority to adjudicate in all matters. While the truths of faith are still believed[44] and are not contradicted by reason, they are of less and less concern, as reason becomes the central focus. Independent of faith, and really as a necessary step in establishing an epistemology for his philosophy, reason can prove the one God from its own "clear and distinct" ideas.[45]

When one reaches John Locke, reason has become the judge of revelation and faith itself. While reason cannot discover the truths of revelation, revelation, if it is to considered true, must be reasonable.[46] The end product of reason's judgment of revelation is Deism, in which reasonable persons can believe in only the one God, known by reason's reflection on the self or nature. Revelation and faith are finally unnecessary, if not false.

Thus theism triumphs in both philosophical and theological traditions. In both traditions its method of arguing from human existence to God and its concentration on the one God and his existence became virtually self-evident. Theism has become "traditional theism," and even in theology the triune god has become secondary at best.

However, if reason is omnicompetent, then it must also turn its critical ability upon itself and its own truths. In so doing reason finds its own limits. This process culminates in the critiques of Hume[47] and Kant[48] in which the epistemological basis of theism in reason is challenged. The result for Hume is atheism;[49] for Kant it is that religion becomes a matter of practical rather than theoretical necessity.[50] The irony of this is that traditional theism which begins and is used by the theological tradition as an apologetic strategy — to show reason's support of theological truths — ends up by generating atheism.

Schleiermacher's Reconstruction

The final point of our analysis of the tradition of theism is to see how it responds to critique. When atheism destroys one of theism's bases, theism often attempts to re-establish itself upon a new ground. If atheistic critique eliminates its use of reason, theism reasserts itself by using some other human point of contact with God. Kant himself demonstrates this tendency by re-establishing the truth of God on the basis of practical reason after his critique of pure reason. Kant remains a kind of theist.[51]   Theologians, as exemplified by Friedrich Schleiermacher, also attempt to reiterate theism on a new basis.[52]

Schleiermacher accepts Kant's critique of the attempt to found belief in God on reason. But, unlike Kant, he is not willing to relegate faith to the moral realm. Religion "cannot be an instinct craving for a mess of metaphysical and ethical crumbs."[53] Therefore, for the apologetic necessity of responding to the Kantian position and distancing himself from the rationally based orthodoxy of the day, Schleiermacher finds a new basis from which to argue the acceptability of the Christian faith. In this instance it is not the reasonableness of the existence of God that serves as the point of contact available to all. Rather, for Schleiermacher the truth of religion in general becomes the central foundation. This truth is not based on the human capacity of reason, but another element of human life, feeling. Religion, says Schleiermacher, "considered purely in itself, [is] neither a Knowing nor a Doing, but a modification of Feeling . . . ."[54] The truth of religion in general cannot be denied, according to Schleiermacher, because it is a constituent aspect of human being. It belongs inherently to the level of human "feeling" (*Gefühl*), more closely defined as "immediate self-consciousness."[55] Religion is that "consciousness" or "feeling of being absolutely dependent."[56] When religion speaks of God it is not about some metaphysical being outside of humanity that can be proved by reason. Neither is it about a ground for moral activity. Rather its referent is only that modification of feeling, only the "co-determinant" implicit in, or the "Whence" of, the feeling of absolute dependence.[57] Because this feeling of absolute dependence is implicit in and constituent of human self-consciousness,[58] religion is an integral part of human being.

It is only after this proof of the truth of religion in general that Schleiermacher speaks about the Christian faith. For him it is the highest expression of the feeling of absolute dependence and therefore the highest form of religion.[59] And it is distinguished from all other religions "by the fact that in it everything is related to the redemption accomplished by Jesus of Nazareth."[60] Schleiermacher claims that for the

Christian all "religious moments," that is, all expressions of the feeling of absolute dependence, "come into existence through that redemption."[61] Christian theology, then, does not speak of metaphysical realities. Rather it is the articulation of the feeling of absolute dependence as it is related to redemption in Jesus. "Christian doctrines are accounts of the Christian religious affections set forth in speech."[62] Proper theological statements must be utterances drawn from the Christian self-consciousness.[63]

At first Schleiermacher's approach to theology looks new. But, both methodologically and in its doctrine of God, it is essentially an altered form of traditional theism. Methodologically, there is the apologetic attempt to ground the acceptability of the Christian faith in some prior truth available to all. Schleiermacher substituted the proof of the truth of religion in general for the proof of the existence of God as the epistemological basis of Christian belief. This truth is established prior to faith by appealing to a general human capacity. In this case, it is human feeling instead of human reason. Speech about God, therefore, is an inherent human possibility and proceeds by the same theistic process of abstracting the attributes of God from human experience in the world. For Schleiermacher, theology abstracts god-language from human self-consciousness of absolute dependence instead of from nature.

Likewise, the content of the doctrine of God in Schleiermacher's theology is indistinguishable from traditional theism. As in the theological tradition before him in which the general truth of God's existence and the natural knowledge of him tend to dominate the doctrine of God, it is Schleiermacher's general definition of religion that controls his theology. In spite of his attempt to establish redemption in Jesus as the center of the Christian faith, it is his conception of the feeling of absolute dependence that remains his central criterion. For Schleiermacher, the identity of Jesus and his redeeming work are not defined by the specifics of his story in the New Testament. Rather, these are defined in terms of the feeling of absolute dependence; and only those aspects of Jesus' existence which demonstrate this definition are important. The cross and resurrection, for example, add nothing to the nature of his redemption or his lordship.[64] Rather, what identifies Jesus as the Redeemer is "the constant potency of his God-consciousness,"[65] his informing every moment with the feeling of absolute dependence.[66] And his redeeming work is accomplished in that he "assumes believers into the power of His God-consciousness . . . ."[67]

Similarly, in developing the doctrine of God, the specifics of Jesus' existence play little if any role. Rather, the doctrine is developed by defining the attributes of God on the basis of the feeling of absolute dependence.[68] Because it is the feeling of *absolute* dependence, God must be conceived of as one,[69] as absolute causality,[70] omnipotent,[71] eternal,[72] omniscient,[73] immutable,[74] omnipresent,[75] infinite,[76] simple.[77] Schleiermacher's doctrine of God turns out to be indistinguishable from the common theistic concept of the one God viewed in absolutist terms. Only later does Schleiermacher deal with God's holiness, justice and mercy.[78] And only at the end of the *Christian Faith* does he finally discuss "Divine Love" and "Wisdom."[79]

Finally, one further signal of the way in which Schleiermacher's general definition of religion controls his theology and of his location in the tradition of theism is his treatment of the doctrine of the Trinity. Based on his methodology, Schleiermacher includes the doctrine of the Trinity only at the end of his theology as an appendix. It has no primary relevance for the Christian faith, because it says nothing that is not said in other, essential doctrines. The doctrine of the Trinity is merely a synthesis. Schleiermacher writes,

> But this doctrine itself, as ecclesiastically framed, is not an immediate utterance concerning the Christian self-consciousness, but only a combination of several such utterances.[80]

It is impossible to move from Christian self-consciousness to trinitarian distinctions in God.

> Who would venture to say that the impression made by the divine in Christ obliges us to conceive such an eternal distinction [a trinitarian distinction in God] as its basis [the impression, or Christian self-consciousness]?[81]

In spite of his new basis for doing theology and regardless of the differences between Schleiermacher and previous theology, he has but re-established theism, its methodology and its doctrine of God, on new grounds.

But the theism of Schleiermacher and his followers, like that of previous generations, also fails as an apologetic strategy and ends up generating atheistic critiques from various positions. In the next chapter we will see that, far from serving its intended apologetic task, this theistic theology as well, becomes the occasion for criticism and negation which leads to atheism. In Chapter II, we will first see how traditional theism is criticized because its *method* is mistaken epistemologically. Then in the succeeding chapters, we will see how atheism arises in three different protests against the theistic *conception* of God. In each case, the question will be whether the doctrine of the Trinity can provide a cogent response to these forms of atheism.

NOTES

[1] For theologians that speak of the crisis in theism and make use of these various terms, see for instance Schubert Ogden, *The Reality of God* (New York, 1966), pp. 16, 17, 19, 44; John Macquarrie, *Thinking About God* (New York, 1975), pp. 88, 90, 94, 106; Moltmann, *CG*, pp. 107ff, 149ff; Heinrich Ott, *God*, trans. Iain and Ute Nicol (Richmond, 1971), pp. 62ff.; Wolfhart Pannenberg, *Basic Questions in Theology*, trans. George H. Kehm (Philadelphia, 1971), II, 234ff.

[2] See, for instance, Charles Hartshorne and William L. Reese, *Philosophers Speak of God* (Chicago, 1953).

[3] Welch, *In This Name*, p. vii.

[4] See Justo L. Gonzalez, *A History of Christian Thought*, 3 vols. (Nashville, 1970), I, 270ff.

[5] Welch, *In This Name*, p. vii.

[6] Rahner, *The Trinity*, pp. 16ff. See also Jüngel, p. 4, and Moltmann, *CG*, pp. 239ff.

[7] Rahner, *The Trinity*, p. 16.

[8] For Averroes' use of Aristotle and Thomas' response to the Averroists, see Etienne Gilson, *Reason and Revelation in the Middle Ages* (New York, 1938), pp. 37-84. See also F.C. Copleston, *Aquinas* (Baltimore, 1955), p. 11.

[9] See Copleston, pp. 55-61.

[10] Thomas Aquinas *Summa Theologica* 1.2.2. (Hereafter cited as *Summa*.)

[11] *Ibid.*

[12] *Ibid.*

[13] Rahner, *The Trinity*, p. 17.

[14] *Summa* 1.2.2.

[15] *Ibid.*, 1.2.3.

[16] On this see R. W. Jenson, *The Knowledge of Things Hoped For* (New York, 1969), p. 69. This part of the discussion of Aquinas is indebted to Jenson.

[17] *Summa* 1.12.12.

[18] *Ibid.*, 1.2.2.

[19] *Ibid.*, 1.12.12.

[20] *Ibid.*, 1.4.3.

[21] On this see *Ibid.*, 1.13.5.

[22] *Ibid.*, 1.3.

[23] *Ibid.*, 56f. Aquinas says it: "The manner in which God does not exist can be shown by excluding what is incompatible with God, such as composition, movement, and the like."

[24] See *Summa* 1.3-1.11 and 1.25.

[25] See *Summa* 1.12.12; also Jenson, p. 70.

[26] *Ibid.*, 1.1a.1. See Jenson, p. 61.

[27] Thus, Gunton, *Becoming and Being: The Doctrine of God in Charles Hartshorne and Karl Barth*, p. 3.

[28] See Gilson, pp. 84ff.

[29] See Gonzalez, II, 308-310; also Gilson, pp. 85ff.

[30] See *CD* I/1, 478; also *CG*, pp. 208ff. This discussion is indebted to Karl Barth's analysis of these issues in the *Church Dogmatics*.

[31] See Moltmann, *CG*, pp. 231ff.

[32] See *CD* I/1, 419. In his Table Talk, at least, Luther could even follow the tradition of the *vestigium trinitatis* found in nature (See *Ibid.*, I/1, 386).

[33] Quoted in Welch, *In This Name*, p. 19. Welch points out that Luther's statement was referred to with approval by nineteenth century theologians like Ritschl.

[34] See Wilhelm Pauck, ed., *Melanchton and Bucer*, The Library of Christian Classics, XIX (Philadelphia, 1969), pp. 21f. See also *CD* I/1, 476 and Moltmann, *CG*, p. 237.

[35] See Gonzalez, III, 95f; also *CD* II/1, 259 and *CG*, 237.

[36] See Gonzalez, III, 126.

[37] *CD* I/1, 477.

[38] See Gonzalez, III, 126.

[39] See *Calvin: Institutes of the Christian Religion*, ed. John T. McNeill, trans. Ford Lewis Battles, 2 vols. The Library of Christian Classics, XX (Philadelphia, 1960). Calvin first discusses natural knowledge of God found in the "minds of men" (Chapter III), and in the creation and order of the universe (Chapter IV). Even though for Calvin this natural knowledge does not bring salvation, but rather renders humans inexcusable in their sin, it does nevertheless offer a type of proof for God's existence. A "sense of divinity" is so deeply and universally a part of human being that Calvin concludes, "Actual godlessness is impossible" (pp. 45f). In the discussion of how God is known in creation Calvin concentrates on the "one God" (p. 58) and his wisdom, power and goodness (pp. 51-63). Only later (Chapter XIII), and still under the heading of "The Knowledge of God the Creator," does Calvin discuss the Trinity.

[40] See Moltmann, *CG*, p. 239; also *CD* II/1, 261.

[41] See *CD* II/1, 261.

[42] See Hans Küng, *Does God Exist?* (New York, 1980), pp. 20ff, for Descartes' indebtedness to Thomas.

[43] See Elizabeth Anscombe and Peter Thomas Geach, eds. and trans., *Descartes: Philosophical Writings*, The Library of the Liberal Arts (Indianapolis, 1971), p. 157; also Küng, p. 18.

[44] See Küng, pp. 16f, on Descartes' continued sincere religious belief.

[45] See Descartes' two proofs of God in the *Meditations on First Philosophy* in Anscombe, pp. 76-91 and 103-108, and how they guarantee the reliability of reason, pp. 101-124; also Küng, pp. 14f.

[46] See John Locke, *Essay Concerning Human Understanding*, ed. A. D. Woozley (New York, 1964), pp. 432f.

[47] See David Hume, *The Natural History of Religion*, ed. A. Wayne Colver (Oxford, 1976).

[48] See, for instance, Immanuel Kant, *Prolegomena to Any Future Metaphysics*, The Library of Liberal Arts (Indianapolis, 1950), particularly pp. 96, 102ff.

[49] On Hume's attack on religion see Peter Gay, *The Enlightenment*, 2 vols. (New York), I, 404-419.

[50] See Immanuel Kant, *Religion Within the Limits of Reason Alone*, trans. T.M. Greene and H.H. Hudson (New York, 1960), pp. 4-6.

[51] Theodore W. Jennings, Jr., *Beyond Theism: A Grammar of God-Language* (New York, 1985), p. 20, makes a similar point. D. Bonhoeffer in *Letters and Papers from Prison*, ed. Eberhard Bethge, trans. Reginald F. Fuller (New York, 1953), p. 218, is more critical of Kant. "In the last resort," Bonhoeffer says, "Kant is a deist."

[52] In the concluding chapter we will see again attempts to reconstitute theism on a new basis in contemporary theology.

[53] Friedrich Schleiermacher, *On Religion: Speeches to its Cultured Despisers*, trans. John Oman (New York, 1958), p. 31.

[54] Friedrich Schleiermacher, *The Christian Faith*, ed. H.R. Mackintosh and J.S. Stewart (Philadelphia, 1976), p. 5.

[55] *Ibid.*, pp. 5-7.

[56] *Ibid.*, p. 12.

[57] *Ibid.*, pp. 16ff.

[58] *Ibid.*, pp. 16, 26f.

[59] See *Ibid.*, pp. 34ff: Schleiermacher argues that monotheistic religions, because they "express the dependence of everything finite upon the one Supreme and Infinite Being," are the highest forms of religion. And, after comparing Christianity to Islam and Judaism, he concludes:

> "And so this comparison of Christianity with other similar
> religions is in itself sufficient warrant for saying that Chris-
> tianity is, in fact, the most perfect of the most highly
> developed forms of religion" (p. 38).

[60] *Ibid.*, p. 52.

[61] *Ibid.*, p. 56. See Richard R. Niebuhr, *Schleiermacher on Christ and Religion* (New York, 1964), pp. 210ff, where he stresses Schleiermacher's "Christo-morphic" theology. As we will see below, however, this is a Christocentrism of a particular type, one that focuses on the God-consciousness of Jesus rather than the concrete elements of his history.

[62] *Ibid.*, p. 76.

[63] *Ibid.*, pp. 125f, 131f.

[64] See *Ibid.*, pp. 417f, 436f, 458ff. Schleiermacher has a tendency to spiritualize the suffering of Jesus. The essence of his suffering was his "sympathy with misery" (p. 436) or his "sympathy with sin" (p. 458). ". . . from merely natural evils He never suffered . . . ."(p. 457), and one should not attribute "a special reconciling value to this physical suffering" (p. 437). Most significantly, Christ's suffering could not include any real separation from God, which "from the nature of the case could in Him be only sympathy"(p. 460). Such suffering must be rejected for it would indicate a break in his perfect God-consciousness. For this reason Schleiermacher rejects Matthew 27:46 — "My God, my God why hast thou forsaken me?" — as representing Christ's suffering. If historical it is only quoted from Psalm 22 "with reference to what follows" (p. 460).

[65] *Ibid.*, p. 385.

[66] See *Ibid.*, pp. 17, 22, 388.

[67] *Ibid.*, p. 425.

[68] See *Ibid.*, p. 194:

> "All attributes which we ascribe to God are to be taken as
> denoting . . . only something special in the manner in which
> the feeling of absolute dependence is to be related to him."

[69] *Ibid.*, pp. 229f.

[70] *Ibid.*, pp. 200f.

[71] *Ibid.*, pp. 201f, 203ff.

[72] *Ibid.*, pp. 201f, 203ff.

[73] *Ibid.*, pp. 202, 219ff.

[74] *Ibid.*, p. 206.

[75] *Ibid.*, pp. 206ff.

[76] *Ibid.*, pp. 230f.

[77] *Ibid.*, p. 231. We must note that not all theologians of the traditional theism stress these absolutist attributes. A notable example is Albrecht Ritschl [*The Christian Doctrine of Justification and Reconciliation* Vol. 3, trans. H.R. Mackintosh and A.B. Macaulay (Edinburgh, 1900; Clifton, N.J., 1966)] who places a primary emphasis on God's love expressed in his work of justification and reconciliation (See p. 13). However, in his stress on the one God and his grounding of theology in moral value he remains a theist. The doctrine of the Trinity is excluded from his theology.

[78] *Ibid.*, pp. 325-354.

[79] *Ibid.*, pp. 727-752.

[80] *Ibid.*, p. 738.

[81] *Ibid.*, p. 739. Parentheses mine.

CHAPTER II

THE DOCTRINE OF THE TRINITY
AND THE EPISTEMOLOGICAL QUESTION

The epistemological position of traditional theism attempts to justify knowledge of God through a process of abstraction from nature or human self-consciousness. Ludwig Feuerbach challenges this epistemology by developing the claim that since language about God is drawn from nature or human self-consciousness it does not succeed in speaking about God, but only about the world or humanity. Thus an epistemological examination of traditional theism results in the confirmation of atheism. This chapter will propose that the doctrine of the Trinity provides the context for a response to atheism's critique of the epistemological foundation of belief. We will first examine Feuerbach's critique of theism showing that his atheism is generated by, and responds to, the method of traditional theism. We will then argue that Barth's development of a trinitarian conception of God may be understood as an incorporation of, and response to, Feuerbach's critique. This discussion will show (1) that in forming his theology Barth is constantly aware of Feuerbach's critique. Demonstrating this awareness (2) is the doctrine of the Trinity which as developed by Barth serves an apologetic function in that it incorporates Feuerbach's major epistemological position — its demand for both the sensuousness and the subjectivity of the object of knowledge. We will see (3) that this trinitarian appropriation of Feuerbach's epistemology enables Barth to use the doctrine of the Trinity as the basis for argumentation against other theological systems, namely, those which remain tied to what has previously been described as traditional theism. Barth's doctrine of the Trinity, then, (4) allows Barth to move beyond Feuerbach. On the one hand it includes a "yes" to Feuerbach. It calls theologians to take Feuerbach's critique seriously, to realize that he makes a positive theological contribution, to recognize that the God of traditional theism is a product of human projection. However, this is not the final word. On the other hand the doctrine of the Trinity also includes a "no" to Feuerbach. Feuerbach's critique remains tied to traditional theism. But according to Barth's doctrine of the Trinity, there is a God who is not a projection, even in terms of

Feuerbach's own criteria. If Feuerbach's arguments can be developed on the basis of and included in trinitarian faith, and if the doctrine of the Trinity meets Feuerbach's epistemological demands, Feuerbach's atheism is itself called into question.

Feuerbach's Critique

It is fitting that the chapters which examine various forms of atheistic critique begin with Ludwig Feuerbach. As Hans Küng points out, "From that time [of the writing of Feuerbach's critiques of religion] onward there has been no form of atheism that did not draw on Feuerbach's arguments."[1] Feuerbach has been the fountainhead of modern atheistic critiques of religion. This is true particularly of the tradition of protest atheism with which this essay is concerned. Feuerbach anticipates the other forms of atheism which will be discussed in the following chapters. His atheism is a protest against the suffering human situation as seen religiously and therefore a call for political action. Nevertheless, his critique of religion is founded upon an epistemological argument. It is this that we first take up.

Because his critique is well known, no extensive treatment of his philosophy or the development of his thought is necessary in this context.[2] Whatever shifts in emphasis may be detected in his different writings on religion — The Essence of Chritianity and The Essence of Religion, for instance — his central concepts and criticisms remain stable. His anthropological standpoint and his sensualistic epistemology are throughout the key to his critique.[3] Feuerbach himself claims this in the Essence of Religion.[4]

One reason that Feuerbach's atheism is so powerful lies in the fact that he did not merely dismiss religion as nonsense. Religion, for him, is far from "an absurdity, a nullity, a pure illusion." "But I by no means say (that were an easy task!): God is nothing, the Trinity is nothing, the Word of God is nothing, &c."[5] Feuerbach does not want to destroy religion but to "let religion speak for itself."[6] When one listens to it, though, when one examines its epistemological grounds, it is discovered that what religion means is not what believers think it means.

Of utmost importance for understanding Feuerbach's critique (and the trinitarian response) is the recognition that its positive foundation is Feuerbach's sensualistic epistemology. Feuerbach rejects idealism or any kind of speculative thinking or claim to knowledge. Thinking that leads to knowledge must be concrete, sensuous, materialistic. Feuerbach exclaims,

> I unconditionally repudiate absolute, immaterial, self-suffic-
> ing speculation . . . . I differ *toto coelo* from those
> philosophers who pluck out their eyes that they may see
> better; for my thought I require the senses, especially sight; I
> found my ideas on materials which can be appropriated
> only through the activity of the senses. I do not generate the
> object from the thought, but the thought from the object;
> and I hold *that* alone to be an object which has an existence
> beyond one's own brain.[7]

Using this key, Feuerbach attacks not only religion but speculative
philosophy. He extensively criticizes his teacher, Hegel — as well as
"the entire modern philosophy from Descartes and Spinoza" — for an
"unmediated break with sensuousness."[8] When philosophy begins with
thought and attempts, then, to have knowledge of reality, it "overleaps
its boundaries."[9] It confuses what it thinks for what is real and thereby
controls the object of knowledge. According to Feuerbach it is this of
which Hegel is guilty and which calls for a reversal. If objectivity of
thought and truth are to be achieved, the objects of our thought must be
primary, must control our knowledge of them. Sensual experience must
take precedence; thinking must follow sensation of the concrete object.
"In sensation," Feuerbach declares, "I am determined by objects, in
thought I determine the object."[10] Therefore, according to Feuerbach to
arrive at the truth two interdependent requirements are necessary.
Thinking must be done concretely, based on a sensuous object. And that
object must maintain its subjectivity in human thinking about it.
Thought must give up control of its objects and allow to objects their
proper autonomy as independent subjects.[11] Edward Sawyer is correct in
his analysis of Feuerbach when he says, "Sensation must not be a
predicate of the idea; the idea must be a predicate of sensation."[12] In an
important passage in *Principles of the Philosophy of the Future*, Feuerbach
summarizes,

> In thought, I am absolute subject; . . . I am intolerant. In
> the activity of the senses, on the other hand, I am liberal; I
> let the object be what I myself am — a subject, a real and
> self-actualizing being. Only sense and perception give me
> something as subject.[13]

This means for Feuerbach that thinking is done by the whole person,
located in sensuous reality. "Before you think the quality you feel the
quality."[14] It also goes some way in explaining Feuerbach's famous
aphorism, "You are what you eat."[15]

More importantly, in light of this sensuous epistemology, the western philosophical tradition must be criticized for its false starting point, for this tradition begins in thought rather than in sensuous reality. Hegel's approach, according to Feuerbach, takes an absolute standpoint by beginning in thought. By presupposing that the absolute spirit is[16] and that, through the dialectical process, it is becoming conscious in finite human spirit, finite human consciousness is elevated to infinite, absolute spirit.[17] But according to Feuerbach's critique this is abstract speculation. The secret of this philosophy is theology.[18] On the basis of a sensuous epistemology a reversal is necessary in which the absolute standpoint is given up. Instead of thinking of the human consciousness, presupposing an abstract infinite consciousness, thinking must proceed from the concrete, finite human consciousness. The concrete basis for thought about the infinite consciousness is the sensuous human consciousness. The sensuous basis for thought about the Absolute Spirit is the concrete human spirit. By this reversal the infinite consciousness is dissolved into the finite. The idea of the Absolute arises out of sensuous reality. "Consciousness of God is self-consciousness, the knowledge of God is self-knowledge."[19]

From this perspective it is not difficult to understand why Feuerbach, over against Hegel, agrees with Schleiermacher and the theological trend of the nineteenth century in locating religion in human self-consciousness, in feeling. The "foundation of Religion is a feeling of dependency . . . ."[20] Schleiermacher, in locating religion in feeling, was recognizing the concrete, sensuous, human basis of religion. However, any "Whence" that is claimed for this consciousness or feeling that lies beyond humanity or nature, Feuerbach denies as mere abstraction and speculation. Feuerbach criticizes Schleiermacher because he could not overcome his "theological embarrassment" and draw the "necessary consequences."[21] " . . . when once feeling has been pronounced to be the subjective essence of religion, it is also the objective essence."[22] Not only Schleiermacher but theology in general refuses to admit that "religion being identical with the distinctive characteristic of man, is then identical with self-consciousness — with the consciousness which man has of his nature."[23] While theology admits the concrete, sensuous ground of religion in human self-consciousness, it then posits another subject of that self-consciousness, God. But this is possible only on the basis of abstract, speculative thinking. And it is against this speculative leap, against this abstract theology, that Feuerbach's critique is directed. Starting from human self-consciousness, theology has no epistemological basis to speculate about a being distinct from that consciousness. If religion wishes to speak about something real and concrete, it must speak about the concrete subject of that self-consciousness, humanity. "Theology is anthropology."[24] Or if humanity turns its attention to nature and attempts to speak of God from that concrete point, then it must realize that it is in reality speaking about nature. "Theology is . . . anthropology and physiology."[25]

It is on the basis of this sensuous epistemology, therefore, that Feuerbach establishes his atheism and his contention that religion and theology which ground the conception of God in human self-consciousness (or nature) are the true teachers of atheism and worshippers of humanity.

> It is not I, but religion that worships man, although religion, or rather theology, denies this; it is not I, an insignificant individual, but religion itself that says: God is man, man is God; it is not I, but religion that denies the God who is not man. . . . I have only found the key to the cipher of the Christian religion . . . . If therefore my work is negative, irreligious, atheistic, let it be remembered that atheism . . . is the secret of religion itself; that religion itself . . . in its heart, in its essence, believes in nothing else than the truth and divinity of human nature.[26]

This means that religion, as it is usually understood, is an illusion, because its object is thought to be God, a being distinct from humanity. According to Feuerbach's epistemology, however, any speech about a god distinct from humanity must be an illusory projection. It is merely an abstraction from the concrete, sensuous existence of humanity. God as an independent being is the result of abstracting attributes from human nature and experience and projecting these attributes outside of human existence and viewing them as if they existed independently. Sensuous thinking, though, knows that these projections speak only of their sensuous ground — humanity. Therefore Feuerbach asserts, "Man has given objectivity to himself, but has not recognized the object as his own nature . . . ."[27] "Man . . . projects his being into objectivity and then again makes himself an object to this projected image of himself thus converted into a subject."[28]

This means that there is no real difference between God and man. ". . . the antithesis of divine and human is altogether illusory . . .,"[29] Feuerbach declares. However, it cannot be denied that human beings do encounter a distinction between themselves as limited individuals and what they perceive as the absolute greatness of God. To be true to his epistemology, Feuerbach must find a sensuous, concrete basis for this supposed distinction. He establishes this by claiming that the supposed distinction between the divine and the human ". . . is nothing else than the antithesis between the human nature in general and the human individual . . . ."[30] According to Feuerbach the essence of humanity is not found in individual humans abstracted from their concrete relationships with others.[31] Rather, humanity's true nature is found in the community of humankind, in concrete I-Thou relationships.[32] It is the predicates of humanity as a whole that constitute the essence of humanity and that are projected outward as God. "The mystery of the inexhaustible fullness of the divine predicates is therefore nothing else than the mystery of human nature considered as an infinitely varied . . . phenomenal being.[33] Each person is a new predicate. The concrete, sensuous determination of the distinction between the divine and the human, then, lies in the distinction between the predicates of humanity as a whole which are projected and the individual person who as a single individual cannot possess all these varied attributes.

Feuerbach develops a response to what he perceives as a common theological defense against his projection theory of religion. Feuerbach claims that theologians themselves admit that the attributes of God are human projections, but attempt to escape his conclusion by denying that the subject of these predicates is projected.[34]   Both Thomas and Schleiermacher make such an argument. Thus Thomas' distinction between God's essence which is unknown and what can be predicated of God on the basis of his creation[35] functions to distinguish the reality of God from predicates which are, in a certain sense, "projected" analogies. Likewise, Schleiermacher claims that the attributes of God "denote not something special in God" but have to do with the feeling of absolute dependence.[36] According to Feuerbach, though, if one is to be concrete, if one wishes to talk about a real being, this separation between the predicates and their subject is impossible. "Only when God is thought of abstractly, when his predicates are the result of philosophic abstraction, arises the separation between subject and predicate . . . ."[37]   Furthermore, Feuerbach claims that no being can exist without attributes. "To deny all the qualities of a being is equivalent to denying the being himself."[38]   Therefore, the theology that does this is itself "a subtle, disguised atheism".[39] A God that has no attributes can mean nothing to human beings.

It is clear from this analysis that Feuerbach's critique presupposes and arises in the context of traditional theism — its method and its conception of God. As with theism, Feuerbach's critique has in view and is dependent upon the method of developing the conception of God by abstracting attributes from the world and predicating them of God.[40]

"Only from man does God derive all his determinations," Feuerbach declares.[41]

> Thou believest in love as a divine attribute because thou thyself lovest, thou believest God is a wise benevolent being because thou knowest nothing better in thyself than benevolence and wisdom.[42]

As with theism, predicates of human beings are predicated of God in their perfect, absolute degree. This perfection of God's attributes is achieved through a *via negativa*, again as we saw operative in traditional theism.[43]

Following this method, Feuerbach arrives at a doctrine of God that we have already seen is typical of traditional theism. On the one hand, this God is seen as the end and goal of humanity. Echoing theism from Thomas through Schleiermacher (and beyond), Feuerbach declares, "God is what man would like to be."[44] Humankind's highest wishes, its noblest goals, its greatest loves — which individual humans do not yet possess — have been attributed to and are therefore found in God. On the other hand this conception of God as absolute perfection results in a definition that is the antithesis to humanity. The more the perfection of the human attributes are abstracted and projected outward, "the greater is the apparent difference between God and man."[45] This is so because through the *via negativa* what is given to God is denied to humans. God is impassible, humans suffer; God is omnipotent, humans do not have the power to change themselves or the world. So, according to Feuerbach, the more perfect God becomes, the more base humanity is: "Man is wicked, corrupt, incapable of good; but on the other hand, God is only good — the Good Being."[46]

In view of the fact that Feuerbach in his critique remains within the context of traditional theism, certain questions arise. Is Hans Küng entirely correct when he claims that Feuerbach propounded "an atheism that cannot in any way be subsequently theologically reinterpreted and appropriated"?[47] It is certainly true that Feuerbach did not "atheistically believe in God" and that his "consistent atheism represents a permanent challenge to any belief in God."[48] Nevertheless, inasmuch as Feuerbach is tied to traditional theism, might not there be options other than Feuerbach's for continued theological speech? Is it not possible, on the one hand, to "appropriate" Feuerbach's critique, that is, to accept his conclusions over against any theology that speaks of God in a traditional, theistic manner, and yet, on the other hand, still find a basis for theology that would call into question the appropriateness of Feuerbach's conclusions? Is it possible for theology to meet Feuerbach's epistemological criteria without becoming anthropology? That is, can theology have a concrete object other than collective humanity which remains subject of our knowledge of it, so that it is not a human projection but controls our thinking about it? If this can be accomplished, it would constitute an answer to Feuerbach that accepts his critique and yet moves beyond the conclusion offered by him. The doctrine of the Trinity as formulated by Karl Barth proposes affirmative answers to these questions. If these answers are cogent then the trinitarian formulation can be used as the basis of Christian apologetics in the face of Feuerbach's epistemological critique of theology.

Barth's Relationship to Feuerbach

From early in his career Barth took Feuerbach seriously. While he did not wish to give Feuerbach the final word, Barth nevertheless agreed with Feuerbach over against the theological tradition. "Theology has long since become anthropology,"[49] Barth quotes Feuerbach favorably. In his 1920 essay on Feuerbach, which became the introductory essay to the reissue of the English translation of Feuerbach's book *The Essence of Christiantity*, Barth emphasizes the importance of Feuerbach and urges theologians to study him.[50] Barth asks,

> . . . are we capable of admitting to Feuerbach that he is
> entirely right in his interpretation of religion in so far as it
> relates not only to religion as an experience of evil and
> mortal man, but also to the "high," the "ponderable," and
> even the "Christian" religion of this man?[51]

> Whoever is concerned with the spirit, the heart, and con-
> science and the inwardness of man must be confronted with
> the question of whether he is really concerned with God and
> not the apotheosis of man.[52]

Nevertheless, the usual position of commentators on Barth is that his response to Feuerbach was either a failure or non-existent. For instance, in their book *Philosophers Speak of God*, Charles Hartshorne and William Reese view Barth's reply to Feuerbach as a failed "measure of desperation."[53]   And Edward Sawyer sees in Barth's response a "retreat to the circle of faith" which forgoes "combat in the arena of argumentation."[54] John Glasse in his article "Barth on Feuerbach" goes some distance in refuting these critics in stressing that Barth carried on an extended dialogue with Feuerbach and did reply to him in a way that was at least partially successful.[55] While he correctly indicates that the central issue that Barth sees between Feuerbach and theology is always

the question of theological method, Glasse discovers in Barth two
different responses — the first a failure, the second more successful.[56]
According to his interpretation, Barth formulates an early response to
Feuerbach in the nineteen-twenties. This answer remains the major one
until the nineteen-fifties when Barth addresses Feuerbach in a new
manner in *Church Dogmatics* IV/2 and 3. In the first response, Glasse
argues that Barth answers Feuerbach by an appeal to a general anthropology, available to everyone.[57] As Glasse correctly points out, Barth
responds by appealing to an anthropology which he believes is more
concrete and realistic than Feuerbach's. Feuerbach's anthropology
remains abstract. He was able to identify the human and the divine
because he failed to see death and evil as it occurs in the concrete solitary
human individual. Taking these elements of the essence of each human
being into account, it is ludicrous to identify the divine and the human.
Therefore, Barth believes that we should be able "to laugh in his
(Feuerbach's) face at this point."[58]

In contrast to this early response based on general anthropological
considerations is Barth's christological answer, which Glasse asserts was
not formulated until *Church Dogmatics* IV/2 and 3. Here Barth gives up
any answer based on a general anthropology and now grounds his answer
in the "character of God himself."[59] To the question of how Jesus Christ
reveals God, Barth speaks of "'the manifest radiance' of the assertion
that Jesus Christ reveals . . . ." Glasse explains,

> . . . Barth proceeds by exhibiting respects in which the life
> of Jesus Christ is "the manifest declaration of God." For
> example, the meaning of the assertion itself holds that the
> acting Subject of the life of Jesus Christ is the God who is
> eloquent and radiant *in himself.* He is Son, as well as
> Father, that is to say what the Triune God is in his own life,
> he is also *in his revelation to us.* Again, this God who acts in
> Jesus Christ is gracious in himself, and such grace inherently
> involves disclosure, self-impartation, revelation. On the
> basis of this gracious radiance of his own, then, he manifests
> himself to us.[60]

According to Glasse it is evident that Barth is now answering
Feuerbach on the basis of the sovereignty and subjectivity of the God
who reveals himself. Therefore, as Glasse points out correctly, Barth
maintains that Feuerbach's question cannot arise for Christians. For to
ask if God revealed in Christ is only our projection or is really the truth is
to attempt to establish its truth on the basis of something else, something
external to the revelation of God. We could answer it only on the basis

of human criteria and competence. God's sovereignty and subjectivity would be destroyed and Feuerbach's conclusion would be inevitable.[61] Therefore, Feuerbach's question evaporates and is replaced by the real question. This question is not asked by us, but addressed to us. "On the contrary, when we confess Him, He Himself is the One who asks."[62]

Glasse is correct in pointing out that in his early essay Barth does develop an answer based on a general anthropology.[63] In this answer there has been no real shift in theological method. Barth remains tied to doing theology on an anthropological basis. Moreover, Glasse has made a contribution by indicating that Barth does make another, and this time, cogent response to Feuerbach and that this response has to do with the character of God. Nevertheless, several severe problems remain with Glasse's analysis.

First, in no case can Barth's essay from the nineteen-twenties be considered his definitive response to Feuerbach. This was written while Barth was still attempting to rethink theological methodology, which, again according to Glasse, is the main issue between Barth and Feuerbach. But even in this early essay, the anthropologically based response is not the only one. Barth also asserts strongly that a new theological method is necessary.

> In order to construct an adequate defense against Feuerbach, one would have to be sure that along the whole line the relation to God is one that is in principle uninvertible: . . . . so long as the relation to God is not unconditionally inconvertible for us, and does not remain so under all circumstances we shall have no rest in this matter.[64]

It is this methodological shift, articulated early on, that is the center of Barth's central response and that is at issue in the discussion in *Church Dogmatics* IV/3, First Half. These sentences from 1920 anticipate the latter discussion.

The second and major problem in Glasse's analysis, though, is his claim that it was not until the nineteen-fifties and *Church Dogmatics* IV/3, First Half, that Barth explicitly gave his basis for his most important theological response to Feuerbach. Glasse claims against Barth,

> For over four decades his discussions of Feuerbach failed to state clearly his grounds for supposing that his talk of God was anything other than illusory projection. Finally, by adapting Anselm's argument to the case of Feuerbach in 1959, Barth rid himself of this central omission.[65]

Glasse claims that until that time Barth had based his whole polemic
against Feuerbach on the earlier anthropologically based critique.

This position is simply untenable for several reasons. First, we
should mention Barth's christologically based discussion on Christian
anthropology found in *Church Dogmatics* III/1 and III/2. It is evident
here that Barth already has given up any general anthropological considerations in discussion with Feuerbach or in any of his theological
anthropology. His thinking is based on revelation, the Word of God.[66]
He is secure enough in his position that he no longer opposes
Feuerbach's anthropology by appealing to a "solitary individual"
human. Rather, his own position leads him to give up talk of the real
human as a "solitary individual" and to agree with Feuerbach that the
real mark of humanity is the I-Thou relationship,[67] terminology which
was first developed by Feuerbach. Surprisingly, both Feuerbach and
Barth tie the human I-Thou relationship to the doctrine of the Trinity.
For Feuerbach the trinitarian formulation is the projection of the I-Thou
relationship which constitutes true humanity. "Participated life is alone
true, . . . this simple thought, this truth, natural, immanent in man, is
the secret, the supernatural mystery of the Trinity." "God the Father is
I, God the Son, Thou."[68] For Barth, the relationship between the
Trinity and the human I-Thou relationship flows in the opposite direction. For Barth the *imago dei* in humanity is its creation in the I-Thou
relationship. That is, humanity's constitution in an I-Thou relationship
is a repetition of the trinitarian encounter in God's own being.

> Man is the repetition of this divine form of life; its copy and
> reflection . . . . The analogy between God and man, is
> simply the existence of the I and the Thou in confrontation.
> This is first constitutive for God, and then for man created
> by God.[69]

Again, opposed to the claims of Glasse, already in these volumes of the
Church Dogmatics from the nineteen-forties, Barth has given up the
earlier method of response to Feuerbach and has also already developed
his christological basis for discussion with him. Because he is certain that
in light of his theological method, even at this time he "need fear no
Feuerbach,"[70] Barth is not concerned about the similarities between his
and Feuerbach's anthropology. He, in fact, can speak approvingly of
Feuerbach (along with Confucius and Buber) for seeing that true
humanity is found in the I-Thou relationship.[71]

But this discussion of the basis for Barth's theological anthropology
is merely indicative of what Glasse has not seen about Barth's relationship to Feuerbach that is apparent right from the beginning of the

Church Dogmatics. The christologically based response, which Glasse sees emerging only in *Church Dogmatics* IV/3, First Half, is based on, and indeed is already in place in, the prolegomena, *Church Dogmatics* I/ 1. Perhaps because in his discussion of Feuerbach's critique he never analyzes its epistemological ground — even though he uses trinitarian language in explicating Barth's response — Glasse fails to realize that Barth's whole discussion of the doctrine of the Trinity and, indeed, its very location at the beginning of his theology is constitutive of his answer to the question of whether the God about which theology speaks is merely a human projection. In Barth's theology the doctrine of the Trinity answers the epistemological demand for a sensuous object and on this basis also comprehends the subjectivity of God. It is, therefore, the fulfillment of Barth's statement in his article of 1920, quoted above, that for an "adequate defense" the "relation to God" must be "uninvertible". Glasse did not see this connection and therefore failed to realize that the doctrine of the Trinity is essential for understanding Barth's relationship to Feuerbach. We will see that time and again Barth relates the doctrine of the Trinity to discussions of Feuerbach's critique and indicates how trinitarian thinking might respond to it. If this is the case, then Barth's *Church Dogmatics* in its entirety is grounded epistemologically in a way that responds to Feuerbach.

The Basis of the Apologetic:
Revelation, the Trinity and Sensuous Epistemology

If an adequate response to Feuerbach is to be developed, one must come to terms with Feuerbach's epistemological demand that knowledge be grounded on a concrete, sensuous object, which, as such, remains subject over human thinking about it. For Barth the doctrine of the Trinity has to do with the epistemological problem of the knowledge of God.[72] The discussion of the location of and the method of developing the doctrine of the Trinity involves the Feuerbachian issue, "the question as to the meaning and possibility of theology as distinct from a mere cosmology or anthropology."[73] We will see in this section that the doctrine of the Trinity as formulated by Barth is based on the claim that God reveals himself in Jesus and thereby is known in a sensuous, concrete object. In the next section we will see how trinitarian thinking, therefore, preserves the subjecthood of theology's object of knowledge. It is in this way that trinitarian thinking is to be understood as a response to Feuerbach.

For Barth the question of the formulation of the doctrine of the Trinity is one with the question of the correct understanding of revelation. Barth had seen already in his teachers one option for understanding God's subjectivity and concreteness in his revelation. Wilhelm Herrmann, for instance, placed great emphasis upon the self-revelation of God.[74] "We cannot know God otherwise than that he reveals himself to us ourselves by acting upon us."[75] Here Herrmann is attempting to safeguard God's subjectivity in revelation. God is never experienced in objectifiable terms, nor is God an object of our cognition. Rather, theological statements are grounded in human subjective religious experience, where God has revealed himself. Thus, Herrmann wants to develop a dynamic conception of revelation based on "God's free action upon us,"[76] which also guards theology from abstract thinking. According to his position, theology would have a concrete basis from which to speak — God's action on the human self. But it becomes clear that in God's self-revelation Herrmann is mainly concerned with the human self, which is the locus of revelation. The way in which this theology becomes anthropology and moves directly into Feuerbach's critique is not difficult to see. Herrmann has fulfilled Feuerbach's epistemological call for a sensuous basis to thinking; but the human self is that basis. Therefore, the subjectivity of God is dissolved into the human subjective experience and theology becomes anthropology. We should perhaps note the role and position of the doctrine of the Trinity in Herrmann's theology. Herrmann concluded that his doctrine of revelation must lead to the doctrine of the Trinity, although it does not arise from religious experience. It is, rather, a "reflection on faith" belonging near the end of dogmatics.[77]

To reformulate theology so that it meets Feuerbach's demands and yet has a basis other than anthropology from which to speak about God requires, Barth discovers, a transformation of the conception of revelation and consequently of theological method. If theology is to be "so practiced as not to be subject to that [Feuerbach's] base suspicion,"[78] it must not speak of God as does traditional theism, by developing a conception of God which is abstracted from the world or human self-consciousness and therefore reveals only the world or humanity. Barth says,

> If we really dare to go back to the sphere of what God is in Himself, it must have nothing whatever to do with the absolutizing of human nature and being. Indeed, it must not be that we try arbitrarily to withdraw from our own sphere — and therefore from the sphere in which we have to do only with ourselves — as if it lay in our discernment and power to set up or even to choose another.[79]

Therefore Barth reverses the interpretation of Herrmann's self-revelation of God. Against Herrmann, the "self" of the "self-revelation" of God is not to be taken anthropologically, but as designating the divine self. "It becomes obligatory to ask whether dogmatics does not have to begin where Herrmann ends."[80] The doctrine of God, his triune nature, is not to be drawn from a reflection on faith or religious experience. On the contrary, God is the very possibility of faith and religious experience. Barth exclaims, "A wholly different 'self' has stepped into the scene with *his* own validity. An *a priori* of the so-called religion becomes visible above all that has been or can be experienced, above all circles and correlations."[81] This divine self, Barth is asserting, is a subject, and even in revelation maintains its subjectivity in its relation with the world and, therefore, cannot be confused with it.

Early on Barth believed that this divine self was brought to speech in the doctrine of the Trinity. It is the triune God who is "eternally Subject and never object," who "determines himself and is knowable exclusively through himself in 'pure act' (*actus purissimus*) of his triune personality."[82] Barth wrote to Eduard Thurneysen in 1924:

> A Trinity of being, not just an economic Trinity! At all costs the doctrine of the Trinity! If I could get the right key in my head there, then everything would come out right . . . .[83]

> I understand the Trinity as the problem of the inalienable subjectivity of God in his revelation and I cannot withhold my approval from Athanasius who in general must have been quite a man. The moderns are naturally sad brothers at this point, too! Sabellians and other undesirabilities.[84]

The doctrine of the Trinity, Barth believed, was the key that prevents any confusion of the world and humanity with God. As Eberhard Jüngel explains, the doctrine of the Trinity is Barth's hermeneutic investigation into how theology can legitimately speak of God without this speech being merely anthropology.[85]

This means that when the claim is made that trinitarian thinking can provide a response to these Feuerbachian issues, it is not just any method of developing the doctrine of the Trinity that is meant. The doctrine of the Trinity, like any other doctrine, can be developed improperly. It can be formulated on the basis of abstraction and speculation and therefore be subject to Feuerbach's critique. Several methods of developing the trinitarian doctrine are then to be rejected. Barth rejects, for instance, the quest for and theologizing from the so called *vestigia trinitatis*,[86] through which theologians argue for God's triune nature on the basis of tripartite divisions of aspects of creation. Barth concedes that it was not originally the intention of the theologians employing the *vestigia* to speak speculatively or anthropologically about God. Rather, they were searching for "language" for "the mystery of God made known to them by revelation."[87] Nevertheless, inasmuch as it is admitted that there are *vestigia trinitatis* in the world — in nature, culture, history, religion, the human soul — apart from God's revelation in Christ and that these become an independent basis for talk about God and for developing the doctrine of the Trinity, then Feuerbach's reversal of theology to anthropology can be asserted.[88] Barth asks whether on the basis of the *vestigia trinitatis* finally "the doctrine of the Trinity" might not have to be "adjudged to be the bold attempt of man's understanding of the world and, in the last resort, of self . . . ."[89]

For this same reason Barth rejects also the theological tradition (including Protestant orthodoxy) that deduces "the doctrine of the Trinity . . . from the premises of formal logic."[90] These theologies begin elsewhere than with the doctrine of the Trinity, speak of it speculatively and lead to Feuerbach.

As opposed to this, the necessary shift in method that is required is for theology to speak about God only on the basis of God's concrete revelation in Jesus of Nazareth. We will see that for Barth it is this that gives rise to the correct understanding of the doctrine of the Trinity. Barth believes that in this way he can maintain the concreteness and subjectivity of God in his revelation so that theology and anthropology do not become confused.

Barth, like Herrmann, bases his theology on the revelation of God.[91] "Revelation is *Dei loquentis persona.*"[92] But this revelation, this word of God, is not found in nature or human self-consciousness, feeling or any subjective human experience. Rather, it is found in a particular concrete historical event, namely the history of Jesus of Nazareth. As soon as one begins to analyze God's revelation, however, questions arise which lead inevitably to the doctrine of the Trinity. "Revelation" is "the root of the doctrine of the Trinity."[93] The question about the self-revealing God is inseparable from the question of how the revelation takes place and from the question of the result of this revelation, "the effect of this event upon the man whom it befalls."[94] The answer to these interconnected and inseparable questions is:

> God reveals Himself. He reveals Himself through Himself.
> If we wish really to regard revelation from the side of its subject, God, then above all we must understand that this subject, God, the Revealer, is identical with His act in revelation, identical with its effect.[95]

This brief statement demonstrates how the doctrine of the Trinity arises from an analysis of revelation.[96] Conversely, the doctrine of the Trinity is an analytic statement that provides the conceptual clarification for understanding revelation. It is God who reveals Himself. And when He reveals Himself He reveals nothing but Himself. And it is God who makes this revelation real in human life. The God who reveals Himself in the event of Jesus is God in the "threefold mode of being" as "Revealer, Revelation and Revealedness."[97] God is triune.

It should be clear that the claim that the doctrine of the Trinity functions apologetically does not mean that it is only developed for apologetic reasons, that it becomes central only because it responds to challenges to faith. Rather, for Barth a theology that is based on a proper understanding of revelation and therefore grounds itself in the concrete event of Jesus Christ is led, when analyzing that revelation, to the doctrine of the Trinity. It is, on the other hand, precisely because the doctrine of the Trinity clarifies and names the God who reveals himself in Jesus that it may have an apologetic function. As we will see in the case of Feuerbach, the doctrine of the Trinity properly identifies the God who is misidentified by him.

Since the doctrine of the Trinity names the God who reveals himself and reveals nothing but himself, it will follow that God is who he is in his act of revelation. God is not only himself but also his self-revelation.[98] The doctrine of the Trinity means that revelation is identical with God himself,[99] that it is a "repetition of God,"[100] "God a second time."[101] But this revelation is not found in nature or human self-consciousness. It has nothing to do with "an abstract metaphysic of God, the world or religion, claiming to hold good always and everywhere."[102] Rather this revelation is a concrete event, the concrete history of the life, death and resurrection of Jesus of Nazareth, recorded in "the tiny sheaf of news" of the New Testament.[103] At this concrete point God is known by human beings in a sensuous way. As Barth asserts,

> . . . He makes himself present, known, and significant to
> them as God. In the historical life of men He moves into a
> place and a very definite place at that and makes Himself
> the object of human contemplation, human experience,
> human thought, human speech. He makes Himself an
> authority and an agent, and a concrete authority, an histori-
> cal agent at that . . . . He exists as God for them exactly as
> quite other things or persons exist for them . . . and con-
> cretely exists in definite form.[104]

Therefore, fulfilling Feuerbach's demands, we have a sensuous foundation for knowledge of and speech about God that is neither anthropology nor cosmology. For Barth the doctrine of the Trinity always refers to the God who is known concretely and sensuously in Jesus. As a consequence the doctrine of the Trinity is weighted toward the center — the person of God the Son.[105]

In the trinitarian context, therefore, God's revelation is concrete in every aspect and in a way that cannot be circumvented. Barth makes this clear at several points. In terms of the appearance of the revelation itself there can be no understanding of its meaning abstracted from its form; its content cannot be distinguished from the manner in which it is given.[106] Since it is the man Jesus who is God's revelation, the "what" of this revelation cannot be separate from the "how" of its appearance. Rather, the form is constituent of the content, the how is constitutive of the what. Barth declares, ". . . the event of revelation as described for us in Scripture has everywhere a natural, bodily, outward and visible component . . . ."[107]

> That this revelation happens, and in a particular way, is not an accident, in view of the fact that it is the revelation of this God that is involved. It is also and precisely in the That and the How of this revelation that He shows Himself as this God.[108]

> The distinction between form and content cannot be applied to the biblical concept of revelation. Hence, where according to the Bible revelation is an event, there is no second inquiry as to what its content might be.[109]

God's revelation in Jesus, therefore, includes not only that he appeared as a human, nor only the content of the message that he spoke, but also the whole form of life and practice that Jesus concretely lived. To understand it otherwise, to separate the content of revelation from the form of its occurrence, would again destroy revelation's sensuous basis and render it an idealistic abstraction.

The concreteness of the revelation of the triune God, furthermore, does not only include both the revelation's form and content, it means also that God's whole being is given concretely in revelation. Because the doctrine of the Trinity is the reflection on the God who is who he is in his act of revelation,[110] the doctrine of the Trinity also indicates that the triune God can never be thought of apart from that concrete event of revelation. This means that God is not some abstract being lying beyond or behind this concrete event of Jesus. There is not some other reality behind or beyond this revelation to which one can appeal, because this event is God Himself happening among humankind. Modalism is rejected, for there is no fourth person acting beyond the triune God. Barth states it:

> The reality of God in his revelation cannot be bracketed by an "only", as though somewhere behind His revelation there stood another reality of God . . . .[111]

Barth expresses this same point in the language of essence and act. Again we are in the context of the doctrine of the Trinity that brings to speech the God who is identical with his act of revelation, who is what he does.[112] This means, Barth says, that "God's essence and His operation are not twain but one."[113] For this reason, there can be no inquiry into the essence of God apart from his act. Indeed, Barth says, "Essence follows act."[114] God's essence is constituted by his action and is therefore only known through his concrete action.

Because the doctrine of the Trinity comprehends the God who gives himself fully in the sensuous event of Jesus and is who he is only in that concrete action, it keeps theology down to earth and concrete in its thinking, and yet in such a way as not to be based on general humanity, human self-consciousness or nature. And because the triune God has given himself sensuously in Jesus, "we have no need to project anything into eternity, for at this point eternity is time, i.e., the eternal name has become a temporal name and the divine name a human."[115]

However, the relationship of the doctrine of the Trinity to concrete theology must be extended further. For Barth it is not enough to say that God gives himself fully in his revelation, although this is certainly true. Rather, if we are to comprehend how this can be and if God is not to be ultimately an abstraction, God must be conceived as concrete in his own being. This contention is developed by Jüngel when he says,

> If the concreteness of God's self-communication to man is to be thoroughly comprehended, then the self-relatedness of God's being in the differentiation of the three modes of being must likewise be comprehended as fellowship in which the being of God takes place concretely.[116]

This claim is important because it expresses the ontological foundation of the concreteness of God in his revelation. If God is so concretely given in his revelation that he can be known on no other basis, then God must be conceived as concrete in his own being, as including in his being no abstract reality that does not express itself in his concrete act of revelation. Turning to a discussion of God's inner being does not mean that theological language suddenly becomes abstract and lacking a sensuous ground. Barth always moves from God's concrete act in revelation to God's being in itself, from the economic to the immanent Trinity.[117] Therefore, the concreteness of the triune God is ascertained from the fact that God himself is what he is in his revelation. Because God is concrete in his revelation, he is so in himself. Conversely, because what God is in himself is the ontological foundation for what he is in his revelation, God must be concrete in himself if his revelation is to be concrete. The question of the concreteness of the being of God is answered in Barth's theology by the doctrine of *perichoresis*.[118]

The doctrine of *perichoresis* guarantees the concrete unity of the three persons of the Trinity in their relationships with one another. In revelation the distinctions in God as Revealer, Revelation and Revealedness are made clear concretely. But it is precisely at this point that the concrete unity of the three modes of existence is comprehended, for in this revelation not just the Second Person but also the First and Third Persons of the Trinity are at work: *Opera trinitatis ad extra sunt indivisa.*[119] The entire Trinity in all three modes of being is involved in any external act of God. It is, after all, these three modes of being in their relationship to one another that are God.[120] This means that there is always a *perichoresis*, "a passing into one another," of the divine persons,[121] "a complete participation of each mode of being in the other modes of being."[122] So no person of the Trinity is an abstraction, existing in abstraction from the other two. Rather they are each known only in their concrete relationship with one another. " . . . none of the three is knowable without the other Two, but each of the Three only with the other Two."[123] "None would be what it is — not even the Father! — apart from its co-existence with the others."[124] The concrete basis of this claim is God's revelation in Jesus. We perceive the Son, but always as being the revelation of the Father and only through the work of the Spirit towards us. The Father cannot be known abstractly but is always the Father of the Son who, in turn, is the concrete Jesus of Nazareth. The Son, however, cannot be known apart from the one he called Father. Likewise, the Spirit is always only the Spirit of the Father and the Son, without which they are not known. At no point, then, is God's being abstract, but is, rather, entirely concrete. It is constituted concretely by the relationship among the three modes of its being. This is comprehended because the three modes of being that are God's essence are revealed only in concrete relationship with one another.

The first and most important aspect of a trinitarian based response to Feuerbach has thus been developed. The doctrine of the Trinity as formulated by Barth shows that theology can agree with Feuerbach's epistemological position that thinking be sensuous if it is to be true. The doctrine of the Trinity is the interpretation of the God who is a concrete, sensuous object in Jesus and is known only on that basis. It has nothing to do with the abstract God, conceived on the basis of human self-consciousness or the world, who is in reality only an anthropology or cosmology. However, like the traditional theism of his day, Feuerbach knew only this method of conceiving God and therefore saw only this abstract God who, from the trinitarian position which is always concrete, he was correct to criticize as a projection. On the one hand, therefore, the doctrine of the Trinity enables the positive responses of accepting both his epistemology and, on this basis, his rejection of the abstract God. However, in addition to this yes there is also a no to Feuerbach. For again, like the theologians of his day, he was unable to see the triune God who is known as a sensuous object. Therefore, the doctrine of the Trinity makes it possible to claim that Feuerbach's critique was founded on a misidentification of God, and thus to question the validity of its conclusion over against the God who is triune.

The Subjectivity of the Triune God

We have not yet given a full response to Feuerbach. For in order for thinking to be truthful, Feuerbach insisted not only on a sensuous object of knowledge, but also that the object remain a subject determining human thinking about it and negating all abstract, speculative thinking which attempts to control it. We have seen that the doctrine of the Trinity as developed by Barth interprets the God who is known con-cretely as a sensuous object. But this doctrine of the Trinity also reflects the God who is and remains subject over all human knowledge of him. We will now examine how this is developed in Barth's theology and, therefore, how the doctrine of the Trinity responds to Feuerbach at this point as well.

According to Barth, the doctrine of the Trinity has to do with the fact that "God reveals Himself as Lord."[125] This is so because there is no point in the process of revelation in which God is not subject. He is both the Revealer and the Revelation. This claim is related to the triune God's concreteness in revelation. Since the doctrine of the Trinity names the God who becomes a concrete object in Jesus and in such a way that God is not another reality beyond this revelation, and since this means that this God is not known apart from his concrete revelation but only there and in that form, the triune God is therefore subject and sovereign over any knowledge of him. Thinking about the triune God must be deter-mined, not by human ideas and desires, but only by God's concrete appearance. The doctrine of the Trinity speaks of the God who is subject in human knowledge of him, because, in being fully concrete, his revelation is grounded solely in itself. It has, as Barth says, "its reality and truth wholly and in every respect — i.e. ontically and noetically — within itself."[126] All conceptions of God, therefore, that are abstracted from human self-consciousness, the world or any point other than God's concrete revelation, represent attempts to control God and deny his subjectivity.

The doctrine of the Trinity declares that the subjectivity of God does not end with the revelation event however. The triune God is "the Subject of revelation" and always "remains indissolubly Subject."[127] "God reveals himself as Lord" means that his subjectivity extends also over the impact of this revelation on human beings. God is Revealer, Revelation and *Revealedness*, Father, Son and *Holy Spirit*. Jüngel says, in interpreting Barth, that the doctrine of the Trinity speaks of the God who is "the subject, predicate and object of the revelation-event."[128] The doctrine of the Trinity therefore interprets the God who not only reveals himself concretely but makes that revelation concrete and real in the lives of human beings, "a concrete revelation to concrete men."[129] This God "is not only Himself but also what He creates and achieves in men."[130] Even in the "subjective side in the event of revelation," where humans come to know the truth of God's revelation and experience it in their own lives, it is God who is subject.[131]

The God of the doctrine of the Trinity, then, has nothing to do with an abstraction from human self-consciousness or experience. At no point are knowledge and speech about God autonomous human possibilities. Barth writes, "God reveals Himself as the Spirit, not as any spirit, not as the discoverable and arousable subsoil of man's spiritual life, but as the Spirit of the Father and the Son . . . ."[132] The doctrine of the Trinity, says Jüngel, means that there is no human "synergism" in the attainment of the knowledge of God.[133] Rather, knowledge and speech about God are possible only on the basis of God's action, which is God Himself distinguishing Himself from Himself, making His revelation real for human beings. This trinitarian thinking prevents theology from becoming a human projection. It also offers the basis for joining Feuerbach in claiming that theologies that proceed otherwise, from nature or self-consciousness, end as anthropology or physiology. Traditional theistic theologies violate the principle of God's subjectivity over all knowledge of him and therefore are subject to critique by Feuerbach (as they are also critiqued by trinitarian thinking). It is therefore no accident that these theistic theologies subordinate or eliminate trinitarian conceptions.

The subjectivity of God is developed further by Barth in several additional ways. The triune God remains subject in his freedom to determine his own being. "Revelation in the Bible means the self-unveiling, imparted to men, of the God who according to His nature cannot be unveiled to men."[134] Again, this means that God cannot be known by humans on the basis of some general revelation. Rather in revealing himself, in becoming a concrete object of knowledge, "God does what man himself cannot do in any sense or in any way."[135] On the basis of this concrete revelation, therefore, we know that God remains subject in that he determines his own being. God's self-unveiling depends upon his own being as the triune God, upon his eternal decision to distinguish himself from himself.

> He who reveals Himself here as God is able to reveal Himself; already the fact of His revelation declares that it is His property to distinguish Himself from Himself, i.e. in Himself and hiddenly to be God and yet at the same time in quite another way, namely, manifestly, i.e. in the form of something He Himself is not, to be God a second time.[136]

Because God determines his own being, is subject, no *a priori* presuppositions about divinity hold. No abstractions from the world or human experience account for knowledge here. For it cannot be decided before-hand, before God's sovereign revelation, what God can or cannot do and be. God can and does determine himself to become something quite different from himself. He has the freedom to "become so unlike Himself that He is God in such a way as not to be bound by his secret eternity and eternal secrecy . . . ."[137]

This leads to a further statement of God's subjectivity. For as God is subject in the free determination of his being, he is also subject in that it is always his free choice to reveal himself. God is not bound by either external or internal necessity to reveal himself. "God gives Himself to man entirely in His revelation. But not in such a way as to give Himself a prisoner to man. He remains free, in operating, in giving Himself."[138] "God's presence is always God's decision to be present . . . , God's self-unveiling remains the act of sovereign divine freedom."[139]

This freedom from any necessity to reveal himself is conceptualized most clearly in the relationship of the economic to the immanent Trinity. We have already seen that, following his sensuous epistemology, Barth always moves from God's concrete act in revelation to God's being in itself, and, therefore, from the economic to the immanent Trinity.[140] But it is the latter that is ontologically prior to and the basis for the former.

> As and before God seeks and creates fellowship with us, He
> wills and completes fellowship in Himself. In Himself He
> does not will to exist for Himself, to exist alone. On the
> contrary, He is Father, Son, and Holy Spirit and therefore
> alive in His unique being with and for and in another.[141]

Before the Trinity is economic it is immanent. This distinction conceptualizes God's freedom and subjectivity in his relation to everything that is
not God and brings it to its highest point. It means that God does not
need the world or humanity to be who he is. Before he creates fellowship
with us, he is already who he is; he is already in fellowship in the concrete
relation of the three modes of his being. His fellowship with humanity is
based on who God is already in himself in this fellowship between
Father, Son, and Spirit.[142] Even to say "God is Love" does not necessarily require human beings to be the object of God's love.

> It is not part of God's being and action that as love it must
> have an object in another who is different from Him. God is
> sufficient in Himself as object and therefore as object of His
> love. He is no less the one who loves if He loves no object
> different from Himself.[143]

Barth's point in the discussion from which this quotation is taken is
that God is the one who loves us, but "in freedom."[144] God is sufficient
in himself, needing neither the world nor human beings to be what he is.
This does not imply that God is closed in upon himself, but rather
asserts that His relationship to the world or human beings is one of pure
subjectivity and therefore pure freedom. It also means, therefore, that
God remains distinct from the world and humanity and cannot be
grasped or made an object of human contemplation or be conceived as a
mere projection. In the triune God's relation to us no reversal is possible.

In summary, we have demonstrated that the doctrine of the Trinity, as developed by Barth, serves always to maintain God's subjectivity.
It is the way of speaking of God, proper to God's concrete revelation,
that prevents us from assuming that God could become an object of
human speculation. Jüngel has compared the function given by Barth to
the doctrine of the Trinity with Bultmann's program of demythologiz-
ing. Without evaluating how Bultmann succeeds, it can be said that
both he and Barth seek a way to bring God to speech without objectify-
ing God as an it or a He. The "significance of the doctrine of the Trinity
consists for Barth," Jüngel writes, "in the fact . . . that God becomes
'not it or He'; 'he remains a Thou.'"[145] Because God is who he is
immanently before he is who he is for us, he remains a Thou, always

subject, his own origin. "As Father, Son and Spirit God is, so to speak, ours in advance."[146]

For Barth, then, the doctrine of the Trinity is here again capable of responding to Feuerbach. Feuerbach claims that an object must remain subject if the object is to be other than an anthropological projection. The doctrine of the Trinity comprehends the God who is always subject in revelation, in the achievement of revelation in human beings, in the decision to reveal himself, in the determination of his very being, in himself as immanently triune. Thus this trinitarian conception finds itself in agreement with Feuerbach. And this means that traditional theism, based on *a priori* assumptions about God drawn from the world or self-consciousness, must be criticized for not allowing God to remain subject. Its doctrine of God is in danger of being only a human projection and, therefore, open to a Feuerbachian interpretation. However, Feuerbach must be criticized too, because the trinitarian apologetic goes beyond him. For in comprehending the subjectivity of God, the doctrine of the Trinity fulfills Feuerbach's epistemological demands and prevents the being of God from "being understood as a human construction."[147] Feuerbach never saw the God who is subject. Like his theological antagonists, the only doctrine of God he had in view was the abstract God of traditional theism who could not remain subject. In negating this God as an objective reality Feuerbach believed that his critique concluded the issue. However, in accepting Feuerbach's epistemological concerns Barth's trinitarian theology has moved beyond Feuerbach's critique.

The Trinitarian Appropriation
of Feuerbach's Critique of Theology

Barth's controversy with both the theology of the nineteenth century and Thomistic theology is well known.[148] This controversy is signified by the location of the doctrine of the Trinity.[149] While Schleiermacher places the doctrine at the end of the *Christian Faith*, outside of his theology proper as an appendix, and while Thomistic theology locates it only after the articles on the One God, Barth, unlike the theistic tradition, begins with the doctrine of the Trinity, claiming that it is the controlling doctrine of his whole system.[150] Barth effects this reversal because, for him, the eclipse of the trinitarian doctrine in the theological tradition signifies what is wrong with these theologies. Dealing with the Trinity as these theologies do is indicative of an improper theological method and, therefore, an incorrect theology — a theology whose object lacks the necessary sensuous basis. These systems are attempting to do theology "irrespective of the concrete givenness of what 'God' means for a Christian."[151] For this reason, the theistic theological tradition must be asked if it is really speaking about the "God" of the Christian church, or only projected humanity.[152] If theology begins elsewhere than with the doctrine of the Trinity, Barth claims, there is a

> very serious risk, in the case of the doctrine of the Holy Scriptures as well as in the doctrine of God, of getting lost in considerations and seeing oneself forced to conclusions totally irrelevant to the ostensibly concrete object of both doctrines, if one first discards His concreteness, as it is actually made plain in the trinitarian form of the Christian concept of God.[153]

The doctrine of the Trinity is the answer to the question of who God is. Therefore, if theology is to avoid the danger of saying things that do not apply to its object, it must first inquire into the God about which it is speaking. The doctrine of the Trinity, then, should stand at the beginning of theological thinking.

> And again, it is difficult to see how what is significant for this God should be made clear, if, as has been done repeatedly in old and new Catholic and Protestant dogmatics, we reserve the question to which the doctrine of the Trinity is the answer (namely, who God is) and deal first with his existence and His nature, as if this That and What could be determined otherwise than on the presupposition of the Who.[154]

Here Barth is making a fundamental point of theological epistemology over against these theologies. Apart from the "Who", the "That" and "What" cannot be determined. The "Who" is determinative for where and how God can be known. We have seen that the doctrine of the Trinity is tied to the Christian concept of revelation, God's word to human beings in Jesus of Nazareth. "The doctrine of the Trinity arises from an analysis of revelation."[155] Therefore, it delineates the Who of the Christian doctrine of God and also "marks off the Christian concept of revelation as Christian."[156] Again, therefore, according to Barth a dogmatics must begin with the doctrine of the Trinity, for if it does not it will speak about God from some point other than God's concrete revelation. The point at issue here is that Barth ties the eclipse of the doctrine of the Trinity in theology to the attempt to speak of God apart from his revelation and therefore abstractly. According to Barth, this method, whether looking to nature or human self-consciousness, led to theological disaster, to theism and ultimately to

Feuerbach. Although at first it may not be evident and although the theologians did not intend it, "the continuity of the way cannot be disputed."[157] Time and again Barth traces the consequences of this method in various theological traditions. Barth attacks Thomistic theology for not taking God's triune nature seriously enough. This allows this theology to speak of God's essence before his acts on the principle "*operari sequitur esse*" — that is, it speaks of God's essence prior to and apart from his revelation by abstracting from the world. Barth criticizes this method of abstraction and asks Feuerbach's question, "Is not the *Deus Dominus et Creator* of this doctrine the construct of human thinking?"[158]

Perhaps the best example of this process is found in Barth's discussion of the problem of the personality of God in modern theology. Barth writes,

> Its origin is to be found deep in the doctrine of God of the time of orthodoxy, and even of the Middle Ages. We have already mentioned the common practice in this doctrine of placing the doctrine of the Trinity after the development of a concept of the nature and attributes of God in general. This arrangement led to the temptation of speaking of God apart from His revelation and therefore apart from His being as the One who loves, on the basis of a free appraisal of what can be called divine. The result was an involuntary movement away from the school of Scripture into that of heathen antiquity. The nature of God was defined as a neuter furnished with every conceivable superlative, as the *ens perfectissiumum* and the *summum bonum*, which as such, as the *actus purus* of the spirit, is also the *primum movens*. And it was no easy matter to bring together the concept of the existence of this *Deus unus* and that of the biblical *Deus triunus*.[159]

This extended quote demonstrates clearly again what Barth sees as the methodological problem of much theology and how it is connected with the doctrine of the Trinity. Theologies that start elsewhere than with the doctrine of the Trinity are led to speak of God "apart from his revelation." According to Barth's analysis this type of theology ends as anthropology because its intended object is neither concrete nor subject. Humans decide by a "free appraisal" what words to speak about God. What God can or cannot be is decided on the basis of "speculative considerations."[160] The words spoken about God, perhaps based on a reading of the Christian self-consciousness or on the basis of a reasoned investigation of nature, end up as attributes abstracted from human existence which are taken to the superlative degree. According to Barth the eclipse of the doctrine of the Trinity in this way leads to what was described in Chapter I as traditional theism. For Barth, this theistic theological method means a reversal has taken place. Theology finds itself talking about human capacities, to be sure taken to the highest degree, but human capacities none the less.

The result of the method of this traditional theism is that theology opens itself up to the atheistic critique of Feuerbach. And we have seen that Barth is in total agreement with Feuerbach at this point. These theologies that attempt to speak of God apart from his revelation and therefore begin elsewhere than with the doctrine of the Trinity are anthropology. God-talk on this basis is merely the best ideals and wishes of humanity projected into eternity. In *Church Dogmatics* I/2, Barth says, "Yet we are bound to agree with L. Feuerbach in his objection to theology, that the essence of such thought and language consists practically in man creating God for himself after his own image."[161] In the same excursus on the problem of the personality of God mentioned above, Barth traces the problem through the nineteenth century, concluding that these theologies "had the fatal peculiarity that they exposed the distinctly postulary character of the whole modern doctrine of God in what is undoubtedly a very compromising way."[162] Barth then goes on to quote Feuerbach extensively and approvingly, demonstrating the indefensible position into which these theologians had strayed. He summarizes his analysis:

> We can see how here the mystery of the modern doctrine of God — that the being of God is the predicate of the human subject — was long ago carelessly exploded by a philosopher who derived from the school of idealism, but was no longer interested in the church.[163]

Then Barth wonders why these theologians had failed to listen to Feuerbach:

> We may well wonder that his objection did not make more impression on those who denied the personality of God in so far as he also and particularly attacked their positive assertions. But we must wonder even more how its defenders, with their references to the longing of the human heart, the infinite value of human personality, . . . with their quite open and express projection of human self-consciousness into the transcendent, could expose themselves so openly to this objection of Feuerbach without apparently taking any account of its existence.[164]

The solution to this problem could have been found if, instead of basing the discussions of the personality of God on "speculative considerations," the theologians would have worked "on the basis that God is actually present in His revelation."[165] This means that the doctrine of the Trinity should control thinking at this point. Barth ends this excursis by claiming that what personality is for God is understood only on the basis of the doctrine of the Trinity: "The important and true thing intended by the concept of personality . . . is, of course, connected not merely closely, but indissolubly, with the doctrine of the Trinity."[166] It is the triune God who is the personal God.

What is clear here is that Barth's critique of the theological tradition is based upon trinitarian thinking. He sees the doctrine of the Trinity as enabling him to appropriate Feuerbach's critique against other theologies, and yet still providing a basis for speaking of God.

Conclusion: The Apologetic Function of the Doctrine of the Trinity in Responding to Feuerbach's Epistemological Critique

This chapter has indicated the manner in which the doctrine of the Trinity as developed by Barth responds to Feuerbach's epistemological critique of theology and can therefore serve an apologetic function. This apologetic is not a "measure of desperation."[167] It does not mark a "retreat to the circle of faith" which foregoes "combat in the arena of argumentation,"[168] thereby failing to deal with Feuerbach's "arguments" for the "leading substantive propositions" that he asserts.[169] Neither is it the case, as Glasse has claimed, that for "over four decades his discussions of Feuerbach failed to state clearly his grounds for supposing that his talk of God was anything other than illusory projection," and, therefore, that Barth finally dealt with the issue only in the nineteen-fifties in *Church Dogmatics* IV/3.[170] All these charges can mean only that the critics have not understood the function of the doctrine of the Trinity in Barth's theology. Barth's response to Feuerbach is not different from his revolution in theological method, signified by the formulation and position of the doctrine of the Trinity in the *Church Dogmatics*. The theological necessity for the doctrine of the Trinity does not exclude but enables its apologetic function.

One reason critics miss this apologetic function is that according to Barth the doctrine of the Trinity arises from founding theology solely in God's revelation in Jesus of Nazareth and thus arises from a standpoint within the circle of faith. This constitutes a methodological reversal of traditional theism and its strategy of apologetically arguing for the acceptability of belief on some generally available basis before entering the circle of faith. In rejecting this strategy it appears that Barth has withdrawn from debate with Feuerbach and others to an esoteric analysis of the Christian conception of revelation and God. The doctrine of the Trinity, after all, attempts to be the "interpretation of revelation." And because revelation itself is God's self-interpretation, the doctrine of the Trinity is, therefore, also an interpretation of God's being. As Barth says, "From the doctrine of the Trinity we actually gather who the God is who reveals Himself . . . ."[171] We have seen it is for this reason that Barth insists that a dogmatics must begin with this doctrine. Since the God who reveals Himself is identical with His revelation and His revealed-ness, it is necessary to speak of God in a threefold way. The one God is "the Revealer, the Revelation and the Revealedness" or "the revealing God, the event of revelation and its effects on man"[172] or the Father, the Son, and the Holy Spirit. The doctrine of the Trinity holds together the conception of this one God in God's "three modes of being."

But Barth's methodological shift and his consequent emphasis on the doctrine of the Trinity do not constitute a retreat or a refusal to confront Feuerbach's arguments. On the contrary, they constitute the basis of Barth's response to Feuerbach. Allowing the doctrine of the Trinity to govern theology shows that Barth's *Church Dogmatics*, from the beginning (1932), includes a response to Feuerbach. For his trinitarian based theology attempts to demonstrate why theology cannot be anthropology or physiology. As Jüngel says, "It protects the Christian doctrine of God from becoming mythological or slipping into metaphysics." The doctrine of the Trinity serves "the critical-polemical function" of preventing the "doctrine of God from being a human construction."[173]

The second reason that it appears to some that Barth refuses to argue with Feuerbach (Sawyer) or responds only to Feuerbach's major conclusions and not his arguments for them (Glasse), is that, far from having to oppose the epistemological basis of Feuerbach's critique, the development of the doctrine of the Trinity allows Barth to accept Feuerbach's epistemological demands. Feuerbach's claim that religion is merely a projection, an illusory wish fulfillment, is based on the epistemological position that thinking is concrete, that knowledge must have a concrete object. The doctrine of the Trinity makes this same claim. Theology must be founded on the basis of God's concrete revelation in the concrete man Jesus. God can give himself concretely because the being of the triune God is concrete in itself. Feuerbach also holds that the concrete object must remain subject and oppose *a priori* thinking about it. Thus, the doctrine of the Trinity also stands for the subjectivity of God in his revelation.

Trinitarian thinking, then, does not mean simply the rejection of Feuerbach's atheism, but is able to incorporate the truth of that atheism. Apologetically, it allows theology to say "yes," to say it is in agreement with the critique. Against traditional theism of whatever variety, trinitarian theology brings the charge of abstract thinking, which makes God into object and finally only a projection of humanity. Thus, the doctrine of the Trinity enables the appropriation of Feuerbach in the name of theological truth.

But there is a further apologetic function of the doctrine of the Trinity. Is it impossible to go beyond Feuerbach? Is theology limited only to the possibilities that Feuerbach saw? The doctrine of the Trinity means the answer must be "no." The Christian faith does not die with abstract theology. Nor does it rise and fall with traditional theism. Therefore, Feuerbach does not have the final word. The doctrine of the Trinity can serve as the basis for the further apologetic function of asserting that knowledge of God is possible within the epistemological rules set by Feuerbach. The doctrine of the Trinity provides the concrete basis for speech about the God who remains subject and cannot be a human projection.

For this reason the methodological shift signified by the doctrine of the Trinity in Barth's theology is not a retreat from argument with Feuerbach, but a way of engaging him. The doctrine of the Trinity illumines certain misunderstandings held by Feuerbach. It means that Feuerbach's reading of the Christian concept of God was a case of mistaken identity. The only concept of God he knew was the abstract God related to the method of traditional theism, the God abstracted from nature or human self-consciousness. He was able to point out the truth of this method and this God, but never move beyond them. Although he rejects this God — and for this he should be commended — he remains tied by theism to his theological adversaries. The doctrine of the Trinity, however, shatters the alternative between theism and atheism. It correctly identifies the Christian concept of God that is not sensuously grounded in general humanity or nature. It and the theological method that it signifies, therefore, involve the assertion that Feuerbach, like his adversaries, was looking in the wrong place to find the true Christian God, the concrete Trinity who is always subject.[174]

To explain this claim, a word must be said about Barth's extended response to Feuerbach in *Church Dogmatics* IV/3, First Half. We have seen that Barth responds to Feuerbach here on the basis of the "manifest radiance" of God's revelation in Jesus. Again, this radiance is explicated by reference to "the trinitarian being of God" who gives himself "concretely" and is always a "subject" in this giving.[175] For this reason, Barth declares, "Questions like that of Feuerbach will not be even remotely possible."[176] Because if God's revelation is concrete in Jesus and if in it God is always subject, then (as Barth had said already in *Church Dogmatics* I/1[177]) this revelation cannot be judged on any other ground without denying revelation. That is, to raise Feuerbach's question about whether or not the truth of the Christian revelation is merely ascribed or projected means that the concreteness and subjectivity of the revelatory event has been negated. Then "our answer will follow the lines laid down by that of Feuerbach when he put these questions,"[178] and our answer will have an anthropological basis only. For, Barth writes, "we can ascribe to Him only the majesty which we have first ascribed to ourselves by thinking we can and should assign ourselves the competence to put such questions."[179]

What Barth only hints at, but what is implied in this analysis, is another "no" to Feuerbach. For the claim can be made that Feuerbach, like his theistic theological adversaries, was unable to be true to his own epistemological criteria. He did not allow the concrete appearance of Jesus, God in his sensuous revelation, to remain subject over his thinking. Rather, he asked his own question which controlled and determined the object he was attempting to know. According to trinitarian thinking, as well as Feuerbach's epistemological position itself, Feuerbach was guilty of an idealistic projection whose concrete basis was anthropology and which, therefore, could lead only to the inescapable anthropological answer. Because in this instance Feuerbach was not true to his own epistemological demands, it can be said again that he never comprehended or encountered the triune God of the Christian faith.

Barth concludes his discussion:

> How sad it is that the worthy Feuerbach, like so many other unbelievers and believers, seems not to have had any knowledge of this freeing and freedom, and thus seems to have interpreted the glory of God merely as the self-glorification of man, and the light of the life of Jesus Christ merely as the shining of a light supposedly immanent in man himself, and finally, therefore, to have evaded rather than accepted encounter with it![180]

NOTES

[1] Küng, p. 204. Küng also writes, "For the first time in the history of humanity, we are faced with a fully considered, absolutely determined, unreservedly professed and — this, too, is important — *planned atheism*, kept up to the very end . . . ,"(p. 211). Although the major portion of this sentence is correct and indicates the importance of Feuerbach for understanding modern atheism, the assertion that Feuerbach was the "first" "in the history of humanity" is an overstatement. One need only think of David Hume, for instance. On the extent and depth of Hume's atheism see Gay, I, 401-419.

[2] See Edward Hill Sawyer, *Secularization and the Problem of God in Ludwig Feuerbach's Philosophy of Religion* (Th.D. Dissertation, Graduate Theological Union, 1970), for the development of Feuerbach's thought.

[3] See Gregor Nüdling, *Ludwig Feuerbachs Religions-philosophie* (Paderborn, 1961), p. 71. See also, Sawyer, pp. 131-133.

[4] Ludwig Feuerbach, *The Essence of Religion*, trans. Alexander Loos (New York: Asa Butts & Co., 1873) p. 72, note 1. See also Ludwig Feuerbach, *Lectures on the Essence of Religion*, trans. Ralph Manheim (New York, 1967), pp. 19ff. (Hereafter cited as *Lectures*.) Here, responding to his critics, Feuerbach claims that his method did not change between *The Essence of Christianity* and *The Essence of Religion*. Only his subject matter was altered. In the former he deals with God as a moral being and therefore primarily with anthropology, in the latter with God physically and therefore primarily with nature (p. 20f). Here, Feuerbach alters his famous line to read: "Theology is . . . anthropology and physiology" (p. 21). That is, the secret concrete basis of religion lies in humanity and nature. While he connected Christianity to humanity, like natural theology , Feuerbach links nature to religion in general. Nevertheless, there is no great difference in the problem with or Feuerbach's approach to either. Both speak of an abstract, projected deity. In Feuerbach's critique of each, a sensualistic theory of knowledge is operative and anthropology, including its material context, is primary. Finally, nature is a basis of religion because of *human* dependence on it (p. 37).

[5] Ludwig Feuerbach, *The Essence of Christianity*, trans. George Eliot (New York, 1957), p. xxxviii.

[6] *Ibid.*, p. xxxvi.

[7] *Ibid.*, p. xxxiv.

[8] Ludwig Feuerbach, "Zur Kritik der Hegelschen Philosophie," *Sämtliche Werke*, II, ed. Wilhelm Bolin and Friedrich Jodl (Stuttgart-

Bad Cannstatt, 1959), 184. (Hereafter cited as "Kritik.") See Sawyer, pp. 91ff, for an extended analysis of Feuerbach's critique of Hegel.

[9] Ludwig Feuerbach, *Principles of the Philosophy of the Future*, trans. Manfred H. Vogel (Indianapolis, 1966), p. 44. (Hereafter cited as *Principles*).

[10] Ludwig Feuerbach, "Vorläufige Thesen zur Reform der Philosophie," *Sämtliche Werke*, II, 235 (Hereafter cited as "Thesen"), quoted in Sawyer, p. 122.

[11] See Feuerbach, *Principles*, p. 51.

[12] Sawyer, p. 123.

[13] Feuerbach, *Principles*, p. 40.

[14] Quoted in Sawyer, p. 121, from "Thesen", p. 229.

[15] Quoted in Barth, "An Introductory Essay," trans. J.L. Adams in *The Essence of Christianity*, p. xiv. This essay is also found as "Ludwig Feuerbach" in Barth, *Theology and Church*, trans. Louise Pettibone Smith (New York, 1962), pp. 217-237.

[16] See Feuerbach, "Kritik," p. 181. See also Sawyer pp. 91ff.

[17] See Küng, p. 199.

[18] See Sawyer, p. 98ff.

[19] Feuerbach, *Essence of Christianity*, p. 12.

[20] Feuerbach, *Lectures*, p. 25. See also *Essence of Christianity*, p. 9.

[21] See Ludwig Feuerbach, "Zur Beurteilung der Schrift: 'das Wesen des Christentums'," *Sämtliche Werke*, VII, 266, where Feuerbach indicates how his critique of Schleiermacher differs from that of Hegel.

[22] Feuerbach, *Essence of Christianity*, p. 10.

[23] *Ibid.*, p. 2. See also pp. 29-30.

[24] Feuerbach, *Lectures*, p. 17. See also Barth, "An Introductory Essay," p. xv.

[25] Feuerbach, *Lectures*, p. 21.

[26] Feuerbach, *Essence of Christianity*, p. xxxvi.

[27] *Ibid.*, p. 13. See also p. 16.

[28] *Ibid.*, pp. 29f.

[29] *Ibid.*, pp. 13f.

[30] *Ibid.*

[31] See *Ibid*, p. xxv.

[32] See *Ibid.*, p. 66. In this chapter on the Trinity, Feuerbach says, "But religion is man's consciousness of himself in his concrete or living totality, in which the identity of the self-consciousness exists only as the pregnant, complete unity of I and thou."

[33] *Ibid.*, p. 23.

³⁴ See *Ibid.*, pp. 14ff. Also see Claude Welch, *Protestant Thought in the Nineteenth Century* (New Haven, 1972), p. 175.

³⁵ *Summa* 1.12.12.

³⁶ Schleiermacher, *The Christian Faith*, pp. 194ff.

³⁷ Feuerbach, *Essence of Christianity*, p. 20.

³⁸ *Ibid.*, p. 14.

³⁹ *Ibid.*, p. 15.

⁴⁰ See Sawyer, p. 145, who concurs with this interpretation that Feuerbach's critique is dependent on the similarity and correlation of human and divine attributes.

⁴¹ Feuerbach, *Principles*, p. 48.

⁴² Feuerbach, *Essence of Christianity*, p. 18.

⁴³ See *Ibid.*, p. 27.

⁴⁴ Feuerbach, *Principles*, p. 48.

⁴⁵ Feuerbach, *Essence of Christianity*, p. 26.

⁴⁶ *Ibid.*, p. 28.

⁴⁷ Küng, p. 211.

⁴⁸ *Ibid.* It is significant that in light of this latter evaluation, Küng throughout his discussion on Feuerbach and other atheists attempts to show how they fail to "substantiate" their atheism (See p. 403). Feuerbach, according to Küng, cannot "prove" his position (p. 206). Küng asks, ". . . has not atheism lost credibility" (p. 207)? How then does Feuerbach remain a permanent challenge? Küng, it seems to me, finally does not take the challenge of Feuerbach seriously enough. In pointing out the flaws in Feuerbach's arguments, he does not adequately come to terms with the real questions. Küng, like Feuerbach, remains within the context of traditional theism. He offers no re-evaluation of theology that really responds to Feuerbach's critique, but rather only shows the weakness of Feuerbach's presuppositions.

⁴⁹ Barth, "Introductory Essay," p.xxi.

⁵⁰ See H. Richard Niebuhr's "Forward" in Feuerbach, *Essence of Christianity*, p. viii.

⁵¹ Barth, "Introductory Essay", p. xxix. Barth's attitude toward Feuerbach throughout his theology is related to his distinction between human religion (including Christianity) and a Christianity based on God's word.

⁵² *Ibid.*, p. xxv.

⁵³ Hartshorne and Reese, p. 448.

⁵⁴ Sawyer, p. 224.

⁵⁵ John Glasse, "Barth on Feuerbach," *Harvard Theological Review*, LVII/2 (April, 1964), 69-96.

⁵⁶ *Ibid.*, p. 73.

[57] *Ibid.*, p. 79.

[58] See *Ibid.*, p. 76. The quotation is from Barth, "Introductory Essay," p. xxviii.

[59] *Ibid.*, p. 88.

[60] *Ibid.*

[61] See *CD* IV/3, First Half, 73-75.

[62] *Ibid.*, p. 77. See Glasse, p. 90.

[63] Glasse, p. 82.

[64] Barth, "Introductory Essay," pp. xxiii-xxiv.

[65] Glasse, p. 94, n. 49.

[66] In *CD* III/2, 19, Barth writes, "Man is made an object of theological knowledge by the fact that his relationship to God is revealed to us in the Word of God. . . . thus theological anthropology cleaves to the Word of God and its biblical attestation." See also p. 20.

[67] See *CD* III/1, 184ff, 192ff, 196ff; III/2, 203, 222ff, particularly 244ff. Glasse (p.84) mentions this shift in Barth's position, but does not understand how it affects his own argument.

[68] Feuerbach, *Essence of Christianity*, p. 67.

[69] *CD* III/1, 185. See also p. 196.

[70] *CD* IV/3, First Half, 85.

[71] *CD* III/2, 277f.

[72] See *CD* I/1, 348, 432; *CD* II/1, 67-69, 78-83, for example.

[73] *CD* I/1, 385.

[74] See Barth's "The Principles of Dogmatics According to Wilhelm Herrmann" in *Theology and Church*, pp. 238-271, for what follows. Jürgen Moltmann in *Theology of Hope*, trans. James W. Leitch (New York, 1967), pp. 50-58, (Hereafter cited as *TH*), and Christopher Morse, *The Logic of Promise in Moltmann's Theology* (Philadelphia, 1979), pp. 42-43, also discuss Barth's relationship to Herrmann on the issue of revelation. I, like Morse, am indebted to Moltmann for this analysis.

[75] Quoted in Barth, *Theology and Church*, p. 247. See also Moltmann, *TH*, p.52, and Morse, p. 43.

[76] See Morse, p. 43.

[77] See Barth, *Theology and Church*, pp. 253-256.

[78] *Ibid.*, p. 229.

[79] *CD* II/1, 73.

[80] Barth, *Theology and Church*, p. 256. See Morse, p. 43.

[81] Barth, *Theology and Church*, p. 256.

[82] *Ibid.*

[83] Karl Barth, *Revolutionary Theology in the Making: Barth-Thurneysen Correspondence*, 1914-1925, trans. James D. Smart (Richmond, 1964), p. 176.

[84] *Ibid.*, p. 185.

[85] See Jüngel, p. 25.

[86] See *CD* I/1, 383-399.

[87] *Ibid.*, p. 390.

[88] See *Ibid.*, p. 394, where Barth explicitly mentions Feuerbach as the end result of one instance where the *vestigia trinitatis* is claimed.

[89] *Ibid.*, p. 385.

[90] *CD* II/1, 261.

[91] Barth's breakthrough in his understanding of revelation came through his interpretation of Anselm. See Karl Barth, *Anselm: Fides Quaerens Intellectum. Anselm's Proof of the Existence of God in the Context of His Theological Scheme*, trans. Ian W. Robertson (London, 1960). We saw above that Glasse asserts the importance of Anselm for Barth's response to Feuerbach. The problem with Glasse's view is his belief that Barth applies this new understanding of revelation to the case of Feuerbach only in 1959. We will see however that it is ingredient in Barth's response to Feuerbach from the inception of the *Church Dogmatics*.

[92] *CD* I/1, 349.

[93] *Ibid.*, pp. 355, 357, 359.

[94] *Ibid.*, pp. 339-340.

[95] *Ibid.*, p. 340.

[96] See *CD* I/1, 354, 356; also Gunton, p. 129.

[97] *CD* I/1, 339, 344. It should be noted here that Barth prefers to use "mode of being" instead of "person" when referring to the Father, Son or Spirit. He does this to avoid the confusion of a trinitarian person with the modern notion of person which carries the connotation of an individual personality. According to Barth there is only one personality in God, not three. See Barth's discussion in *Ibid.*, pp. 408-414.

[98] *Ibid.*, p. 343.

[99] *Ibid.*, p. 349.

[100] *Ibid.*, p. 343.

[101] *Ibid.*, p. 363. See also p. 414: "But this one God is God three times in another way . . . ."

[102] *Ibid.*, p. 374.

[103] Karl Barth, "The Christian Understanding of Revelation," *Against the Stream: Shorter Post-War Writings 1946-52*, trans. E. M. Delacour and S. Godman, ed. R. Gregor Smith (London, 1954), p. 211.

[104] *CD* I/1, p. 362.

[105] *Ibid.*, p. 361.
[106] *Ibid.*, pp. 342, 351.
[107] *CD* II/1, 262.
[108] *CD* I/1, 342.
[109] *Ibid.*, p. 343.
[110] See *Ibid.* Here Barth says, "Revelation in the Bible is not a minus, it is not another over against God. It is the same, the repetition of God."
[111] *Ibid.*, p. 548. There should be no confusion between the heresy of modalism and Barth's use of "modes of being or existence" to refer to the trinitarian persons (See above n. 97). To protect the unity of God, modalism spoke of the triune persons "only as phenomenal forms under which God's real single essence was concealed as something different and higher . . . " (*CD* I/1, 405). This has the effect of denying God's revelation, since God is actually different from the way in which he appears to us. Barth also wishes to protect God's unity. Hence, he prefers mode of existence or being to person, which in the modern sense implies a distinct center of personality and willing. To apply this term to God uncritically would suggest tritheism (See *Ibid.*,pp. 410-11). For Barth, however, God's unity, his one personality, is not above or behind God's three modes of existence. Rather, it is precisely in God's being in three modes that his personhood and unity are discovered (See below, n. 124 and *CD* I/1, 412): " . . . the one personal God is what He is not in one mode only, but . . . in the mode of the Father, in the mode of the Son, in the mode of the Holy Spirit" (*CD* I/1, 413). God, therefore, is not different from his triune revelation.
[112] See Gunton, pp. 147, 170.
[113] *CD* I/1, 426.
[114] See *CD* II/1, 83. This is the basis of Barth's rejection of Thomism.
[115] *Ibid.* See also, I/1, 439, 350f; II/1, 51, 83.
[116] Jüngel, p. 32. On page 30, he also says, "If we are enabled to formulate this self-giving of God in which he is ours as concrete event, then we must also formulate the being of God in the event of the self-relatedness of this being as concrete being."
[117] See *CD* I/1, 382.
[118] See Jüngel, pp. 29-41, for a discussion of the relationship of the concreteness of the God's being to *perichoresis*.
[119] See *CD* I/1, 416.
[120] See Jüngel, p. 32.
[121] *CD* I/1, 425.
[122] *Ibid.*, p. 424.

[123] *Ibid.*, p. 425.

[124] *Ibid.* This is related to Barth's distinction between "person" and "personality" and why he does not use "person" but "mode of being" in his trinitarian language. There is in the modern sense only one person or personality in God, constituted precisely by the concrete relationships of the three modes of being.

[125] *Ibid.*, p. 351.

[126] *Ibid.*, p. 350.

[127] *Ibid.*, p. 438.

[128] Jüngel, p. 16.

[129] *CD* I/1, 374.

[130] *Ibid.*, p. 343.

[131] *Ibid.*, p. 515.

[132] *Ibid.*, p. 381.

[133] Jüngel, pp. 18, 20.

[134] *CD* I/1, 362.

[135] *Ibid.*, p. 363.

[136] *Ibid.*

[137] *Ibid.*, p. 367.

[138] *Ibid.*, p. 426.

[139] *Ibid.*, p. 369. See Jüngel, p. 19.

[140] See *CD* I/1, 382.

[141] *CD* II/1, 275.

[142] See K. Barth, *The Humanity of God*, trans. John Newton Thomas and others (Atlanta, 1974), p. 50. See also Morse, p. 122.

[143] *CD* II/1, 280.

[144] See Jüngel, pp. 34ff, where he makes a similar point.

[145] *Ibid.*, p. 22.

[146] *CD* I/1, 440. See also Jüngel, p. 25.

[147] See Jüngel, p. 25.

[148] For Barth's controversy with the nineteenth century see, for example, Hans W. Frei, *The Doctrine of Revelation in the Thought of Karl Barth, 1909 to 1922: The Nature of Barth's Break with Liberalism*, (Ph. D. Dissertation, 1956). Pages 174-202 of this dissertation appear as Frei, "Niebuhr's Theological Background in *Faith and Ethics: The Theology of H. Richard Niebuhr*, ed. Paul Ramsey (New York, 1965), pp. 40-53.

For Barth's controversy with Thomism see Gunton, pp. 117, 127.

[149] See *CD* II/1, 261, for instance. Here Barth claims that non-trinitarian theologies are finally subject to Feuerbach's critique.

[150] See *CD* II/1, 261.

[151] *CD* I/1, 347.

[152] See *CD* II/1, 80, for instance.

[153] *CD* I/1, 345-346.

[154] *Ibid.*, p. 345.

[155] *Ibid.*, pp. 353f. See Welch, *In This Name*, pp. 162, 171.

[156] *CD* I/1, 346.

[157] *CD* I/2, 7. See Glasse, p. 83, n. 28, where he also refers to Barth's dispute with the method of these theologians and how they end at Feuerbach. Glasse fails to notice that their failure of method is related to the eclipse of the doctrine of the Trinity in their theologies. See also *CD* II/1, 467.

[158] *CD* II/1, 82.

[159] *Ibid.*, pp. 287-288.

[160] *Ibid.*, p. 293.

[161] *CD*, I/2, 6.

[162] *CD* II/1, 292. For Barth, as this analysis shows, it is not a great distance from Thomism to nineteenth century philosophy, that is, from starting with nature to starting with human self-consciousness. The method remains the same. In this he also agrees with Feuerbach.

[163] *Ibid.*, p. 293.

[164] *Ibid.*

[165] *Ibid.*

[166] *Ibid.*, p. 297.

[167] Hartshorne and Reese, p. 448.

[168] Sawyer, p. 224.

[169] Glasse, p. 93.

[170] *Ibid.*, pp. 95, 83.

[171] *CD* I/1, 358.

[172] *Ibid.*, p. 343.

[173] Jüngel, p. 21.

[174] See Robert W. Jenson, "Response," *Union Seminary Quarterly Review*, Vol. XXVIII, No. 1 (Fall, 1972), pp. 31-34. In his response to John E. Smith's interpretation of Barth in the same volume, (John E. Smith, "The Significance of Karl Barth's Thought for the Relation Between Philosophy and Theology," pp. 15-30) where Smith claims that Barth's method involves a retreat from discussion with philosophy, Jenson makes points similar to mine here. He claims that Barth is not "a 'compartmentalizer' who breaks off communication." Rather, like "all thinkers of the Western tradition," Barth claims that his adversaries "have performed a misidentification." They are "looking in the wrong place" (p. 33). Barth, of course, believes that the correct identification of human problems and their answers takes place in the context of the

revelation of God in the history of Jesus Christ and, therefore, in the context of the triune God.

[175] *CD* IV/3, First Half, 80, 81, 83, 79.
[176] *Ibid.*, p. 80.
[177] *CD* I/1, 350.
[178] *CD* IV/3, First Half, 73.
[179] *Ibid.*
[180] *Ibid.*, p. 82f.

CHAPTER III

TRINITARIAN THEOLOGY AND ATHEISM
FOR HUMANITY'S SAKE

The most profound form of atheism is not based on epistemological concerns only, but rather is a protest against God in light of the human condition. In this chapter and the next we will examine two different forms that this protest takes and the trinitarian responses to them. This chapter will focus on the more general protest which is grounded positively in a general humanism. It therefore takes an atheistic position against the God whose divinity is constituted at human expense, who, for example, is conceived as strong only as humans are seen as weak. Although the theological method of sensuous trinitarian thinking is itself part of the response, for this form of protest atheism a more complete response is achieved by a turn from a concentration on method to what that method means for the doctrine of God. In other words, this chapter represents a move from epistemological to ontological categories. In analyzing this atheism and the trinitarian response we will again draw material from Ludwig Feuerbach and Karl Barth respectively.

Feuerbach's Humanistic Protest

Although the major portions of Feuerbach's writings are devoted to a critique and reinterpretation of theology and religion on the basis of a sensuous epistemology, the aim of his atheism is not epistemology but the affirmation of humanity. His is an atheism of protest against God on behalf of humankind. Feuerbach is attempting to cure human pathology[1] that is found in "theism," in religious projection. The sickness that Feuerbach perceives is alienation. Humans are alienated from their own best attributes because these have been projected outward and attributed to God. According to theological interpretation what God is humans cannot be. Thus, Feuerbach asserts, "God is and has exactly what man is not and has not. Whatever is attributed to God is denied to man and contrariwise . . . ."[2]   God is constituted, then, only at the expense of humanity. "If you want to have God, therefore, give up man."[3] God gains his being and attributes only by robbing humanity.

> To enrich God, man must become poor; that God may be all, man must be nothing . . . . Man gives up his personality; but in return, God, the Almighty, infinite, unlimited being, is a person; . . . Religion further denies goodness as a quality of human nature; man is wicked, corrupt, incapable of good, but on the other hand, God is only good — the Good Being.[4]

For Feuerbach, these attributes, seen in God in their perfect degree, are real and are not to be denied. However, these attributes do not belong to a being distinct from humanity. They are qualities of humankind. The intention of Feuerbach's atheism is to heal the human pathology of alienation by restoring to humanity what rightfully belongs to it. To accomplish this, God must be negated by criticizing the wedge that theism and its abstract thinking have driven between God and humanity. Feuerbach's sensuous, concrete thinking is the tool that exposes the fallacy of theism. It shows the cure for theological speculation and leads human beings to recognize their true unalienated value, qualities and selves. This means Feuerbach's denial of religion has a positive aim: human wholeness and dignity. Therefore he says,

> Certainly my work is negative, destructive; but, be it observed, only in relation to the unhuman, not to the human elements of religion.[5]

> Thus my purpose is far from negative. It is positive; I negate only in order to affirm; I negate the fantastic hypocrisy of theology and religion only in order to affirm the true nature of man.[6]

Feuerbach claims that it is really belief in God itself that is negative, for it denies the value of the world and humanity.

> What is truly negative is theism, the belief in God; it negates nature, the world and mankind: *in the face of God, the world and man are nothing.* . . . For the true theist the power and beauty of nature, the virtue of man, do not exist; a believer in God takes everything away from man and nature in order to adorn and glorify God.[7]

Thus, Feuerbach's critique is a positive negation of the negative. If belief in God negatively alienates persons from the true worth of this world and themselves, its negation by atheism positively restores this value to its rightful place. Feuerbach writes,

... hence theism sacrifices the real life and nature of things and of men to a being who is a mere product of thought and imagination. Thus atheism is positive and affirmation, it gives back to nature and mankind the dignity of which theism has despoiled them; it restores life to nature and mankind, which theism had drained of their best powers.[8]

It is the positive aspect of Feuerbach's atheism, his concern for the concrete human condition, that gives it its true profundity.[9] For it is not an atheism based on speculative negation — atheism that has little to do with concrete life, but is interested only in a correct epistemology. Feuerbach himself rejects any merely negative atheism as worthless:

And it is perfectly true that if atheism were a mere negation, a denial without content, it would be unfit for the people . . . ; but only because such atheism is worthless.[10]

But Feuerbach's atheism is always a protest against God on behalf of humanity, a negation understood only on the basis of his affirmation. It is this understanding of Feuerbach that allows us to see him as the fountainhead and anticipation of modern protest atheism.

However, it is clear in this context also that Feuerbach's critique presupposes traditional theism. The theological method that he attacks is the theistic one in which the conception of God is formulated by abstracting attributes from the world in a *via negativa*. Feuerbach declares,

Religion abstracts from man, from the world; but it can only abstract from the limitations, from the phenomena; in short, from the negative, not from the essence, the positive, of the world and humanity: . . .[11]

Thus, Feuerbach always has in view the theistic one God who is defined not only as the perfection but also as the antithesis of humanity and the world. As such, the God rejected by Feuerbach is thought of in the typically theistic fashion as endowed with all the absolutist attributes.

Since Feuerbach remains within the context of traditional theism, however, trinitarian theology can again make a response in two directions. We saw in Chapter II that the doctrine of the Trinity as developed by Barth signals a transformation of theological method. We will see momentarily that this method also indicates a transformation in the doctrine of God. The doctrine of the Trinity therefore indicates agreement with Feuerbach on the rejection of traditional theism but also demonstrates that Feuerbach himself never moved beyond it. Trinitarian thinking advances beyond Feuerbach by placing his protest in the new context of the doctrine of the Trinity.

The Doctrine of the Trinity and
the Identity of God

The major response to Feuerbach in this section will be developed by examining the modification of the traditional attributes of God that takes place in trinitarian theology. However, this modification is based upon the trinitarian theological method which in itself is a constituent part of the response to Feuerbach's protest. Thus we will first look briefly at this methodological aspect.

Trinitarian Method as Response

As discussed extensively in Chapter II, trinitarian theology as developed by Barth does not use the method employed by traditional theism in which one arrives at the concept of God by abstracting attributes from the world through a *via negativa*. Rather, the doctrine of the Trinity and the theology related to it speak of God only on the basis of the concrete event in which God gives himself to be known, namely on the basis of his revelation in Jesus of Nazareth. It is this concrete self-giving of God in his revelation that the doctrine of the Trinity comprehends. But this methodological shift means that, unlike the God of theism, the triune God does not rob humanity in order to constitute the divine glory. The doctrine of the Trinity enables a response to this charge, for, in this context, God is not defined at the expense of humanity, as everything humans are not. Far from this, the doctrine of the Trinity interprets the God who defines himself precisely by becoming human in Jesus, by giving himself to human beings.

But if the doctrine of the Trinity demands a new theological method in which the concept of God is not developed on the basis of the world or the self-consciousness, but on the basis of the concrete history of Jesus, it must be asked what conception of God emerges. This method brings about a "revolution in the concept of God"[12] which, as it signals the rejection of the God of traditional theism, also shows that God is not enriched by demeaning humanity. The trinitarian doctrine of God therefore is the second and major basis of a response to atheism grounded in humanism.

The Attributes of God

This trinitarian revolution in the concept of God is seen clearly in the rejection of the use of the static, substantial categories of traditional theism's conception of God in which, by abstracting from and in opposition to the world and humanity, God is seen for instance as the "unmoved mover" and the "supreme being." According to trinitarian thinking this illegitimately brings *a priori* notions into the conceptualization of God because it splits apart God and God's concrete action. It is abstract thinking open to the charge of projection which also demeans humanity. Rather, as developed by Barth (and, as we will see, by Moltmann as well), trinitarian theology sees God as an event, as a being in act, as a being in becoming. Barth develops this along by now familiar lines of argument. Because "God is who he is in his works,"[13] because God truly gives himself in his revelation, because in the event of revelation God is God a "second and third time" — that is, because God is triune — any discussion of God's being must include this act of revelation because that is precisely what God is in himself. ("In the light of what He is in his works it is no longer an open question what He is in Himself."[14]) This means that there is no possibility of going behind God's action to find a God who is not active, a static unmoved mover perhaps. Barth writes,

> We are dealing with the being of God; but with regard to the being of God, the word "event" or "act" is final, and cannot be surpassed or compromised. To its very depths God's Godhead consists in the fact that it is an event . . . .[15]

Only the doctrine of the Trinity can grasp concretely God as a being in act. As we saw in Chapter II, God's act of revelation, when analyzed, necessitates conceiving God in a trinitarian manner, as Revealer, Revelation and Revealedness. And this Trinity is not only economic. Because the movement of revelation is God and because it is God's free decision, revelation finds its basis in God's decision to move in himself, to put himself in relationship to himself, to become God "three times in another way,"[16] and, therefore, to be an event, a being in becoming.[17] This "movement is expressed conceptually by the eternal relation of the Son to the Father in the Spirit."[18] God's being is not a static substance, however supremely conceived; but in revelation and immanently it is an event, an event brought to speech by the doctrine of the Trinity. Trinitarian theology, then, is distinct from traditional theism and at the same time responds to protest atheism. For, according to the doctrine of the Trinity, God's being is not a static substance, taken from the world, which leaves the world and humanity tossed in a sea of arbitrary change while taking rest and immutability for itself. Rather, God's being is a dynamic event of self-giving to the world.

This discussion of the event character of God's being signifies the method that must be used in developing all the traditional attributes of God. If these attributes are to be employed at all, they must be reconceived on the basis of the concrete method indicated by the doctrine of the Trinity. This makes manifest traditional theism's and atheism's misidentification of God. As Barth says,

> We have to be ready to be taught by him that we have been too small and perverted in our thinking about him within the framework of a false idea of God . . . . We may believe that God can and must only be absolute in contrast to all that is relative, exalted in contrast to all that is lowly, active in contrast to all suffering, inviolable in contrast to all temptation, transcendent in contrast to all immanence, and therefore divine in contrast to everything human, in short that He can and must be only the "Wholly Other." But such beliefs are shown to be quite untenable, and corrupt and pagan, by the fact that God does in fact be and do this in Jesus Christ.[19]

At no point, therefore, is the triune God glorified at humanity's expense. He does not take the supreme term while leaving its opposite for men and women. Rather, in his triune self-giving, God shows that he overcomes these *a priori* distinctions between "the divine" and "the human" by comprehending both. In this "He shows Himself to be more great and rich and sovereign than we had ever imagined."[20] For example, the normal conception of the infinity of God, which in theism is derived in dialectical relationship with human finitude, limited by space and time, must be rejected.[21] Infinity of this sort, which attempts to show God's greatness, not only is really nothing but anthropology, but also ultimately confines and imprisons God's being. It excludes God from the finite. On the other hand, the doctrine of the Trinity which includes the revelation in Jesus in God's being speaks of the God who is finite as well as infinite. The infinity of the triune God, therefore, "does not involve any contradiction that it is finite as well."[22] Again the response to this atheism is that God has not robbed humanity for his own glory. He has not constituted his being in infinity while leaving finitude for humanity.

Associated with God's infinity are his omnipresence and his eternity. But these doctrines too cannot be developed abstractly as is done in traditional theism. Rather they must be reformulated.   God's omnipresence cannot mean his non-spatiality. "Non-spatiality means existence without distance, which means identity."[23] This contradicts God's triune nature. Rather, God's omnipresence is his decision to be present both to himself and to reality distinct from himself. God opens up space in himself as he relates himself to himself as Father, Son and Holy Spirit. And, on the basis of this, he creates in himself space for created reality. As Barth says,

> God's triunity is the space which is exclusively His own space, and as such can become and give itself to be the space of all spaces. As Father, Son and Holy Spirit, God uses and has and is space for Himself. But in His being as Father, Son and Holy Spirit. . . . He uses and has and is also space for all this which is distinct from Himself. . . . Yet these spaces can be spaces by Him and in Him, enclosed by His space. . . . He is present to them all and in them all He is omnipresent.[24]

Likewise, God's eternity cannot be abstractly defined as in the *via negativa* of theism where by a negation of time it comes to mean mere timelessness.[25] This would again negate the triune God revealed in Jesus Christ. "A correct understanding of the positive side of the concept of eternity, free from all false conclusions, is gained only when we are clear that we are speaking about the eternity of the triune God."[26] God is eternally Father, Son and Holy Spirit. Yet it is precisely in this that it is seen that time is important for God. God makes time.[27] And in his revelation in Jesus Christ God takes time for us and "takes time to Himself."[28] If God becomes temporal in his revelation, temporality cannot be excluded from God's eternity. "True eternity includes this possibility, the potentiality of time."[29] In fact, time finds its basis in the time opened up in God's triune being. Again Barth explains this by reference to God's triune being: In the inner movement of the Trinity there is "a before and an after."

> God is once and again and a third time . . . . the fact that God has and is Himself time, and the extent to which this is so, is necessarily made clear to us in His essence as the triune God. This is His time, the absolutely real time, the form of the divine being in its triunity . . . .[30]

This investigation could continue at length. Barth, following this trinitarian method, also rejects the traditional concept of God's immutability, which is abstracted from the world and placed in opposition to changing reality. Barth claims this leads to Feuerbach and atheism.[31] He defines immutability as constancy. The triune God changes, but is the same in every change.[32] But whatever attribute of God is under discussion, the direction of development must be the same. Theology founded on the doctrine of the Trinity as formulated by Barth develops its conception of God from concrete revelation. This shatters the abstract, metaphysical method of traditional theism. But the difference is not only in theological method. By following the method of trinitarian theology, a revolution in the concept of God is accomplished which makes it clear that the triune God is distinct from and opposed to the God of theism.

The Trinitarian Response

At this point trinitarian theology is able to respond to protest atheism grounded in humanism. On the one hand, it affirms this protest. The God that is conceived of at the expense of the world, the God that robs humanity to glorify himself, the God whose attributes are in opposition to the qualities of creation, must be denied. Traditional theism is wrong and, at this point, atheism is right. However, on the other hand, trinitarian theology says no to atheism. For atheism, like theism, misidentifies God and therefore negates a God who is not God; it never sees the triune God. This God is not opposed to everything worldly and human, but gives himself in an event — a human event — and, in so doing, makes space for and includes the finite in his own space, and gives us time as he takes time for us and includes our time in his own being.

Moreover, on the basis of trinitarian thinking Barth develops two other important points that respond to Feuerbach's humanistic protest. First, Barth comes to speak of the "humanity" and "humanism of God."[33] "It is precisely God's *deity* which, rightly understood, includes his humanity."[34] "In Him [Jesus Christ] the fact is once and for all established that God does not exist without man."[35] This is certainly not to be taken in the Feuerbachian sense that God is merely a projected humanity. God's humanity is not robbed from humankind. Rather it is realized concretely in the human history of Jesus. Since the man Jesus is God the Son, "when we look at Jesus Christ we know decisively that God's deity does not exclude, but includes His *humanity*."[36] In fact, the triune God's deity is not constituted as Feuerbach claimed by diminishing humanity, but is seen precisely in his being human.[37] Far from robbing from humanity, God, in being human, gives himself to, identifies with and thus opposes any diminution of humanity.

Second, on this basis Barth also speaks of the glory of man: "The incarnation of Christ is the great glorification of man. In it, every man is

ennobled in principle."[38] The triune God honors and shows the high
position of humanity by becoming human. Indeed, the true worth of
humanity is seen in that it is only in God's humanity that we know him.
"We can meet God only within the limits of humanity determined by
Him."[39] Furthermore, the highest glory of humanity comes in that in
Jesus the Son humanity finds its way into the very being of God.[40] This
means that the triune God brings humanity into unity with him and that
true humanity is constituted only in this fellowship. "Basically and
comprehensively, therefore, to be a man is to be with God."[41]
Humankind's ontological determination is to be in fellowship with God.
Hence: "Godlessness is not, therefore, a possibility, but an ontological
impossibility for man. Man is not without, but with God."[42] For Barth
this does not mean "that godless men do not exist." Yet they, along
with all humanity, "are actually with Jesus, i.e., with God."[43] The
denial of this relationship with God is a denial of true humanity and its
real worth and honor.

It is important to understand that in its union with God humanity
is not absorbed and lost in the divine. Rather, it is a fellowship in which
human beings maintain (indeed are given) their independence and
freedom in relation to God.[44] A dominant metaphor of the relationship
with God which is determinative of humanity is "covenant partner."[45]
The triune God establishes the partnership, but in a way that enables
humanity its distinct free work.

> And so "man goeth forth unto work and to his labour until
> the evening" (Ps. 104[23]); to which it belongs that he can
> use his senses and understanding to perceive that two and
> two make four, and to write poetry, and to think, and to
> make music, and to eat and drink, and to be filled with joy
> and often with sorrow, and to love and sometimes to hate,
> and to be young and to grow old, and all within his own
> experience and activity, affirming not as half a man but as a
> whole man, with head uplifted, and the heart free and the
> conscience at rest: . . . . It is only the heathen gods who envy
> man. The true God, who is unconditionally Lord, allows
> him to be the thing for which He created him.[46]

We see in this discussion a reversal of Feuerbach's concept of God.
For in his revelation in a human person and in his assumption of
humanity into his being, the triune God reveals and gives to humanity it
true value and glory. Thus, instead of demeaning humankind, trinitarian
thinking affirms that humanity is a "gift" that comes from God.[47]
Moreover, we also see that humanism cannot know the true dignity and
glory of humanity, since it cannot know the honor which humanity

receives in God's becoming human or in his determination of humanity to be with him. Feuerbach attempts to honor humankind by recovering its projected attributes. But this is an honor that is bestowed only idealistically, for it is accomplished by an alteration of conceptions. On the other hand, in the trinitarian perspective human honor and dignity are bestowed, not merely in thought, but concretely in the appearance of Jesus. In this event God honors humanity in a concrete way by becoming human, by taking humanity into his own life and by showing that the destiny of humankind is unity with him.[48]

Our analysis has indicated again a reversal of traditional theism and a response to Feuerbach. Since the doctrine of the Trinity brings to speech the God who does not demean but in a concrete way gives real value to humanity; since in this context God is defined not as the antithesis of the world and humanity, but as earthly and human; since the doctrine of the Trinity, therefore, signals the rejection of traditional theism; we can maintain that the protest of Feuerbach's atheism against traditional theism remains and is taken up into trinitarian thinking. But, in the context of the triune God, the unbelief of atheism must be supported by other arguments if it is to be intelligible.

The method that we have employed here to determine the concept God and the content of the divine attributes will be important in the next chapter as well in which a specific form of protest atheism and the trinitarian response to it will be examined.

NOTES

[1] See Feuerbach, *Lectures*, p. 35, where he describes religion as a human pathology as well as anthropology.

[2] Ludwig Feuerbach, *The Essence of Faith According to Luther*, trans. Melvin Cherno (New York, 1967), p. 33. See also *Lectures*, p. 160: "The activity of God negates the activity of the world, and conversely. If I have done a certain thing, God has not done it; and if God has done it, I have not; one possibility precludes the other."

[3] Feuerbach, *The Essence of Faith According to Luther*, p. 160.

[4] Feuerbach, *The Essence of Christianity*, pp. 26-28.

[5] *Ibid.*, p. xxxvi.

[6] Feuerbach, *Lectures*, p. 23.

[7] *Ibid.*, pp. 282-283.

[8] *Ibid.*, p. 283.

[9] See Barth, "Introduction," p. xiv-xv; also, Claude Welch, *Christian Thought in the Nineteenth Century* (New Haven, 1972), p. 177.

[10] Feuerbach, *Lectures*, p. 282.

[11] Feuerbach, *The Essence of Christianity*, p. 27.

[12] This phrase is Moltmann's (See *CG*, pp. 4, 145, 201). Its importance for him will become evident in the next chapter.

[13] *CD* II/1, 260.

[14] *Ibid.*

[15] *Ibid.*, p. 263.

[16] *CD* I/1, 414.

[17] See Jüngel on this, particularly pp. 92ff.

[18] Gunton, p. 168. See also, *CD* II/1, 293.

[19] *CD* IV/1, 186.

[20] *Ibid.*

[21] See *CD* II/1, 467. Barth claims that as usually defined this notion leads to Feuerbach's question.

[22] *Ibid.*

[23] *Ibid.*, p. 468.

[24] *Ibid.*, p. 476.

[25] See *Ibid.*, p. 617. See also *CD* I/2, 66: "The God thus addressed is, of course, the eternal God, but not the timeless God of the Greeks."

[26] *CD* II/1, 615.

[27] See *CD* I/2, 53.

[28] *CD* II/1, 616.

[29] *Ibid.*, p. 617: God's time, of course, does not suffer from "the defects of our time." And yet this very time with its defects "is not so alien to Him that He cannot take it to Himself in His grace, ..."

[30] *Ibid.*, p. 615. This discussion of the trinitarian understanding of God's eternity will be continued in the next chapter.

[31] See *Ibid.*, p. 494.

[32] See *Ibid.*, pp. 493-499.

[33] See Barth, *The Humanity of God*, pp. 46-52, 60.

[34] *Ibid.*, p. 46.

[35] *Ibid.*, p. 50.

[36] *Ibid.*, p. 49.

[37] *Ibid.*, pp. 51, 49.

[38] Quoted in Heinz Zahrnt, *The Question of God*, trans. R. A. Wilson (New York, 1966), p. 103, from Barth's discussion of 1947 (*Der Götz wackelt*).

[39] Barth, *The Humanity of God*, p. 54. See also *CD* II/1, 53.

[40] See Barth, *The Humanity of God*, p. 50.

[41] *CD* III/1, 135.

[42] *Ibid.*, p. 136.

43 *Ibid.*

44 On this and other points in this paragraph, see Zahrnt, p. 104.

45 See *CD* III/1, 203ff; and also *CD* III/3, 87.

46 *CD* III/3, 87.

47 Barth, *The Humanity of God*, pp. 53, 54.

48 Karl Barth criticizes extensively anthropologies which are not christologically based and which are, therefore, "abstract" (See *CD* III/2, 71-132). In his criticism he challenges philosophical, existential and theistic conceptions. While he is very clear on how these positions claim too much for humanity, he is not as forceful on how, from a trinitarian perspective, they fail to give humanity its true dignity and honor.

CHAPTER IV

PROTEST ATHEISM, THEODICY AND THE TRINITY

A more radical form of protest atheism which is also rooted positively in humanism represents perhaps the most serious challenge to the Christian faith. This atheism is born out of the theodicy question and involves a protest against and a negation of God based on the experience of human suffering. This chapter will examine this form of protest atheism and the responses to it made possible by the doctrine of the Trinity. Here the dialogue with protest atheism will be developed with Jürgen Moltmann as well as Karl Barth. It is generally agreed that Jürgen Moltmann is closely related to Karl Barth theologically.[1] Moltmann's theology, like Barth's, is christologically based. He therefore follows Barth's methodology, deriving his theology from the concrete history of Jesus centered in the cross and resurrection. Moltmann, however, goes beyond Barth by demonstrating explicitly how the trinitarian conception of God responds to atheism grounded in human suffering. For this reason Moltmann will become primary in this chapter.

Once again we will see that trinitarian thinking does not merely reject protest atheism. In fact it agrees with it and takes up its protest against human suffering. However, the claim will again be made that this protest atheism misidentifies the correct Christian concept of God inasmuch as it remains within the context of traditional theism. Once again, on the basis of the doctrine of the Trinity, theology says a yes and a no. It incorporates the protest but moves beyond it by placing the questions raised by this atheism in the context of the triune God.

Protest Atheism's Basis in Suffering

Atheism that arises as a protest against suffering finds expression in the writings of atheists like Albert Camus, the critical theory of Max Horkheimer and Theodor Adorno and some of the characters in the novels of Fyodor Dostoevsky.[2] Following Feuerbach, its denial is a protest against God who is rich at human expense. It is based upon the perception of the extent and persistence of human pain and suffering. In the face of such misery, protest atheism says no to any God who would continue to allow such conditions. How, this atheism asks, can one believe in God, who, though supposedly perfectly just and omnipotent, remains unmoved by and fails to respond to injustice and human agony, who is impassible while his creatures suffer? That creation includes these conditions is incomprehensible already, but that there is a just God who would allow them to persist is a contradiction. For the sake of humanity and the human feeling for justice, God must be rejected. "It is why," says Adorno, "one who believes in God cannot believe in God, why the possibility represented by the divine name is maintained, rather by him who does not believe."[3] "The only excuse for God would be for him not to exist."[4] In light of this positive concern for humanity's condition, any merely speculative atheism dwindles to insignificance.

The protest of this atheism can arise from human suffering in various contexts. One of the themes of Camus is natural evil, human suffering resulting from natural causes. In the *Myth of Sisyphus,* Camus analyzes the absurdity of the world, the "vast irrational" in which "hope has no further place"[5] and death reigns.[6] The essay "Summer in Algiers" exemplifies Camus' understanding of this absurdity. In Algiers people spend their days tanning themselves in the sun, that is, enjoying the beauty of nature. And yet it is that very sun, nature itself, that will kill them. "One realizes that he is born of this country where everything is given to be taken away."[7] Camus articulates the condition of absurdity clearly in the comment, "I know no more hideous spot than the cemetery on the Boulevard Bru opposite one of the most beautiful landscapes in the world."[8] The extent of the absurdity of creation and the depth of natural evil, however, is most forcefully perceived in the suffering of children. One must protest against God for the innocence of children seems manifest. Camus dramatizes the atheistic response in *The Plague.* Here, after watching the torturous death of a child, Dr. Rieux, an atheist, rails at Father Panelous, "Ah! That child, anyhow, was innocent, and you know it as well as I do! . . . And until my dying day I shall refuse to love a scheme of things in which children are put to torture."[9] In view of the absurd creation which includes the suffering of innocent children, Camus claims one must say no to God.

However, as absurd as natural evil is, the major compelling force behind protest atheism is the injustice and suffering inflicted on humans by other humans. The focus is not mainly nature but the political, social and economic context. Two points of human suffering that intensely focus the issue are once again the suffering of innocent children and the Holocaust. In Dostoevsky's *The Brothers Karamazov,* Ivan, perhaps more forcefully than any other figure in literature, represents the case of atheistic protest. Ivan, in conversation with his pious brother, Alyosha, vividly describes several episodes of horror in which children were tortured or killed. In one account he tells of a five year old little girl who was beaten and kicked by her "cultivated parents." Afterwards, she was locked up for the cold night in a privy where her mother "smeared her face and filled her mouth with excrement." The child responded by praying "to dear kind God to protect her."[10] Ivan demands an answer to the question of why such atrocity is permitted. Nothing he concludes is worth that child's prayer. He then culminates his tales of horror with the story of a serf boy who accidentally hurt the paw of one of his master's hunting dogs while throwing stones in play. Upon discovering this, the master had the boy stripped and hunted down by the dogs. The dogs tore the boy apart in view of his mother. Ivan cries for justice and "not justice in some remote infinite time and space, but here on earth," a justice he could see himself. He rejects any future or higher harmony that necessitates the sufferings of children. If it is this that God requires for harmony, one must "renounce the higher harmony altogether."

> It's not worth the tears of that one tortured child who beat itself on the breast with its little fist and prayed in its stinking outhouse, with its unexpiated tears to 'dear kind God'! It's not worth it, because those tears are unatoned for. They must be atoned for, or there can be no harmony.[11]

Ivan concludes,

> I want to forgive. I want to embrace. I don't want more suffering. And if the sufferings of children go to swell the sum of sufferings which was necessary to pay for truth, then I protest that the truth is not worth such a price. I don't want the mother to embrace the oppressor who threw her son to the dogs! She dare not forgive him! . . . Is there in the whole world a being who would have the right to forgive and could forgive? I don't want harmony. From love of humanity I don't want it. . . . too high a price is asked for harmony, . . . And so I hasten to give back my entrance ticket, . . . And that I am doing. It's not God that I don't accept, Alyosha, only I most respectfully return Him the ticket.[12]

Here, then, is protest atheism presented concisely. The transcendent ground of this world cannot be worshipped or believed in. God's ticket must be rejected. For this God does nothing to bring justice to the victims of suffering, to atone for their agony or to end human misery altogether. Beyond this, however, is the central symbol of human suffering in the modern world and, hence, the major basis for this form of atheistic protest: the Holocaust. The ghastly horror of Auschwitz and other concentration camps where millions were tortured and exterminated in view of the cultured world, according to these atheists, has shattered traditional metaphysical thought. Because Auschwitz took place also in full view of God, God too is called to account for his inaction. These events, writes Adorno, "test whether God would permit this without intervening in his wrath."[13] God failed the test. Therefore, there is no way that this radical evil and tremendous human suffering can be reconciled with the existence of God. The grounds for belief and worship have been destroyed.

> After Auschwitz, our feelings resist any claim of the positivity of existence as sanctimonious, as wronging the victims; they balk at squeezing any kind of sense, however bleached, out of the victims' fate. . . . [These events] make a mockery of the construction of immanence as endowed with a meaning radiated by an affirmatively posited transcendence.[14]

On behalf of humanity and the suffering it endures, because God does nothing to prevent the history of human suffering and can therefore only be conceived of as unjust, God must be negated.

"That's rebellion," murmurs Alyosha in response to Ivan's protest. From the viewpoint of protest atheism, he is right. It is a "metaphysical rebellion," says Camus, "by which man protests against his condition and against the whole of creation."[15] This rebellion is not at all an inability to believe in the existence of God on the basis of speculation or formal epistemological considerations, although these might be used to support the protest. Rather, it is saying "no" to any God who could abide human misery. It is a "handing back the ticket" rather than an absolutely positive belief in the nonexistence of God. As Camus puts it:

> The metaphysical rebel is therefore not definitely an atheist, as one might think him, but he is inevitably a blasphemer. . . . he blasphemes . . ., denouncing God as the father of death and as the supreme outrage . . . . The rebel defies more than he denies.[16]

Protest Atheism and Traditional Theism

A cogent response to protest atheism requires an understanding of the theological context in which its questions about human suffering are framed. Protest atheism is formulated within the context of traditional theism and is tied to its method.[17] Theism and protest atheism are related methodologically in that both draw conclusions about God by a process of abstracting from the world. Protest atheism never challenges this method. As a result theism's concept of God is likewise never challenged but is presupposed by this atheism. Only theism's interpretation of the world and its conclusion about the existence of its God are disputed. Theism looks at the world, sees it as existing and purposive and concludes that there must be a God who exists and who, as the cause of the world's order, is, for instance, omnipotent, good and just. Protest atheism accepts this concept of God. However, in its own investigation of the world it does not find the evidence to support belief in this God. Purposiveness is not perceived. The order of the world is the actual disorder of suffering and injustice. The conclusion that protest atheism reaches, also by abstracting from the world, is that in view of this suffering and injustice there is no basis for belief. The omnipotent, good and just God could and would act against human suffering. But this God does not act and therefore must be denied. In this manner this atheistic protest presupposes both the method and the doctrine of God of traditional theism.

It is clear then that a significant issue in understanding protest atheism is its focus on certain attributes of God that have been maintained by traditional theism. Because God is omnipotent he must be held accountable for causing suffering or allowing it to continue, for he has the power to overcome it. And because God is just and good he cannot allow evil to continue or to triumph over innocent victims. But this means divine omnipotence and justice are self-contradictory. Because suffering does in fact continue, the omnipotent God cannot be thought of as just.

It is at this point in the atheistic protest that theism's notion of the impassibility of God also becomes an issue. God is negated because the divine does nothing about suffering. But the basis of this inaction is that God, conceived of as everything humans are not, cannot participate in suffering. God, in his own being, does not experience pain and suffering. Thus, God remains above the suffering world, unmoved by it and therefore unresponsive to it. Atheism, again, does not get beyond this conception. Rather, a conception of God taken from traditional theism is presupposed in atheism's rejection of God. Protest atheism claims that an impassible God cannot love or, in fact, be God. "A being without suffering is a being without a heart," writes Feuerbach.[18] Because such a God cannot love, it is an incomplete being, no God at all. Moltmann makes this analysis of the position of protest atheism:

> . . . a God who cannot suffer is poorer than any man. For a
> God who is incapable of suffering is a being who cannot be
> involved. Suffering and injustice do not affect him. And
> because he is so completely insensitive, he cannot be affected
> or shaken by anything. . . . But the one who cannot suffer
> cannot love either. . . . Finally, a God who is only omnipo-
> tent is in himself an incomplete being, for he cannot exper-
> ience helplessness and powerlessness.[19]

This God must be rejected, claims protest atheism, because he does not
exist or act in any meaningful way for human beings.

Protest atheism's rejection of God in the face of human suffering
can function as a negative theodicy.[20] This means that theism and
atheism are related once again, in that each attempts to relate the
suffering of the world to its claim about transcendence. Both exonerate
God and make suffering comprehensible. Theism attempts to overcome
the obstacle of suffering by perceiving purpose in and beneath it, by
demonstrating reasons for it from the viewpoint of a "higher harmony."
Thereby God and human agony are reconciled and the world is claimed
as God's. Suffering is overcome and made comprehensible on the basis
of God. Protest atheism, conversely, believes that, on the basis of the
sufferings of the world, the God who maintains such a world must be
overcome. Suffering and the omnipotent and just God of theism are
incompatible, contradictory terms. Suffering continues; therefore, in the
name of his omnipotence and justice, God must be denied. Again, the
only excuse for God is for him not to exist, and his nonexistence is
precisely what justifies him. Ernst Bloch labels this an atheism "for
God's sake."[21] However, protest atheism, while claiming that suffering
and injustice are unacceptable, joins theism in making the existence of
suffering comprehensible. For without an ultimate ground of power and
justice, one can understand how suffering and injustice persist in the
world.

In all of this the atheistic protest rejects traditional theism as a
"prohibitive and useless answer"[22] to the contradiction between God
and a suffering world. The concept of God developed in traditional
theism cannot stand under the weight of agony and pain in the world. In
its protest this atheism claims to take the problem of human suffering, as
well as the existence of God, more seriously than does theism. Nevertheless, because it is tied so closely to theism, because as Moltmann says,
"atheism demonstrates itself to be the brother of theism,"[23] atheism,
once again like theism, is unable to give an answer to the question of
suffering. All that is left is the rebellion against the absurd and the fight
for justice. For Camus (in at least some of his writings), ingredient in this

rebellion and fight is, at the same time, the decision "to accept such a universe," "a refusal to hope" and "a life without consolation."[24] Here there is no answer to suffering but to take it with resignation while protesting against it.

In distinction from these elements of Camus' thought, the atheism of the Critical School of Horkheimer and Adorno attempts to move beyond resignation. While it rejects God because of suffering and injustice, it refuses to accept "such a universe" or to give up hope. Unlike Mersault in *The Stranger*, it will not become reconciled with "the benign indifference of the universe."[25] Without God, however, Horkheimer and Adorno recognize that human suffering cannot achieve a complete answer and that their hope has no ultimate ground. This means that they believe their hope for the realization of perfect justice in the world is an illusion. For no matter what progress is made, past sufferings and agony remain without atonement. Adorno states it succinctly: "No reforms within the world suffice to do justice to the dead."[26]   And Max Horkheimer writes,

> It is impossible that such justice should ever become a reality within history. For, even if a better society develops and eliminates the present disorder, there will be no compensation for the wretchedness of past ages and no end to the distress in nature. We are therefore dealing here with an illusion . . . .[27]

Like Dostoevsky's Ivan Karamazov, these atheists refuse to accept past and present suffering even if it "may manure the soil of the future harmony of somebody else."[28] Therefore, even if justice is achieved now, it would remain a "finite world of infinite agony" (Adorno). Their atheism, therefore, has no full answer to human suffering. To be sure, the God who allows suffering must be negated; and yet there can be no hope for or satisfaction in the world without transcendence either. Moltmann states this dilemma of atheism: While "suffering is the rock of atheism," as with its brother theism, atheism also ends on the "rock of suffering."[29]

To their credit Horkheimer and Adorno recognize this limit to their protest and therefore attempt to go beyond the usual atheistic position. First, they find the basis of hope, even if uttered negatively, precisely in the limits of their critical theory. This position is articulated by Adorno when he writes, "It lies in the definition of negative dialectics that it will not come to rest in itself, as if it were total. This is a form of hope."[30] Second and more importantly, hope beyond the limits of their critical theory entails some form of transcendence. In spite of their critique of all

forms of transcendence, Horkheimer and Adorno prefer "to read transcendence longingly rather than to strike it out."[31] This holds open the
possibility for the "wholly other" while allowing no satisfaction with
present reality. It means, for instance, that even though perfect justice is
an illusion, its image cannot be "entirely banished."[32] Horkheimer and
Adorno, therefore, place themselves in an odd position. They are atheists
who find nothing in reality with which to identify the longed for
transcendence. And yet this atheism cannot rid itself of the "longing for
transcendence" or the desire for the "perfect justice" which has always
been carried by religion, even if in a distorted way.[33] Adorno expresses
this paradox:

> Even so, nothing could be experienced as truly alive if
> something that transcends life were not promised also; no
> straining of the concept leads beyond that. The transcendent
> is, and it is not.[34]

Here then in Horkheimer and Adorno is an attempt to move
beyond the alternative between traditional theism and traditional atheism,[35] which fail to provide an adequate response to the question of
suffering and the call for justice. But, if, as Horkheimer and Adorno say,
the transcendent is necessary for hope and justice, the Critical School's
proposal is also unable to provide an adequate response to suffering and
injustice. Caught between its longing for and its negation of transcendence, its position offers no positive ground for hope and justice, for any
such ground is negated.

Moltmann finds in their attempt to move beyond theism and
atheism a point on which a dialogue can be produced, through which
perhaps Horkheimer's and Adorno's longed for transcendent might be
given form.[36] But what Moltmann does not indicate is that Horkheimer
and Adorno have not really moved beyond the context of traditional
theism. On the one hand, their longed for transcendent falls victim to a
Feuerbachian critique. For even if allowed a positive status, according to
Feuerbach's sensuous epistemology, this transcendence, like theism's
God, is an abstraction, a projection that is in reality only anthropology.
As this transcendent is conceived now, it is devoid of predicates and,
therefore, again according to Feuerbach, meaningless to human beings
and in truth non-existent. It is obvious that a transcendent of this sort
cannot really serve as a true ground for hope or justice, because it is really
not transcendent at all. On the other hand, Horkheimer and Adorno
remain tied to traditional theism, because it is against its conception of
God that their negation of transcendence is directed in the first place. On
both sides, in their longing for transcendence and in their negation of

transcendence, they remained tied to traditional theism and thus unable to ground adequately their response to human suffering or their hope for justice. What is needed is a new context for understanding God, human suffering and the hope for justice.

The New Context:
Suffering and the Triune God

Trinitarian theology does not give a facile response to the problem of suffering, but on the contrary makes it possible to be as rigorous in an unwillingness to accept human pain as is protest atheism. It is therefore not its protest against human suffering that renders this atheism problematic. Nor does the Critical School's attempt to get beyond traditional theism and atheism need to be criticized. Rather, from the vantage point of the doctrine of the Trinity, atheism's problem lies in its adherence to the method and the conception of God of traditional theism, in its failure to move beyond traditional theism. We have seen that trinitarian thinking entails a transformation of theological method, a revolution in the doctrine of God and, therefore, the rejection of traditional theism. This means that Moltmann's question must be asked: "But if metaphysical theism disappears, can protest atheism still remain alive?"[37] Inasmuch as it remains the brother of theism, this atheism is guilty of a misidentification of the Christian conception of God and, therefore, has based its critique on a misunderstanding. The doctrine of the Trinity, by placing the issue of human suffering in the context of a different methodology and doctrine of God, calls into question the theological presuppositions of protest atheism while at the same time making possible cogent responses to the questions it raises.

We are now in a position to see how the response to atheism grounded on the belief that talk about God necessarily demeans human existence is also ingredient in a response to atheism which is a protest against human suffering. First, at issue in both responses are the attributes of God that have been understood in a certain way by traditional theism and rejected by atheism. For atheism rooted in human suffering, we have seen that the attributes of omnipotence, justice and impassibility are of central concern. Second, the trinitarian method of reconceiving the attributes that has been used thus far must also be used in "revolutionizing" these other three attributes. Because the question of the impassibility of God is essential in understanding the questions of divine omnipotence and justice, it will be the central focus of and vehicle for developing a response to atheism that arises in the context of the theodicy question. We will investigate how it is developed in Barth and developed and expanded in Moltmann.

The Christian doctrine of God's impassibility has its roots in early theology. Early theologians took over the philosophical concept of God for apologetic reasons. By it they were able to distinguish God who is immutable, impassible, etc., from changing, suffering human nature. Hence, they could claim that God was the answer to the human situation: "For where can transitory and mortal man find salvation if not in intransitoriness and immortality . . . ."[38] In this context early theologians made their case for belief in Christ by developing the doctrine of two natures.[39] Christ as fully human identifies with us, but as fully divine brings salvation to our humanity. But this whole process created problems for theology and obstacles to faith. For if God is impassible, how can Jesus be God and how can the unity of the two natures be conceived? While the attribute of impassibility may have an important religious foundation, its uncritical adoption has led to theological disaster and unbelief.

Following the method of trinitarian thinking, however, the notion of God's impassibility is redefined. While it remains true that God is distinct from humanity in that, unlike humanity, he does not suffer unwillingly as the result of some alien cause or deficiency of being, this cannot mean that God cannot suffer in any sense. God's impassibility cannot be absolutized so as to control God, to make him prisoner of his own attribute and to prevent him from actively and willingly opening himself up for suffering, for being affected by others. Both Barth and Moltmann make this point. Moltmann says,

> The justifiable denial that God is capable of suffering because of a deficiency in his being may not lead to a denial that he is incapable of suffering out of the fullness of his being, i.e. his love.[40]

This is similar to Barth's much earlier analysis in *Church Dogmatics* II/1:

> He can feel, and be affected. He is not impassible. He cannot be moved from outside by an extraneous power. But this does not mean that He is not capable of moving Himself. No, God is moved and stirred, yet not like ourselves in powerlessness, but in His own free power, in His innermost being. . . open, ready inclined (*propensus*) to compassion with another's suffering and therefore to assistance, impelled to take the initiative to relieve this distress.[41]

Both Barth and Moltmann then develop a conception of God who can and does suffer.

Barth's Contribution

For Barth, taking God's triune nature seriously entails the rejection of theism's impassible God. For the doctrine of the Trinity means that God is who he is in his revelation in Jesus, that God is given and known concretely in the suffering Jesus. As Barth says,

> . . . . frequently it is not recognized in this concrete-ness . . . . This deity is not the deity of a divine being furnished with all kinds of supreme attributes . . . . Who the one true God is and what He is, i.e., what is His being as God, and therefore His deity, His "divine nature," which is also the divine nature of Jesus Christ if He is very God — all this we have to discover from the fact that as such He is very man and a partaker of human nature, from His becoming man, from His incarnation and from what He has done and suffered in the flesh.[42]

This means nothing other than that the suffering of Jesus must be considered the suffering of God. The passion of Jesus reveals the passion of God. The Gospels always speak of the passion of Jesus "in such a way that this human action and suffering has to be represented and under-stood as the action and, therefore, the passion of God Himself . . . ."[43] In the Christ event, God actively opens Himself for suffering.[44] "He could have remained satisfied with Himself and with the impassible glory and blessedness of His own inner life. But He did not do so."[45] Rather, in the sending of the Son, God "ordained the surrender of something." God surrendered "His own impassibility in the face of the whole world."[46] This is the meaning of Barth's phrase, "God is the one who loves in freedom." In Jesus the Son, God has reached out and made human suffering his own. "He elected our suffering . . . . He elected it as His own suffering."[47]

According to Barth this suffering of God cannot be conceived of as only an external act of God. This is impossible according to the methodology required by trinitarian theology. To think of suffering as only touching God's outward economy but not his inner life would split apart God and his revelation. God would be somewhere behind or above his act in Jesus Christ. Therefore, it cannot be maintained that God is impassible but that as the Son he suffers.[48] There is not some person or mode of being, as Father for instance, in which God does not suffer. To its very depths, God's being is able to and does suffer; God in Jesus is able to and does take the conflict and contradiction of suffering into himself. But, in doing this, God does not come into conflict with himself. Because it involves the whole divine being, suffering does not indicate a contradiction in God. It is, rather, precisely by suffering as the Son that God is God.[49] Barth says, "It is not for us to speak of a contradiction and rift in the being of God, but to learn to correct our notions of the being of God, to reconstitute them in light of the fact that He does this."[50] Jüngel says of Barth that here "Barth's opposition to every form of natural theology received perhaps its most extreme formulation."[51] Another way to put this is to say that in bringing suffering into the being of God, trinitarian theology's rejection of traditional theism, and therefore the doctrine of God presupposed by protest atheism, becomes most sharply focused. Because the triune God is who he is in his revelation, "no concept of God independent of Jesus Christ may decide what is possible or impossible for God."[52] Suffering then is not something added on to or in contradiction with the nature of God, but for the triune God is constituent of God's action on behalf of humanity and therefore ingredient to God's inner being. The suffering of God is not only the identity with human suffering in the suffering Jesus, but also means that this human suffering of Jesus brings suffering into the being of God.

This God who suffers is brought to speech by the doctrine of the Trinity, for this doctrine is able to explicate what the suffering Jesus means for God. The doctrine of the Trinity can comprehend the theological fact that the appearance of Jesus depends upon the relations among the persons in the immanent Trinity. That is, it is founded upon the eternal sending by the Father and the obedience of the Son in the unity of the Holy Spirit. This means that God's suffering is a trinitarian possibility and that it is the doctrine of the Trinity that conceptualizes the God who can and does suffer in the depths of his inner being. Barth's clearest statement of the totality of the triune God's suffering comes in a passage in which he speaks of the element of truth in early patripassian theology:

> For what is represented and reflected in the humiliation of God is the mercy of the Father in which He too is not merely exalted but lowly with His Son, allowing Himself to be so affected by the misery of the creature, of man, that to save it, to endow it with eternal life, He does not count it too high a cost to give and send His Son, to elect Him to take our place as the Rejected, and therefore to abase Him. It is not at all the case that God has no part in the suffering of Jesus Christ even in His mode of being as Father. No, there is a *particula veri* in the teaching of the early Patripassians. This is that primarily it is God the Father who suffers in the offering and sending of His Son, in His abasement.

The suffering is not His own, but the alien suffering of the creature, of man, which he takes to Himself in Him. But He does suffer it in the humiliation of His Son with a depth with which it never was or will be suffered by any man — apart from the one who is His Son. And He does so in order that, having been borne by Him in the offering and sending of His Son, it should not have to be suffered in this way by man. The fatherly fellow-suffering of God is the mystery, the basis, of the humiliation of His Son; the truth of that which takes place historically in His crucifixion.[53]

Barth has developed the basis for a theological response to protest atheism founded upon the question of human suffering. He has done this by rejecting the old answers of traditional theism and opening a new context for addressing the questions and forming the answers. This new trinitarian context implies a theological method that does not rob from humanity to enrich God. Furthermore, this method leads to a new conception of God. God and suffering are no longer defined as contradictory terms. The world's sufferings are no longer seen over against the impassible God who does not act because the deity remains unmoved in heaven. The doctrine of the Trinity, rather, speaks of the God who does act on behalf of human suffering, but precisely by actively opening up the divine life for suffering. The triune God takes human suffering, identifies with it and makes this suffering his own. Human suffering has become God's suffering. The extent to which passibility is attributable to the triune God is perceived in the history of the Jesus. But this is founded ontologically on the passibility of the immanent Trinity, the willingness of the Father to suffer the abasement of the Son and the obedience of the Son in His suffering.

In response to protest atheism, then, the doctrine of the Trinity means that this atheism has, like traditional theism, committed a misidentification of the God of the Christian faith. The triune God means that when human beings suffer, they do not suffer alone. Nothing can separate them from God. For this God, human suffering is so significant that he has acted to make it his own, by risking himself in it. And, if human suffering finds its place in the divine life, then human beings know not only that when they suffer, God is there too, but that they have hope that suffering and death will ultimately be overcome.

Because Barth's material which we have drawn on here is directed mainly against traditional theism, the implications for a response to protest atheism are for the most part not explicitly given by Barth himself. However, in his book *The Crucified God*, Jürgen Moltmann takes up the trinitarian foundation given by Barth and develops it extensively and explicitly in response to protest atheism. In a sense Moltmann's work at this point can be read as an exegesis of the last quotation from Barth. It is to Moltmann that we now turn.

Jürgen Moltmann

For Moltmann, the question of theodicy is unavoidable for any relevant theology. Human suffering is the most profound basis for unbelief and the most serious challenge to Christian faith and theology. Today, as Moltmann sees it, the context of the theodicy question has shifted from natural evil to evil in political, social and economic spheres: "For us it has no longer only the old naturalistic form, as in the earthquake of Lisbon in 1775. It appears today in a political form, as in the question of Auschwitz."[54] It arises out of the "hells of world wars, the hells of Auschwitz, Hiroshima and Vietnam, and also the everyday experiences which make one man say to another 'You make my life hell' . . . ."[55] Christian theology becomes relevant only when it takes the theodicy question as an "absolute presupposition," only "when it accepts this solidarity with present suffering."[56] Because these issues are found in the heart of the Christian faith itself, in the crucifixion of Jesus and his dying cry, "My God, why hast thou forsaken me?", Christian theology must be done "within earshot" of the cross. "All Christian theology and all Christian life," Moltmann says, "is basically an answer to the question which Jesus asked as he died."[57] Only in this way only can the Christian faith be true to its own identity and relevant in the contemporary world.[58]

Moltmann responds theologically to the question of human suffering by developing a trinitarian theology of the cross. If the cross of Jesus stands as the center of the work of Jesus, the question must be asked what this means for the conception of God. The answer is a doctrine of the triune God that revolutionizes the doctrine of God of traditional theism in a way in which its inability to respond to suffering is overcome. In this manner Moltmann is able both to bring suffering into the life of God and to build a foundation for evil's ultimate defeat in the future of the triune God.

But how does Moltmann move from the cross of Jesus to language claiming Jesus as the second person of the Trinity, God the Son? Some commentators have criticized Moltmann for leaving this unclarified or merely assuming it.[59] Another way of stating this question is to ask about the appropriateness of the cross of Jesus as the foundation of Christian theology. How does one speak of God in light of the crucifixion? The key to Moltmann's thinking is his principle of "reading history both forwards and backwards."[60] Although the crucifixion precedes the resurrection historically, the saving significance of the cross is known only by looking back on it in light of the resurrection. Only by reading history from back to front, from the resurrection to the cross, is the identity of the crucified one made clear, is Jesus of Nazareth known to be Jesus the Christ of God. Moltmann supports this with an "analysis of the process of primitive Christian tradition."

> Primitive Christian recollections of Jesus were determined from the start by the experience of his resurrection through God. That was the only reason why his words and his story were remembered and why people were concerned with him.[61]

Using this principle of interpretation, Moltmann's analysis of the crucifixion of Jesus and its finally being conceived as an event "which takes place within God himself," i.e., as a triune event, is comprehensible. Moltmann agrees with Rudolf Bultmann in tying Jesus' preaching to his person. Jesus identifies himself with his preaching in such a way that no division is possible. Moltmann writes,

> Not only is the person of Jesus wholly taken up into his word, but his word in its turn is wholly taken up into his person, and becomes event in it.[62]

This means that, even though Jesus was crucified for religious reasons, as blasphemer against the Jewish law, and for political reasons, as a rebel against the *Pax Romanum*,[63] these do not explain "the true inner pain of his suffering and death."[64] Essentially, Jesus' life was theological, Moltmann claims.[65] His whole existence, word and deed, took place in relationship to the God whom he called "My Father" and whose kingdom of grace he proclaimed as imminent.

> Like no one before him in Israel, Jesus had proclaimed the imminence of the kingdom of God and demonstrated amongst the incurable, the rejected and the hated that it was a gracious imminence, not to judge but to save. In his own relationship to the God of this kingdom, he himself had gone beyond the framework of the tradition of God's covenant with Israel . . . . Note in passing that Jesus often called God exclusively 'My Father.' This is the expression of a fellowship with God which is not mediated through the covenant, the nation and the tradition, and must therefore be termed a direct fellowship . . . . By identifying himself with God in this way, Jesus was clearly assuming that God identified with him and his words.[66]

Moltmann believes that the death of Jesus must be understood in this context, for it was this God who abandoned Jesus on the cross. Moltmann accepts, not as Jesus' literal words, but as the most accurate interpretation of Jesus' death, the death cry of Jesus in Mark 15:34: "My God, why hast thou forsaken me."[67] Thus, the true pain of Jesus' death is that the God whom he called Father, and whom he had preached as close, as one who would not forsake, forsakes him on the cross. "The torment in his torments was this abandonment by God."[68] The event of the cross, then, must finally be understood as "something which took place between Jesus and his God, and between his Father and Jesus."[69] Because Jesus dies on the cross with a cry of abandonment, his message and existence are put in question. And, because Jesus' person and message are one, not only Jesus himself is at stake here, but the truth and deity of his God as well. Moltmann claims, in what he admittedly calls an "exaggerated form," that the cry of Jesus from the cross "means not only 'My God, why hast thou forsaken Me?' but, at the same time, 'My God, why hast thou forsaken thyself?'"[70] Because of the contradiction of the cross, questions arise about the identity of Jesus, the truth of the God he preached and the relationship between Jesus and this God.

Only in the resurrection is the contradiction of the cross overcome and the questions it raises given answer.[71] At this point, Moltmann introduces his principle of reading history forward and backwards. Although the resurrection points to the future triumph of the righteousness of God over all creation, history must also be read backwards from this event. For the "resurrection hope sheds its light not only forward, into God's future, by giving a foretaste of the future in the anticipations of the spirit, but also backwards, into the mystery of the suffering and death of the exalted Lord."[72] The resurrection vindicates Jesus and his message. In it Jesus is revealed as the Christ of God, the Son of God, Kyrios, God's "representative." And if Jesus is this in his resurrection, the question must inevitably be asked, "who was he in his earthly life and in his suffering and death on the cross?"[73] The answer to this question is given by the Christian identification of the crucified Jesus with the resurrected one. If the one who was resurrected, Moltmann argues, is the same Jesus who was crucified, then the Jesus who was crucified is none other than who he is shown to be in his resurrection.

> By his resurrection Jesus is qualified in his person to be the
> Christ of God. So his suffering and death must be under-
> stood to be the suffering and death of the Christ of God.[74]

This means that the resurrection, far from emptying the cross and suffering of Jesus of meaning by turning Jesus into a glorious heavenly figure, reveals that his death is filled with "saving significance." For, again, it shows that the one who was crucified was "the incarnation of the coming God in our flesh and in his death on the cross."[75] Moltmann writes,

> The coming of God has been made flesh in Jesus of Nazareth. The future of the qualitatively new creation has already begun through the history of Jesus' suffering in the history of the suffering of the abandoned world . . . . If, as the Easter vision implies, God has identified himself, his judgment and his kingdom with the crucified Jesus, his cross and his helplessness, then conversely the resurrection of the crucified Jesus into the coming glory of God contains within itself the process of the incarnation of the coming God and his glory in the crucified Jesus.[76]

Implicit in this analysis of the resurrection is also the vindication of the God of Jesus. If the resurrection vindicates Jesus' person and his message, both of which were tied inextricably to the God whom Jesus called Father, then the resurrection of Jesus vindicates this God also. It is this God who raised Jesus from the dead. Again, by reading history from the future into the past, it also means that the God whom Jesus called Father and who raised him from the dead was active in the crucifixion of Jesus. In Jesus' abandonment on the cross, God was not absent but working, and not simply passively allowing it to happen, but actively involved himself. Moltmann supports his position by appealing to Paul

> in II Cor. 5.19ff, when he says 'God was in Christ.' In other words, God not only acted in the crucifixion of Jesus or sorrowfully allowed it to happen, but was himself active with his own being in the dying Jesus and suffered with him.[77]

While the resurrection reveals Jesus to be the Son of God, it also shows this God to be the one who sent his son and gave him up to suffering and death.[78] Therefore, the cross is the point of God's activity and Jesus, the Son of God, is the revealer of God.

> That means that God represents and reveals himself in the surrender of Jesus and in his passion and death on the cross. But where God represents and reveals himself, he also identifies and defines himself.[79]

The consequences of Moltmann's theology that are important for our discussion here are numerous.

First, Moltmann's analysis, like Barth's theology, gives theology a concrete epistemology. All Christian theology, all "Christian statements about God, about creation, about sin and death . . . about history, about the church, about faith and sanctification, about the future and about hope stem from the crucified Christ."[80] Because in the concrete event of the cross God "identifies and defines himself," any "presupposition of a concept of God imported 'from elsewhere'" must be given up "in light of what happened on the cross."[81] When the risen Jesus is seen on the cross, Christian theology says "*this* is God, and God is like *this*."[82]

Second, the crucifixion is identified as an event "which takes place within God himself"[83] and in which God acts on behalf of human suffering by suffering himself. If God is active at the cross, in sending and delivering up his Son, in revealing, identifying and defining himself, then it follows, according to Moltmann's thinking, that God himself is really present here. It can be said with Paul that "God was in Christ."[84] This means that God himself really suffered and experienced death in Christ. In a summary passage, Moltmann writes,

> . . . God was not silent and uninvolved in the cross of Jesus. Nor was he absent in the God-forsakenness of Jesus. He acted in Jesus, the Son of God: in that men betrayed him, handed him over and delivered him up to death, God himself suffers the pains of abandonment. In the death of the Son, death comes upon God himself, and the Father suffers the death of His Son in his love for forsaken man. Consequently, what happened on the cross must be understood as an event between God and the Son of God. In the action of the Father in delivering up his Son to suffering and to a godless death, God is acting in himself.[85]

Third, this means that the God defined by the cross is not the impassible, immutable God of traditional theism, which is presupposed by atheism. On the basis of God's identification with and self-definition in the cross, it follows that this God can and does suffer and change. Like Barth, Moltmann indicates the true element in the traditional doctrines of God's immutability and impassibility: God does not change or suffer under the "constraint from that which is not of God" or from "a deficiency in his being."[86] But this does not mean that there is no possible way for God to change and suffer, that God cannot voluntarily open himself for change and suffering. For at the cross God does precisely this. Moltmann continues the summary passage above:

> [At the cross] . . . he is acting in himself in this manner of suffering and dying in order to open up in himself life and freedom for sinners. Creation, new creation and resurrection are external works of God against chaos, nothingness and death. The suffering and dying of Jesus, understood as the suffering and dying of the Son of God, on the other hand, are works of God towards himself and therefore at the same time passions of God. God overcomes himself,. . . takes the judgment on the sin of man upon himself. . . . The cross of Jesus, . . . therefore reveals a change in God, a *stasis* within the Godhead: 'God is other.'[87]

Finally, to comprehend this whole analysis requires, according to Moltmann, the doctrine of the Trinity. In the final analysis the event of the cross is triune. To speak for now of only the first two persons of the Trinity, if God is defined as the Father of Jesus who sent and delivered him up to the cross and also by the abandonment on the cross of Jesus the Son of this God, if both of these elements reveal and define God, if this cross is an event within God, if here God becomes other, as Moltmann's analysis claims, then at the cross a triune God is revealed and the doctrine of the Trinity is required to comprehend this event. So for Moltmann the doctrine of the Trinity has nothing to do with "impractical speculation" about the nature of God, but is "nothing other than a shorter version of the passion narrative of Christ . . . ."[88] It is made necessary by the cross.

> The theological concept for the perception of the crucified Christ is the doctrine of the Trinity. The material principle of the doctrine of the Trinity is the cross of Christ. The formal principle of knowledge of the cross is the doctrine of the Trinity.[89]

The cross manifests the relationship in distinction and unity between the Father and the Son, shows this relationship to be bonded by the Spirit and brings the movement of this Spirit into the world.[90] This will be examined more closely shortly. But it is for this reason that Moltmann claims that a Christian doctrine of God must be trinitarian and only a trinitarian doctrine of God can be Christian.[91]

At this point a partial response based on the doctrine of the Trinity can be given to atheism grounded on the problem of suffering. The triune God of the Christian faith is a God who acts on behalf of human suffering by suffering himself. If Jesus is the Son, the second person of the Trinity, then at the cross of Jesus God identifies with human suffering. Here God "enters into the situation of man's god-forsakenness."[92] When humans suffer, therefore, they are not alone, but God is suffering with them.

However, Moltmann wants to go further than this. He wants to maintain that God suffers not only in his external works or only as Son, but also in his inner being. Moltmann develops his trinitarian theology of the cross to demonstrate two additional major points. God not only identifies with human suffering at the cross, but (1) at the cross really suffers in himself and in a way that involves his whole triune being. And (2) God's willingness to suffer at the cross reveals that God has opened himself to all the sufferings of history, which he takes up and integrates into his triune life, thereby promising to overcome and transform them.

Moltmann broadens his trinitarian theology of the cross by moving the meaning of the cross beyond a soteriological context only, to its implications for theological concepts. If Jesus is the second person of the Trinity, then at the cross, in his sacrifice and identity with suffering humanity, God is certainly providing the ground of salvation. On the other hand, however, if Jesus is the second person of the Trinity, then the cross has been brought into God's very being and the question becomes: "What does the cross of Jesus mean for God himself?"[93] The cross cannot leave the divine being unaffected. From the perspective of the cross in God, it is seen that suffering and death have been taken into God, and into his inner being, and are not his only in his external works.[94] Moltmann makes this point by criticizing any theology where the distinction between the economic Trinity and the immanent Trinity is used to separate the inner being of God from the way God appears in his acts of salvation. Rather, God is who he is in his relationship to us. Therefore, Moltmann endorses Karl Rahner's thesis: "The economic Trinity is the immanent Trinity, and the immanent Trinity is the economic Trinity."[95] If this is not the case, God becomes some reality other than who he is in his revelation, and once again theology becomes an abstract modalism.

This does not mean that Moltmann does not use the distinction between the immanent and the economic Trinity. He does employ it, at least in works outside *The Crucified God*. But he maintains a strict identity between the immanent and economic Trinity, by following Barth's method of speaking of the immanent Trinity only on the basis of the economic Trinity. This method, again as with Barth, insures the ontological ground of God's revelation in Jesus. Moltmann writes,

> As God appears in history as the sending Father and the
> sent Son, so he must earlier have been in himself. The
> relation of the one who sends to the one sent as it appears in
> the history of Jesus thus includes in itself an order of origin
> within the Trinity, and must be understood as that order's
> historical correspondence. Otherwise there would be no
> certainty that in the messianic mission of Jesus we have to
> do with God himself. The relations between the discernible
> and visible history of Jesus and the God whom he called my
> Father, correspond to the relation of the Son to the Father in
> eternity. The *missio ad intra* is the foundation for the *missio
> ad extra*. Thus theological reflection moves inevitably from
> the contemplation of the sending of Jesus from the Father
> to God himself . . . . From the Trinity of the sending of
> Jesus we can reason back to the Trinity in origin, in God
> himself, so that — conversely — we may understand the
> history of Jesus as the revelation of the living nature of
> God.[96]

By this method the suffering and death that are perceived
externally at the cross must be seen as reflecting God's inner being, and
his whole being. There is a *perichoresis* of suffering among the persons of
the Trinity. Father, Son and Holy Spirit are involved in this suffering.
Once again it is the doctrine of the Trinity that makes comprehensible
the inner suffering of God. Moltmann, like Barth, recognizes the true
element in patripassian thinking, but guards against this heresy by
distinguishing the suffering of the Father from that of the Son. While the
Son suffers dying he does not experience death itself. No one experiences
his or her own death, but only dying. It is the Father who suffers the
death of the Son in giving the Son out of love for humankind.

> The grief of the Father here is just as important as the death
> of the Son. The Fatherlessness of the Son is matched by the
> Sonlessness of the Father and if God has constituted himself
> as the Father of Jesus Christ, then he also suffers the death
> of his Fatherhood in the death of his Son.[97]

In the separation between the Son and the Father, the pain of dying, the
loss of death and the hell of God-forsakenness come upon God himself
and are taken into his inner triune being.

But if the suffering of God is manifest in the separation of the
Father and the Son, in the abandonment of the Son by the Father, how
are these persons united so that they may constitute God? It is the Holy
Spirit that unites the Father and the Son in their separation. Moltmann
seems to parallel Augustine's conception of the Holy Spirit as the "bond

of Love" cementing the union of the Father and the Son.[98] Moltmann develops this on the basis of an exegesis of the New Testament word, *paradidonai,* which means deliver up, abandon or hand over.[99] In certain New Testament texts (i.e., John 3:16, Romans 8:31f), God is the subject of this delivering up. Out of love for humankind he gave up his own Son to God-forsakenness, sin and an "accursed death."[100] In other passages (i.e., Gal. 2:20), however, it is the Son who is subject of this formula and who, out of love for humankind, delivers himself up. This is reflected in the Gospels where Jesus goes willingly the way of the cross. This means that where the Father and Son are the farthest apart they are also the most deeply united in their suffering love for humankind. "In the cross, Father and Son are most deeply separated in forsakenness and at the same time are most inwardly one in their surrender."[101] This community of will that is the basis for the unity of the Trinity in the separation between the Father and the Son and is the basis for this separation in the unity of God's love, Moltmann identifies as the Spirit, the Spirit of suffering love. It is in this Spirit that both the Father and the Son "deliver up."

> The surrender through the Father and the offering of the Son take place 'through the Spirit.' The Holy Spirit is therefore the link in the separation. He is the link joining the bond between the Father and the Son, with their separation.[102]

It is, therefore, this Spirit of suffering love that issues from the cross into the world. What "proceeds from the event between the Father and the Son must be understood as the spirit of the surrender of the Father and the Son, as the spirit which creates love for forsaken men . . . ."[103] In the event between the Father and the Son in the Spirit, God makes room in his own being for suffering and death. In the Spirit which proceeds from this event, God continues to remain open and to identify with human suffering and to integrate the suffering of all creation into his inner being.

Moltmann has shown, then, that the doctrine of the Trinity comprehends the God whose whole being is involved in suffering. This is what is meant, according to Moltmann, by the phrase God is love. God constitutes his being as love in the event of his suffering love at the cross that is manifest as an event between the Father and the Son in the unity of the Spirit. Furthermore, in agreement with Barth at this point, Moltmann asserts that the event character of the triune God cannot be transcended. " . . . 'God' is not another nature or a heavenly person or moral authority, but in fact an 'event.'" For anyone "who speaks of

God in Christian terms must tell the history of Jesus as a history between the Son and the Father."[104] God, therefore, is an event of suffering love. Finally, because the Spirit is still proceeding from the event of the cross, God must be an open and unfinished event. The Spirit of suffering love is still active in the world, bringing all things to God. Moltmann is able in this way to read the Trinity eschatologically. To use one of his favorite phrases: God is not yet all in all. ". . . the Trinity is no self-contained group in heaven, but an eschatological process open for men on earth, which stems from the cross of Christ."[105]

The Apologetic Function of the Doctrine of the Trinity: The Passibility, Goodness and Self-limitation of God

We will now draw the implications of Barth's and Moltmann's trinitarian theologies to show how the doctrine of the Trinity as developed here offers a means of responding to atheism based on the theodicy question. This apologetic function contains two directions which take theology beyond both traditional theism and atheism.

In the first place the doctrine of the Trinity, as it clarifies the Christian concept of God for dogmatics, contains a polemic against the theology of theism. "Is the theistic concept of God applicable to Christian belief in the crucified God?" Moltmann asks.[106] "No" is the proper response from the viewpoint of trinitarian theology. The suffering, loving, dynamically changing triune God of the Christian faith who actively involves himself in human suffering and defines himself in his giving of himself to humankind — in becoming human — cannot be identified with the impassible, immutable God of traditional theism who remains isolated in himself in heaven and who defines himself in opposition to everything human. Trinitarian theology, here, agrees with atheism. The theistic God must be negated, for he is a misidentification of the Christian God and can give only a useless answer to the problem of suffering.[107] This God does not act on behalf of human suffering, because this theistic God cannot suffer himself. It is in this sense that Moltmann uses the expression: "For Christ's sake I am an atheist."[108]

However, protest atheism never gets beyond the theistic conception in its thinking and negation of God. Therefore, while trinitarian theology is clarifying the doctrine of God for the Christian faith and thus saying yes to protest atheism on the one hand, on the other hand the direction of the trinitarian based apology is polemic against and saying no to protest atheism. For, from the trinitarian perspective, protest atheism is based upon a misidentification of God also. God is negated because he does nothing in the face of suffering. Unlike possible human beings, he is impassible and therefore cannot be affected by or respond to human pain. From the perspective of the doctrine of the Trinity, however, a response to the problem of suffering is possible — a response which unlike protest atheism gives a foundation for the hope of justice.

The triune God is not an impassible God who does nothing in view of the terrors of human life. Rather, this God acts. The doctrine of the Trinity comprehends the God who in his inner being is an event, an event that acts concretely in suffering love for suffering humanity. God, here, in his very nature reaches out and identifies with human suffering. In this event God subjects himself to the ambiguities of nature and the suffering which that might entail. More evident is his identification with suffering in the social-political context, where he suffers as an innocent victim without the consolation of "divine" intervention. Here God knows in his own being the suffering of human beings in God-forsakenness. Therefore, the response is possible that when and however humans suffer, they do not suffer alone; God suffers with them. That is, the triune God in opening himself for suffering at the cross answers one of the protests of atheism in that he atones for human suffering. He suffers for humanity in that he suffers with humanity. Therefore, in suffering God is "at one" with humanity. Nothing at all can separate God from humanity.

But so far this constitutes only a partial response to protest atheism. For the triune God does not only identify with human suffering. But, in the identification of the cross of Jesus as a God event, in the identification of Jesus as the second person of the Trinity — the Son who suffers dying and forsakenness by being delivered up by the Father who suffers the death and loss of the Son, both acting in the unity of the Holy Spirit, the Spirit of suffering love — the doctrine of the Trinity claims that God has taken human pain, suffering and death into the very center of his being and life and has made them his own. In making the suffering, death and hell of God-forsakenness at the low point of history his own, the triune God opens his being to all of human history and its suffering. Here we see the universal significance of God's suffering and the deepening of its atoning effect. As Barth says,

> We have already said that in this event God allows the
> world and humanity to take part in the history of the inner
> life of His Godhead, in the movement in which from and to
> all eternity He is Father, Son and Holy Spirit, and therefore
> the one true God.[109]

Moltmann parallels Barth in describing the life of the triune God as the "history of God":

> . . . this history of God contains within itself the whole abyss
> of god-forsakenness, absolute death and the non-God . . . .
> All human 'history, however much it may be determined by
> guilt and death, is taken up into this history of God,' i.e.,
> into the Trinity, and integrated into the future of the 'his-
> tory of God.' There is no suffering within this history of
> God which is not God's suffering; no death which has not
> been God's death in the history on Golgotha.[110]

God has identified — become at one — with the whole history of
human suffering, so that all humans who suffer, past, present or future,
may be at one with the life of God. Nothing at all can separate humanity
from God. In this triune history of God even "Auschwitz is taken up
into the grief of the Father, the surrender of the Son and the power of the
Spirit."[111]

Here the justness and the goodness of the triune God are seen.
Unlike the theistic God presupposed by protest atheism, the triune God
does not fail to act. He does not remain aloof from and unresponsive to
humanity and its suffering. Nor does this God merely offer a higher
position from which suffering can be accepted as meaningful. Rather, the
God brought to speech by the doctrine of the Trinity makes his protest
against human suffering by entering concrete historical practice against
it. And in this practice he identifies with and takes the side of the
innocent victims of suffering and includes them and their suffering into
his own being. In this action on behalf of human misery, God himself
joins the atheistic protest against suffering.[112]

The apologetic function of the doctrine of the Trinity, however, is
not complete with the demonstration of the inclusion of suffering in
God's being. It must also clarify how this inclusion is soteriological, how
it is the basis for the hope of justice and the overcoming of suffering. If
the triune God has included in his life the whole history of death and
suffering, then there is the basis for the hope of transformation in the
future life and history of this God. God has not yet finished his activity.[113] Again at this point the triune God joins the atheistic protest.
There can be a sort of agreement with Horkheimer and Adorno when
they claim that nothing yet corresponds to a transcendent ground for the
hope for justice. The doctrine of the Trinity claims something similar
about God, that God is not yet "all in all."[114] Nothing yet corresponds
to the glory, the full deity of God, not even God himself. We have seen
that the triune God is an open, eschatological process, an event which is
not yet completed.

> This history of God or this history in God begins with the
> sending and delivering up of the Son, continues with his
> resurrection and the transference of the rule of God to him
> and only ends when the Son hands over his rule to the
> Father. The delivering up on the cross is the central point of
> this history in God, not its conclusion.[115]

But while for protest atheism the lack of a fully realized transcendent means the despair of seeing historical justice as an illusion, in
light of the triune God who is still at work and has not yet reached his
future glory, this lack of a completed transcendent reality is the basis for
a positive hope for justice and the transformation of suffering. For the
fullness of God's being is in the future.[116] God has promised there to be
"all in all." And we know that at the cross the triune God has taken all
suffering into his own being and that the Holy Spirit continues the
process of integrating human history and suffering into the life of God.
The victims of suffering are a part of the divine life now and therefore
will be present in God's transformed future as well. Hope is seen in that
the God comprehended in the doctrine of the Trinity is so passible that
he has risked His own being out of love for us. He has demonstrated that
he will not come to his full deity and glory, that he will not be "all in all"
without the justification of all things — without the transformation of
human suffering into joy and human death into eternal life. This is the
foundation of hope for justice and for the transformation of all human
suffering: the continuing history of God that leads to his future. Until
this is accomplished, in the name of the triune God the protest against
suffering and the negation of any divine reality that claims completion
for itself and fulfillment for humanity in the present must continue.

Finally, this leads us to a response to the understanding of God's
omnipotence raised by protest atheism. In each case, God is rejected
because the atheist presupposes that the divine reality is omnipotent. If
God is omnipotent why does he not fully rectify the human situation
now? The first response is that atheism, like traditional theism, misuses
this concept, for it defines God's omnipotence abstractly, as the opposite
of humanity's limited power, as God's ability to do anything he wills. In
the context of the doctrine of the Trinity, however, God's omnipotence
must be defined as were the other attributes, on the basis of his concrete
revelation in the history of Jesus. Two features of conceiving his omnipotence, then, come into view. One is that God's omnipotence must be
eschatologically defined. It is only in the future where God is "all in all."
The other feature is the basis for this. God's omnipotence is truly seen in
that he works through a dying man, through suffering.[117] This means
that the triune God's omnipotence involves a self-limitation out of love

for humanity. The doctrine of the Trinity conceives of God as an event of
suffering love directed toward humanity whose purpose is the liberation
of humanity from suffering and death. Without coming into contradiction, therefore, God can never use coercive force to assure the accom-
plishment of his will. It is Satan who acts in this manner, Augustine
reminds us.[118] The triune God can only overcome suffering by bearing it
in himself in protest against it. The love of God grasped in the doctrine
of the Trinity, then, "cannot command love and counterlove."

> As its purpose is freedom, it is directed towards freedom. So
> it cannot prohibit slavery and enmity, but must suffer this
> contradiction and the grief of protest against it, and mani-
> fest this grief in protest. That is what happened on the cross
> of Christ. God is unconditional love, because he takes on
> himself grief at the contradiction in men and does not
> angrily suppress this contradiction.[119]

In this limitation of God's omnipotence in suffering love, however, the
doctrine of the Trinity also comprehends the ground of human love and
hope for transformation.

> God allows himself to be forced out. God suffers, God
> allows himself to be crucified and is crucified, and in this
> consummates his unconditional love that is so full of hope.
> But that means that in the cross he becomes himself the
> condition of love. The loving Father has a parallel in the
> loving Son and in the Spirit creates similar patterns of love
> in man in revolt. The fact of this love can be contradicted. It
> can be crucified, but in crucifixion it finds its fulfillment and
> becomes love of the enemy. Thus its suffering proves to be
> stronger than hate.[120]

In summary, the doctrine of the Trinity has provided the basis of a
response to the issues raised against Christian belief by protest atheism.
This doctrine not only is an analysis of the God who has become concrete
and sensuous, so that it includes a basis for an epistemology demanded
by Feuerbach. It also means that God's identity is known only in this
concrete event. Therefore, the doctrine of the Trinity comprehends the
Christian God's concrete, sensuous praxis on behalf of human suffering,
the lack of which is criticized by protest atheism. On the basis of
trinitarian theology it can be said that atheism is correct to attack the
God of traditional theism who remains isolated in apathetic impassibility
and omnipotence and who must be rejected because of his injustice.
Although protest atheism remains tied to this misidentified theory of
God, this is not the God toward which Christian faith is directed. Protest

atheism has never perceived the God who has defined himself in his concrete praxis — the triune God who joins the protest and demonstrates his justness by acting against human suffering; who limits his omnipotence, works in suffering love and who will not be fully God while human suffering persists; who surrenders his impassibility and becomes at one with human suffering by identifying with it and by taking suffering and the grief and protest against it into his own life; the triune God who in his promised future, thereby, becomes the ground of hope for the transformation of all suffering, past, present and future. By identifying this God the doctrine of the Trinity "distinguishes" faith from both traditional theism and atheism.[121]

In this chapter the response to the atheism which is a protest against human suffering has been developed for the most part by examining the transformation of the relevant attributes of God which occurs in trinitarian theology. A more complete response involves two further points. We have already mentioned the way in which the triune God joins the protest against human suffering. This needs further analysis and clarification. Moreover, another important point without which a response to the theodicy issue would remain incomplete and of questionable concreteness involves the way in which the triune God engages persons in the protest against suffering. These further points are also necessary to more adequately distinguish the trinitarian response from attempts to reformulate theism. Theists are not necessarily tied to the absolute conception of God, and some have in fact attempted to overcome it precisely in answer to the theodicy question. Edgar S. Brightman suggests a "finite God" as a more coherent way of explaining, among other issues, the problem of evil.[122] Gordon Kaufman, in a chapter entitled "God and Evil" in *God the Problem*, rejects what he refers to as the "abstract" notion of God's omnipotence and modifies it by applying the concept of "agent" to God's activity.[123] In process thought God can be conceived of as passible. Alfred North Whitehead can speak of God as "the great companion — the fellow-sufferer, who understands" and, thereby, indicate God's identification with human suffering.[124]

A major limitation of these positions, however, is that they are subject to Feuerbach's epistemological attack. Their conceptions are abstracted from human experience and are therefore open to the charge that they are mere anthropology.[125] Furthermore, these interpretations do not develop a notion either of God's protest against human suffering or of his engagement of persons in that protest. Trinitarian thinking speaks of God's self-limitation and suffering on the concrete basis of Jesus and therefore can respond to Feuerbach. And, it enables the development of these other two themes. We will, therefore, return to these issues and to the theme of theodicy in Chapter VI, where, in the context of a trinitarian eschatology, they can be developed more fully.

Nevertheless, because both of these issues involve the question of the relationship of practice to belief, we must first turn to a discussion of this.

NOTES

[1] See M. Douglas Meeks, *Origins of the Theology of Hope* (Philadelphia, 1974), pp. 16ff; Carl E. Braaten, "A Trinitarian Theology of the Cross," *The Journal of Religion*, LVI, no. 1 (Jan. 1, 1976), p. 117; G. Clarke Chapman, Jr. "Moltmann's Vision of Man," *Anglican Theological Review*, LVI, no. 3 (July, 1974), pp.313, 315f.

[2] For a work that gives further examples of this type of atheism, see S. Paul Schilling, *God in an Age of Atheism* (Nashville, 1969), pp.33-80.

[3] Theodor W. Adorno, *Negative Dialectics* (New York, 1973), pp. 401f.

[4] A quotation from Stendhal, cited in Moltmann, *CG*, p. 225.

[5] Albert Camus, *The Myth of Sisyphus* (New York, 1955), p. 20.

[6] *Ibid.*, p. 12.

[7] *Ibid.*, p. 109.

[8] *Ibid.*, p. 110.

[9] Albert Camus, *The Plague*, trans. Stuart Gilbert (New York, 1948), pp. 196-97.

[10] Fyodor Dostoevsky, *The Brothers Karamazov*, trans. Constance Garnett (New York, 1957), pp. 250f.

[11] *Ibid.*, p. 254.

[12] *Ibid.*

[13] Adorno, p. 367.

[14] *Ibid.*, p. 361.

[15] Albert Camus, *The Rebel*, trans. Anthony Bower (New York, 1956), p. 23.

[16] *Ibid.*, p. 24-25.

[17] See Moltmann, *CG*, pp. 219ff., for this and what follows.

[18] Feuerbach, *Essence of Christianity*, p. 62.

[19] See Moltmann, *CG*, pp. 222-223.

[20] See *Ibid.*, p. 225.

[21] Cited in *Ibid.*, p. 252.

[22] *Ibid.*, p. 223.

[23] *Ibid.*, p. 221.

[24] Camus, *The Myth of Sisyphus*, p. 44.

[25] Albert Camus, *The Stranger*, trans. Stuart Gilbert (New York, 1946), p. 154.

[26] Adorno, p. 385.

[27] Max Horkheimer, *Critical Theory*, trans. Matthew J. O'Connell and others (New York, 1972), pp. 129-130.

[28] Dostoevsky, p. 253.

[29] See Jürgen Moltmann, *The Trinity and the Kingdom*, trans. Margaret Kohl (New York, 1981), pp. 47-49. (Hereafter cited as *TK.*)

[30] Adorno, p. 406. On the same page he also writes, "To this end, dialectic is obliged to make a final move: being at once the impression and the critique, of the universal delusive context, it must turn even against itself."

[31] *Ibid.*, p. 404.

[32] See Horkheimer, p. 129.

[33] *Ibid.*

[34] Adorno, p. 375.

[35] See Moltmann, *CG*, p. 223ff. Moltmann gives particular attention to Horkheimer.

[36] See *Ibid.*, pp. 223-226.

[37] *Ibid.*, p. 221.

[38] *Ibid.*,p. 228.

[39] On this see *Ibid.*, pp. 227-235.

[40] *Ibid.*, p. 230.

[41] *CD* II/1, 370.

[42] *CD* IV/1, 177.

[43] *Ibid.*, p. 245. See also p. 246: ". . . it is the eternal God Himself who has given Himself in His Son to be man, and as man to take upon Himself this human passion." Also, p. 247: "We are not dealing merely with any suffering, but with the suffering of God . . . ." See also *CD* II/2, 162-168.

[44] God's passion, Barth claims, is always active. His *"passio* in history is as such *actio"* (*CD* I/1, 144). See also *CD* II/1, 371ff and IV/1, 245-246.

[45] *CD* II/2, 166.

[46] *Ibid.*, p. 163.

[47] *Ibid.*, p. 164.

[48] See Feuerbach, *Essence of Christianity*, p. 59, where he makes this mistake. Moltmann points out the problem "which Feuerbach had with Luther's theology of the cross," (See *CG*, pp. 76f, n. 19). In *The Essence of Faith According to Luther*, Feuerbach writes, "Of course you

do not produce God in your sense from yourself; a crucified God is as
ludicrous a contradiction as a painfully punished notion." (Cited in *CG*,
p. 77.) Theistic thinking that claims God is impassible always at least
borders on this notion.

Davis Perkins ["The Problem of Suffering: Atheistic Protest and
Trinitarian Response," *St. Luke Journal of Theology*, XXIII, No. 1
(December, 1979), pp. 14-32] leaves room for the same type of mistake. He wishes to maintain the distinction between what God is in
himself and what God is for us. Therefore, he speaks only about the
economic Trinity and "not at all" about the immanent Trinity.
Although, according to Perkins, he would not claim that the economic
Trinity "exhausts the totality of God," what he does maintain is "that
conversations about the way God is in and of himself are meaningless
and that attempts to deduce an immanent Trinity from the economic
Trinity are futile"(p. 26). Perkins seems to be unaware that developing
the immanent Trinity from the economic Trinity is precisely what
preserves the inexhaustible mystery of God, even as he reveals himself.
But Perkins goes on to locate the trinitarian response to atheism in the
suffering love of God (pp. 28-30). We must ask: does this trinitarian
ability to suffer reach God's inner being? Or, is God's aseity different
from his promeity? Is God in contradiction with himself? Does God
suffer in the economic Trinity, but exist in some other way in himself?
Perkins quotes Moltmann's sentence: "God's being is in suffering and
suffering is in God's being . . . ." But he has no sense of the fact that
Moltmann is speaking of the immanent Trinity (which for him, following Rahner, is derived from, is, the economic Trinity). In any case,
Perkins' statement about the "highly speculative immanent Trinity" (p.
25) suggests that he does not understand how the doctrine of the Trinity
is developed or the role of the immanent Trinity in Barth — whom he
passes over with a single phrase: Barth's use of the doctrine of the
Trinity was to "make it into an overarching formal principle" (p. 14) —
or in Moltmann.

[49] See *CD* IV/1, 246-247: ". . . in this humiliation God is
supremely God . . . . He has maintained and revealed His deity in the
passion of this man as eternal Son."

[50] See *CD* IV/1, 186. See also pp. 183-186, for Barth's discussion
on God's ability to be "God against God" without falling into a
contradiction of his being.

Jüngel, *op. cit.*, p. 84, says,

> "But Barth categorically rejects the consequence of a con-
> tradiction through which God would come into conflict
> with himself . . . . However, Barth's denial of this conse-

quence does not lead to any defusing of his discussion of the suffering of God, but rather, conversely, to a criticism of the traditional metaphysical concept of God according to which God cannot suffer without falling into conflict with his being."

On this see also Gunton, p. 100.

[51] Jüngel, p. 85.

[52] *Ibid.*, pp. 85-86.

[53] *CD* IV/2, 357. It is surprising that Moltmann does not refer to this passage.

[54] Jürgen Moltmann, *Religion, Revolution and the Future*, trans Douglas Meeks (New York, 1969), p. 205. (Hereafter cited as *RRF.*)

[55] Moltmann, *CG*, p. 220.

[56] See Jürgen Moltmann, *Hope and Planning*, trans. Margaret Clarkson (London, 1971), pp. 33-35.

[57] Moltmann, *CG*, p. 4.

[58] See *Ibid.*, pp. 7-31, for Moltmann's discussion of the identity-relevance crisis in the Christian faith.

[59] See George Hunsinger, "The Crucified God and the Political Theology of Violence: A Critical Survey of Jürgen Moltmann's Recent Thought: I," *The Heythrop Journal*, XIV (1973), 277: "He [Moltmann] has not explained how it is epistemologically possible to move from history to eschatology, from the cross as an event between an abandoned man and a silent God, to the cross as an event between God and God."

Also see Roland D. Zimany, "Moltmann's Crucified God," *Dialog*, XVI (Winter, 1977), 51. He criticizes Moltmann's transition when the "Jesus whom he had designated 'Son' only in view of his special relationship with the God whom he called 'father', suddenly becomes the Second Person of the Trinity."

[60] Moltmann, *CG*, p. 162.

[61] *Ibid.*, pp. 161f.

[62] *Ibid.*, pp. 121ff.

[63] See *Ibid.*, pp. 128-145, for Moltmann's discussions of these elements of Jesus' crucifixion. The political dimension of the crucifixion will be examined in Chapter V.

[64] *Ibid.*, p. 145.

[65] See *Ibid.*, pp. 148, 150.

[66] *Ibid.*, p. 147.

[67] See *Ibid.*, p. 149.

[68] *Ibid.*

[69] *Ibid.*

[70] *Ibid.*, p. 151.

[71] See *Ibid.*, pp. 166-178, for Moltmann's discussion of the resurrection.

[72] See *Ibid.*, p. 180.

[73] *Ibid.*, p. 179.

[74] *Ibid.*, p. 182.

[75] *Ibid.*, p. 184.

[76] *Ibid.*, p. 169.

[77] *Ibid.*, p. 190.

[78] See *Ibid.*, p. 191.

[79] *Ibid.*, p. 192.

[80] *Ibid.*, p. 204.

[81] *Ibid.*, p. 190.

[82] *Ibid.*, p. 205. In claiming that it is appropriate to say of Jesus on the cross "*this* is God, God is like this," Moltmann needs to reconsider a criticism found throughout his writings that he has made of Barth's conception of revelation as the "self-revelation of God." Moltmann claims that because Barth identifies revelation in Christ as a revelation of God's being or God's self, it "means the 'pure presence of God', and 'eternal presence of God in time', a 'present without any future'" (Moltmann, *TH*, pp. 57ff). This means, according to Moltmann, that Barth's conception of revelation "shows a tendency towards uneschatological, and then also unhistorical, thinking . . . ." (*Ibid.*, p. 281). For if God's being is fully present in any moment, history has been fulfilled and the *eschaton* has occurred. However, as Moltmann is well aware (See *Ibid.*, pp. 57, 87.), as Barth worked out his *Church Dogmatics* he came to make this same criticism of himself and therefore gave up the notion of revelation as the presence of God "without any future." If this is the case two observations need to be made. On the one hand, Moltmann's criticism will not stand because Barth, based on concrete thinking about God from his revelation in Jesus, comes to identify God's being or self as past, present and future and as in movement from this past to the future. (See the discussion of the eschatological elements in Barth's trinitarian theology in Chapter VI.) Therefore, Barth can still speak of revelation in terms of God's self-disclosure, 'the pure presence of God' or even an 'eternal presence of God in time.' For the self or being of God that is present in revelation is an event with a future and is therefore eschatological. Moltmann can hold to his criticism only if he thinks of "pure presence," "self" or "eternal presence" abstractly and does not see how these terms, for Barth, are defined concretely by revelation in Jesus.

On the other hand, Moltmann is saying something very similar to Barth when he says of Jesus at the cross, "*this* is God . . . ." Doesn't this mean that here we have to do with God's self or being, that here is the 'pure presence' of God? If God is not fully present here, if the cross does not involve the being of God, Moltmann's position in the *Crucified God* would not be intelligible. However, Moltmann does state that the cross is a God-event that defines and constitutes God's being. But Moltmann, like Barth, does not claim that the presence of God at the cross is uneschatological. Rather, it is full of promise for the future, because God's being, even though it is fully present at the cross, is future and is present from its future.

[83] *Ibid.*, p. 152.

[84] *Ibid.*, p. 192.

[85] *Ibid.*

[86] See *Ibid.*, pp. 229, 230. See pp. 227-235 for Moltmann's extended discussion of the immutability and impassibility of God.

[87] *Ibid.*, pp. 192f.

[88] *Ibid.*, p. 246.

[89] *Ibid.*, p. 240f. See also Moltmann, *TK*, p. 83: "The Cross is at the centre of the Trinity." Similarly, in *The Church in the Power of the Spirit*, trans. Margaret Kohl (New York, 1977), p. 95, (Hereafter cited as *CPS*) Moltmann writes, "Christ's surrender of himself to a Godforsaken death reveals the secret of the cross and with it the secret of God Himself. It is the open secret of the Trinity."

It seems to me, that in this discussion, the criticisms of Roland Zimany and George Hunsinger (See note 59) have been overcome. Moltmann perhaps could have been more explicit on the transition from the relationship at the cross between Jesus and the God whom he called Father to the doctrine of the Trinity, but to claim that he does not give the epistemological basis for this move is unfounded.

Moltmann is not alone in seeing the cross as the basis of the doctrine of the Trinity. Eberhard Jüngel also believes that this doctrine arises out of the question of the suffering of God asked in light of the cross:

> "And it cannot be chance that it is precisely the event of the death of Jesus Christ upon the cross which calls the being of God into question and compels a Trinitarian statement of the problem" (Jüngel, p. xiv).

[90] See Moltmann, *CG*, 206f.

[91] Moltmann, *FC*, p. 81.

[92] Moltmann, *CG*, p. 276.

[93] *Ibid.*, p. 201.

[94] See *Ibid.*, p. 207, where Moltmann distinguishes himself from the "death of God" theology. The death of God theology fails because of its lack of the trinitarian dimension. If proper trinitarian conceptions are used one must speak of the "death in God" rather than the "death of God."

[95] *Ibid.*, p. 240. Moltmann's criticism of Barth for his distinction between the immanent and economic Trinity is unwarranted. Barth's distinction is certainly not meant to place a barrier between God's inner being and his acts of salvation. This distinction, for Barth, is to give the latter its ontological foundation and to protect the sovereignty and freedom of God. God's revelation and salvation are freely given. Moltmann makes the same point. God's threefold relationship to us, Moltmann quotes Rahner, "is this Trinity itself, even though communicated as free grace." This is Barth's point exactly. Furthermore, as the next point of text will show, in *The Church in the Power of the Spirit*, Moltmann once again demonstrates that Barth is his teacher here. Moltmann himself uses the distinction between the immanent and economic Trinity and draws on Barth by demonstrating the former as the ontological ground of the latter, while in epistemological terms moving from the latter to the former.

[96] Moltmann, *CPS*, p. 54. Moltmann also makes the same point in relation to the Spirit (p. 55). See also Moltmann, *FC*, pp. 82-85. This method is also a presupposition in *The Trinity and the Kingdom*.

[97] Moltmann, *CG*, p. 243. See also Moltmann, *CPS*, pp. 93-98 and *TK*, pp. 80-83.

[98] See Augustine *On the Trinity* 4.5.

[99] See Moltmann, *CG*, pp. 191, 241ff, for this and for what follows. See also *TK*, pp. 80ff.

[100] On the basis of Moltmann's analysis at this point Carl Braaten's charge that Moltmann does not deal with the concept of substitution might need to be moderated (See Braaten, p. 115). For an interpretation which sees Moltmann using the concept of substitution while avoiding the traditional language, see Richard Bauckham, "Moltmann's Eschatology of the Cross," *Scottish Journal of Theology*, XXX, No. 4 (1977), 307.

[101] Moltmann, *CG*, p. 244. See also Moltmann, *TK*, p. 82, and *CPS*, p. 95.

[102] Moltmann, *TK*, p. 82. See also Moltmann, *CPS*, p. 95.

[103] Moltmann, *CG*, p. 245.

[104] *Ibid.*, p. 247.

[105] *Ibid.*, p. 249. The relationship of eschatology to the doctrine of the Trinity will be discussed more fully in Chapter VI.

[106] *Ibid.*, p. 214.

[107] See *Ibid.*, pp. 250f, 226.

[108] *Ibid.*, p. 195, See also *Ibid.*, p. 251: "Here 'Christian atheism' is in the right."

[109] *CD* IV/1, 215.

[110] Moltmann, *CG*, p. 246. See also *Ibid.*, pp. 276-277.

[111] *Ibid.*, p. 278.

[112] This means that there is truth to Adorno's claim that "the possibility represented by the divine name is maintained, rather, by him who does not believe" (See note 3 above). Adorno is here speaking within the context of traditional theism. Negation of this God on the basis of suffering puts one in a hidden line with the protest found in the triune conception of God.

[113] See *CD* II/1, 619ff, where Barth describes God's eternity as pre-temporality, supra-temporality and post-temporality. Even though God is the former two, he is also the future of all that is. Although God is the who he is, his eternity has a "direction which is irreversible" and, therefore, his post-temporality has "special characteristics" that are not to be confused with his pre- or supra-temporality (p. 639). This will be discussed in some detail in Chapter VI.

[114] See *CD* II/1, 630 and Moltmann, *CG*, p. 255.

[115] Moltmann, *CG*, p. 265.

[116] We will return to Moltmann's notion of the "future as the mode of God's being" in Chapter VI where a detailed account of the "eschatological Trinity" is given.

[117] See *CD* IV/1, 257.

[118] Augustine *On the Trinity* 13.13-18.

[119] Moltmann, *CG*, p. 248.

[120] *Ibid.*, pp. 248f.

[121] This last sentence is a paraphrase of Moltmann. See *Ibid.*, p. 246: "It (the doctrine of the Trinity) protects faith from both monotheism and atheism because it keeps believers at the cross."

[122] Edgar S. Brightman, *A Philosophy of Religion* (New York, 1940), pp. 318-319.

[123] Gordon Kaufman, *God the Problem* (Cambridge, Mass, 1972), pp. 171-200.

[124] Alfred North Whitehead, *Process and Reality* (New York, 1929), p. 532.

[125] Brightman bases his notion on its "empirical adequacy" in relationship to "human experience" (*op. cit.*, p. 321). Kaufman argues that the concept of God as an agent must be "drawn from human experience" (*op. cit.*, p. 179). And Whitehead develops his concept of

God as the "chief" exemplification of metaphysical principes (*op. cit.*, p. 521) which means in "strict analogy with the human self or person." [This phrase is Schubert Ogden's. See *The Reality of God* (New York, 1963), p. 175.]

CHAPTER V

THE TRINITY AND PRAXIS —
THE EPISTEMOLOGICAL QUESTION RECONSIDERED

Our discussion thus far does not yet constitute a complete basis for a response to protest atheism. Protest atheism, at least in Horkheimer and Adorno, has roots not only in Feuerbach but also in the philosophy of Karl Marx and therefore cannot be answered without addressing the issue of human praxis and how it is related to the Christian conception of God. Unless the question of praxis is taken up, atheism is likely to charge that trinitarian theology is merely engaged in a rearrangement of theories about God. This charge already misses the mark, for the triune conception of God is grounded in the concrete, sensuous event of Jesus. Therefore, the doctrine of the Trinity is not speculative theory, but is a theoretical reflection of the concrete, sensuous praxis of God. Nevertheless, the concreteness of the trinitarian formulation must now be shown in the lives of those who have come into relationship with the triune God. Are they also participants in the concrete praxis of God against human suffering? The central questions are these: Does Christian theology serve to overcome in a concrete manner human suffering and oppression? Or, does it support the status quo by rendering human activity meaningless? If God is one who by his own praxis promises to overcome human suffering, is there really any point to human praxis? Does not religious belief function as an opiate and serve to keep change from occurring?

This is not a new challenge to the Christian faith. In the New Testament Paul faced a version of it and so in Romans 6:1ff answers his own rhetorical question: "Are we to continue in sin that grace may abound?" In modern times it is Karl Marx who has raised the charge against Christianity and supported his atheism by a critique of the practice related to faith. For Marx religious belief must be rejected because it serves the unjust status quo. This chapter therefore will consist of a brief analysis of Marx's critique and then will investigate the responses to it, once again on the basis of the doctrine of the Trinity as developed by Barth and Moltmann. The logic of this chapter is built upon what has gone before. The praxological nature of the doctrine of the Trinity begins in the epistemological position accepted from Feuerbach, but goes beyond it. In Chapter II it was seen that the doctrine of the Trinity comprehends the God who gives himself to be known in a concrete, sensuous event. But as we have seen in Chapter IV the location of this event is God's concrete, sensuous praxis on behalf of suffering humanity, with whom God has identified and whom he has consequently taken into his inner triune history. But this can only mean — as we will now see in this chapter — that if one is to know and trust this God, he or she must meet this God where he has given himself concretely to be known, in concrete praxis on behalf of suffering humanity. The doctrine of the Trinity is the doctrine of a revolutionary God who challenges the unjust social context in concrete praxis and leads believers to direct themselves toward the concrete overcoming of human misery. As in the previous chapters, therefore, we will see that this trinitarian response is two-fold. On the one hand, it accepts Marx's critique. Any God that functions as an opiate must be rejected and any theology that is unrelated to praxis on behalf of suffering humanity must be negated. Trinitarian theology, as it again functions to clarify the faith for believers, adds this charge to its polemic against traditional theism. On the other hand, Marx's critique of religion takes place wholly in the context of traditional theism, and, therefore, like the other atheists already discussed, Marx misidentifies the true God of the Christian faith. The doctrine of the Trinity can respond to Marx because it is the concrete reflection of the God who is not an opiate, but is who he is only in concrete praxis on behalf of human suffering and as he leads persons of faith into this praxis. In this chapter, therefore, we will examine the relationship of trinitarian theology to praxis, i.e., to concrete human practice directed toward the transformation of given reality. Then in the following chapter we will analyze the form that this praxis takes.

The Critique of Karl Marx

Here also, in Marx's atheism based on a critique of the praxis related to belief, Feuerbach is the fountainhead. It has already been noted that Feuerbach's epistemological critique of religion was in the service of humanity, reclaiming what rightfully belongs to it.[1] This includes for Feuerbach practical, ethical dimensions. In his *Lectures on the Essence of Religion*, he writes,

> In this book, as in all my writings, my reasons for dealing with the essence of religion were not only of a theoretical or speculative character, but essentially practical. The principle

reason for my interest in religion has always been that, if only in imagination, it is the foundation of human life, the foundation of ethics and politics.[2]

The purpose of his epistemological critique of religion was to redirect the attention of humankind. If religion is shown to be only human, then concern for another world is unnecessary and human interest can be fully directed towards humanity itself. Feuerbach wished

> to transform friends of God into friends of man, believers into thinkers, devotees of prayer into devotees of work, candidates for the hereafter into students of this world, Christians, who by their own profession and admission, are *"half animal, half angel,"* into *men*, into *whole men.*[3]

The practical result of this he saw as the transformation of human life, the conquest of at least "the most glaring, outrageous, heartbreaking injustices and evils from which man has hitherto suffered."[4] "If we no longer *believe* in a better life but decide to *achieve* one, not each man by himself but with our united powers, we will *create* a better life . . . ."[5] It is no wonder that the worker's movement in Germany identified Feuerbach as speaking for them against religion and the "present system of oppression and worthlessness" it supported.[6]

Because of Feuerbach, Karl Marx was a convinced atheist long before he began his political and economic critiques.[7] For Marx, Feuerbach had demonstrated decisively the nature of religion and the validity of the atheistic position. He has Feuerbach in mind when he writes, "For Germany the criticism of religion is in the main complete, and the criticism of religion is the premise of all criticism."[8] Marx takes as self-evident, and therefore never raised critical questions about, the basic direction of the epistemological position of Feuerbach's materialism.[9] Thinking and knowing are based on and determined by concrete, sensuous human existence. Therefore, Marx reiterates Feuerbach's claim that religion is a human projection that is connected with human alienation. He writes,

> Man makes religion, religion does not make man. In other words, religion is the self-consciousness and self-feeling of man, who either has not yet found himself or has lost himself already.[10]

Insofar as Marx's atheism does not advance beyond Feuerbach, it can be given the same trinitarian response that was developed in Chapters II, III and IV. Marx, like Feuerbach, is right to challenge the abstract theology of traditional theism. Trinitarian theology also claims that the

God of traditional theism is a projection of human self-consciousness and, as such, is conceived of as standing in opposition to everything human. But Marx is wrong to identify the God of traditional theism with the God of the Christian faith. For the doctrine of the Trinity as presented in this essay arises not from a process of abstraction from the world or human self-consciousness, but from an analysis of the God who concretely and sensuously gives himself to be known in the man Jesus as he acts on behalf of human suffering. Like Feuerbach, Marx, in his critique of religion, remains wholly within the context of traditional theistic notions of God. He was never inclined to study seriously the self-understanding of the Judeo-Christian tradition, the biblical understanding of God or the message of Jesus.[11] Rather Marx always attacks the timeless, transcendent God who offers happiness and fulfillment to human life, but only in heaven, thereby, rendering historical, sensuous life on earth hopeless, meaningless, abandoned to its misery.

But Marx's atheistic critique moves beyond Feuerbach and therefore requires further analysis if a response is to be given. For while he accepts Feuerbach's basic theory of projection and the atheism consequent upon it, Marx transcends him by establishing praxis as his central concern and as the fundamental basis of his critique of religion. Marx rejects any merely philosophical discussion of atheism.[12] In any discussion of epistemology Marx insists on the unity of theory and practice. The question of truth is profoundly related to the question of praxis, to concrete, sensuous human activity.

According to Marx there are two aspects of the relationship of practice to the truth of a theory, both of which are missed by Feuerbach. The first is the claim that all thought is conditioned by and arises from the concrete situation and practice in which one is involved. Although Feuerbach had wanted an epistemology based on concrete objects, he had not seen that human sensuous activity is objective, is concrete, and therefore stands over against thinking as its concrete basis. Marx writes in his "Theses on Feuerbach,"

> The chief defect of all hitherto existing materialism — that of Feuerbach included — is that the thing, reality, sensuousness, is conceived only in the form of the *object* or of contemplation, but not as *human sensuous activity, practice*, not subjectively. . . . Feuerbach wants sensuous objects really differentiated from thought objects, but he does not conceive human activity itself as *objective* activity.[13]

Marx's distinction here is made clear by comparing his and Feuerbach's views of nature. Feuerbach found in nature the material

basis for understanding human conceptions. For instance, in his interpretations of the Christian sacraments, he reduces their meaning to their
natural qualities: "I, in fact, put in the place of the barren baptismal
water, the beneficent effect of real water."[14] The relationship with nature
in this case is basically one of observation and contemplation. For Marx,
on the other hand, the human relationship with nature is understood in
terms of labor — the human interaction with and transformation of
nature.[15] The real sensuous basis of thought is not merely nature as an
object of observation but productive human engagement with nature.
According to Marx, it is the "material powers of production" that form
and determine the economic, social and political spheres of life which
therefore determine human thought.

> The sum total of these relations of production constitutes
> the economic structure of society — the real foundation, on
> which rise legal and political superstructures and to which
> correspond definite forms of social consciousness. The mode
> of production in material life determines the general
> character of social, political, and spiritual processes of life. It
> is not the consciousness of men that determines their exis-
> tence, but, on the contrary, their social existence determines
> their consciousness.[16]

This means that, according to Marx, Feuerbach had not been
materialistic enough. His view of the real earth and of real human beings
remained abstract. Feuerbach, "in pulling his concept from the heaven
of abstraction down to earth, had merely substituted an abstract earth
for an abstract heaven."[17] What Marx claimed Feuerbach never saw was
that concrete human life consists of sensuous, practical, economic, and
therefore also, social and political activity and relationships. Marx writes,
"But man is no abstract being, squatting outside the world. Man is the
world of man, the state, society."[18] According to Marx this indicates
that Feuerbach had still an abstract anthropology: "Feuerbach resolves
the religious essence into the human essence. But the human essence is
no abstraction inherent in each single individual. In reality it is the
ensemble of social relationships."[19] In this view even Feuerbach's location of humanity in the "I-thou" relationship is not sufficiently concrete.
For Marx social relationships are never merely interhuman, but always
human relationships in their practical, political, economic, social context.[20] Therefore, Feuerbach's "I-thou" relationship remains an abstraction and less than the "real essence" of humanity, for it is not placed in
this concrete social context.

Because Feuerbach is not materialistic enough, does not include praxis in his epistemology, Marx claims that he does not see the real concrete basis for religious projection and the human alienation it represents. "Feuerbach, . . . ," Marx writes, "does not see that the 'religious sentiment' is itself a *social product* . . . ."[21] It was seen in Chapter II that Feuerbach does see religion as a social product in the sense that it originates through the projection of humanity in general and not merely the individual. But again what Marx means by "social product" and what Feuerbach misses are the economic and political circumstances of human beings. Feuerbach had failed to realize, according to Marx, that people project God into heaven (and so alienate themselves) because they are alienated first of all in the economic, social and political sphere where their real lives and essences are determined. Because humans are who they are in the concrete context of their state and society, it is "this state, this society [that] produce religion, a *perverted world consciousness* because they are *a perverted world*."[22] This "perverted world" is seen in a society where workers are alienated from the "fruit of their labor," are forced into a strict division of labor[23] and become merely cogs in the capitalist's machines of production.[24] This means that the worker is alienated in praxis, the very place where human essence is determined. In Marx's view, therefore, far from being merely the projection of the best ideals of humanity, religion is the reflection of, and a perverted answer to, this alienation experienced in concrete existence. God is projected as an attempt to make sense out of this world, to find consolation in it. Marx writes,

> Religion is the general theory of that world, its encyclopedic
> compendium, its logic in a popular form, its spiritualistic
> *point d' honneur*, its enthusiasm, its moral sanction, its
> solemn completion, its universal ground for consolation and
> justification. It is *the fantastic realization* of the human
> essence because the *human essence* has no true reality.[25]

The result of this position is that Marx has a two-fold attitude toward religion. Religion is true to the extent that it is the reflection of, and an attempted answer to, real human problems.

> Religious distress is at the same time the expression of real
> distress and the protest against real distress. Religion is the
> sigh of the oppressed creature, the heart of a heartless world,
> just as it is the spirit of an unspiritual situation.[26]

Religion is false, however, because it offers a wrong answer. It pushes the answer to heaven and offers an "illusory happiness" there, while it does nothing about the concrete situation on earth. In offering this happiness in another world, religion is the "opium of the people."[27] For it directs people's attention away from the conditions of this world; it drugs them into an acceptance of their present condition. If happiness comes in the world above, one can be satisfied with any present situation. Religion, therefore, serves as the ideological framework of the status quo.

This analysis makes it clear that Marx's central charge against religion is related to praxis. It was pointed out above that Marx had no interest in merely philosophical discussions of atheism. It is always the concrete situation that is the basis of religion which remains Marx's concern. What is evil is not that the religious theory of God is incorrect in itself, but that this theory supports the status quo, innervates revolutionary praxis and leaves people in their misery.

Here the other side of the relationship of theory and practice as taught by Marx comes into focus. Marx's epistemology is designed so that theory and practice are always interacting with one another. Not only is sensuous human activity the basis for thinking, but the truth of what is thought must then be tested in practice. In his second thesis on Feuerbach, Marx writes,

> The question whether objective truth can be attributed to human thinking is not a question of theory, but is a practical question. In practice man must prove the truth, that is, the reality and power, the this-sidedness of his thinking.[28]

For Marx, religion is false because it is proved false in practice. The whole point of its critique (and so of atheism) is to change this practice and therefore the human situation of misery.

> The abolition of religion as the illusory happiness of people is required for their real happiness. The demand to give up the illusions about its condition is the *demand to give up a condition which needs illusion*. . . . Criticism has plucked the imaginary flowers from the chain not so that man will wear the chain without fantasy or consolation, but so that he will shake off the chain and cull the living flower.[29]

The truth of atheism, therefore — like the untruth of religion — does not reside in its metaphysical theory, but is likewise proved in practice. It is true because it forces people to remain concrete, down to earth. It enables criticism and transformation of this world. With happiness no longer promised in heaven, true happiness must be found by revolutionary practice on earth, in the political, social and economic setting that forms the world of human beings. Atheism is true because it functions to support revolutionary practice.

Feuerbach had attempted to establish a relationship between his atheism and ethics and politics,[30] but he was not sensuous enough. He did not include praxis — either as the basis of human thought or as the place where thought is verified or falsified — in his epistemological thinking. Thus, he failed according to Marx to see both that religion is a false projection of humanity based on concrete social alienation and that atheism is finally true because it is proved true in practice. Feuerbach, therefore, had believed that because religion is a human projection, human alienation is overcome by reclaiming the religious projection as truly human. But this is idealistic and illusory, for it leaves the concrete social, political and economic alienation unchanged. According to Marx, Feuerbach suffers from the same problem as religion. Feuerbach, like religion and against his own intent, had given an abstract answer to the human situation and missed the real practical application of atheism in the transformation of the political, social and economic misery of humankind. Feuerbach had only interpreted the world in a new way, "the point, however, is to change it."[31]

> Thus the criticism of heaven turns into the criticism of the earth, the *criticism of religion* into the *criticism of right*, and the *criticism of theology* into the *criticism of politics* . . . .[32]

The atheistic critique of Karl Marx, therefore, is directed against religion and the God which are not concerned for the present concrete situation of humanity. It opposes the religious thinking that, by claiming human fulfillment is found in the spiritual dimension of life and consummated above and without earth in heaven, renders sensuous earthly life and activity pointless. This atheism attacks faith which serves as an ideology of the status quo by directing belief towards the spiritual and heavenly realm. Religious interest is turned away from earth and directed to God above the world in heaven, and so does not even have an awareness of the inseparability of religious belief and practical activity.

Once again it is clear that this critique is offered within the theological context of traditional theism — both its theological method and its notion of God. Marx, like theism and Feuerbach, is tied to the method of conceiving God by a process of abstraction from the world. God for him is simply the inverted reflection of the suffering of humanity that takes place in concrete social contexts. God, therefore, is likewise pictured theistically. He can provide an answer — although a false one — because he is not involved in the misery of the world but totally transcends it as the omnipotent guarantor of human happiness in heaven.

We will attempt to demonstrate that the doctrine of the Trinity as formulated by Barth and Moltmann provides the basis of a response to Marx. Negatively, trinitarian theology will show that Marx's critique, in presupposing the theistic conception of God, involves a misidentification of the Christian God. The triune God does not offer satisfaction only in heaven; he does not support the status quo. Positively, it will be seen that the doctrine of the Trinity constitutes a conception of God that enables, indeed demands, an acceptance of Marx's fundamental insights. The triune God leads believers into revolutionary praxis on behalf of the oppressed and poor.

Three central points will constitute the argument for this apologetic function of the doctrine of the Trinity. In this chapter it will be argued that trinitarian theology is capable of recognizing the inseparability of theory and praxis. The doctrine of the Trinity insists that God is inseparable from human practical activity. In the next chapter we will see that this is so because the doctrine of the Trinity speaks of a transcendence that, far from supporting the status quo, stands as a radical critique of present structures and calls for their transformation by human activity. We will then demonstrate that the praxis supported by the doctrine of the Trinity cannot be just any transformation of the status quo, but must always be with and for the poor and oppressed.

Theory, Praxis and the Doctrine of the Trinity

Trinitarian thinking makes it possible for faith and theology to respond to Marx by showing that it includes both poles of the theory-praxis relationship — both the demand that theory be based on praxis and the demand that the truth of a theory be proved in praxis. In the first place, the doctrine of the Trinity is not simply a theory about God but arises out of reflection on praxis. In Chapter II it was seen in response to Feuerbach's epistemological critique that the doctrine of the Trinity is a conception of God that is grounded in a concrete object that determines our thinking about it, namely, Jesus of Nazareth. The doctrine of the Trinity is the name of the God who is who he is in his concrete revelation. And this revelation is not a static entity but an event. As was seen in Chapter IV, in this event God's sensuous activity, his praxis on behalf of human suffering, is perceived. The God who reveals himself in Jesus and who in the Spirit makes that revelation manifest to human beings does not act in this manner only to give the proper knowledge of himself, but to transform the present condition of humanity. The existence of the God revealed here "not only sheds new light on, but materially changes, all things and everything in all things."[33] The doctrine of the Trinity, then, arises from thinking through God's concrete praxis in Jesus to overcome the structures that oppress humankind and means that God's whole being, inner as well as outer, must be conceived of as in praxis.

That the doctrine of the Trinity arises from the praxis of God, however, does not mean that it excludes human praxis. Rather the praxis of the triune God includes in itself human activity towards the transformation of the human situation. The doctrine of the Trinity comprehends the claim that the activity of God coincides with the concrete activity of the human Jesus. The triune God identifies with and opens himself for the human — in this instance, human practical activity of changing the structures that make humans miserable. This means that the triune God keeps human attention and practice focused on the earth. This God is not known in contemplating heaven, but is found in the activity of earthly transformation. And because this is where he gives himself to be known, the doctrine of the Trinity arises out of this context — reflection on human praxis involved in the problem of concrete earthly transformation.

It is not surprising, therefore, that the trinitarian theologies of Barth and Moltmann originate not only out of epistemological considerations but in and from the practical, ethical, political context too.

Karl Barth

The relationship of the theology of Karl Barth to the practical, ethical, political situation has had a long history of discussion and debate. In the United States, following the lead of Reinhold Niebuhr, the dominant opinion has been that Barth's theology is irrelevant to ethical decisions and political activity.[34] In 1959, Niebuhr wrote that Barth was "a very eminent theologian, trying desperately to be impartial in his judgments. The price of this desperation is of course moral irrelevance."[35] Will Herberg[36] and Charles West[37] accuse Barth not so much of irrelevance as of inconsistency, "ineptitude," and "oversimplification of the political issues." Frederick Herzog[38] and James Cone[39] in addressing themes of politics and liberation have accused Barth of a kerygmatic confinement that limits his usefulness in these contexts.

More recently, however, in both the United States and Europe a reevaluation of the relationship between Barth's theology and political praxis has been attempted. In 1969, Reinhold Niebuhr, himself, reversed his evaluation of Barth.[40] Paul Lehmann has argued that

Barth's christocentric method has "made possible a future, not only for
the doing of theology, but for involvement in a revolutionary world
without loss of Christian identity."[41] Barth's theology arises not only in
the context of Feuerbach's critique but is rooted also in the question of
praxis. It is

> an *archimedian theology*, i.e., the source and matrix of an
> unhinging (liberating), forming, and transforming perspec-
> tive which is concrete for our revolutionary time, concrete
> for the permanent revolution always going on in human
> affairs.[42]

According to Lehmann both Bonhoeffer's theology of secularity and
Moltmann's political theology presuppose and are possible only on the
basis of Barth's method.[43] We saw in Chapter II that it is the doctrine of
the Trinity that serves as the framework for Barth's methodology.

The most extensive attempt to interpret Barth's theology as arising
from his political activity has been the work of Friedrich-Wilhelm
Marquardt.[44] In the volume, *Karl Barth and Radical Politics*, edited by
George Hunsinger, it is seen that Marquardt is supported by Helmut
Gollwitzer and followed in the United States by Joseph Bettis and
Hunsinger himself.[45] With varying emphases these interpreters claim
that Karl Barth's theology grew out of, and cannot be understood apart
from, his practical political activity. Karl Barth was a socialist. His break
with liberalism, according to these commentators, is not merely theoretical or epistemological but ethical. Liberal theology did not provide an
adequate basis for Barth's practical activity. Therefore, his turn to and
transformation of theology were an attempt to find a theological basis for
his praxis. To support these claims these writers point to Barth's political
activity and sermons while a pastor in Safenwil;[46] his twice joining the
socialist party in which he was active in the party's left wing;[47] his well-
known resistance to Hitler; and his unwillingness to identify himself
with the capitalist West in a one-sided denunciation of the communist
East. These events and others serve as the praxis that is looking for an
adequate theological foundation. Marquardt and the others, therefore,
exegete passages from Barth — some of which will be examined in this
chapter — in light of this practical background.

Whatever modifications need to be made in some of the more
radical conclusions of Marquardt,[48] the integral relation between Barth's
practical activity and his theology can no longer be denied. Barth himself
makes it clear that his theology did issue from practical, ethical concerns
and the systems of thought related to them. In the first instance, his

critique of nineteeth century theology is based on praxis. Writing about his break with the prevalent theology, Barth wrote,

> One day in early August 1914 stands out in my personal memory as a black day. Ninety-three German intellectuals impressed public opinion by their proclamation in support of the war policy of Wilhelm II and his counselors. Among these intellectuals I discovered to my horror almost all of my theological teachers whom I had greatly venerated. In despair over what this indicated about the signs of the time I suddenly realized that I could not any longer follow either their ethics and dogmatics or their understanding of the Bible and of history. For me at least, 19th-century theology no longer held any future.[49]

Here it is the practical, political activity of these theologians that raises the issue of the inadequacy of their thought — their dogmatics and understanding of the Bible and of history. The failure of their ethics indicated for Barth the failure of their theology. Barth asks,

> Was it — this has played a decisive role for me personally — precisely the failure of the ethics of the modern theology of the time, with the outbreak of the First World War, which caused us to grow puzzled also about its exegesis, its treatment of history, and its dogmatics?[50]

If Barth's break with the former theology is rooted in praxis, so is his attempt to establish theology on a new basis. "I decided for theology because I felt I needed to find a better basis for my social action," Barth said.[51] The essays in George Hunsinger's *Karl Barth and Radical Politics* demonstrate in detail how praxis is formative for Barth's theological reflection and responsible for the various changes that occurred in his theological position. Here we can demonstrate this with a few examples.

In response to the failures of liberal theology, Barth asserts the sovereignty of God. It is the word of God and not human experience that is the theme of theology.[52] In terms of praxis this means that Christian theology stands for

> . . . not the unfolding and fruition of love as we may understand it, but the existence and outpouring of eternal love, of love as God understands it — not industry, honesty, and helpfulness as we may practice them in our ordinary world, but the establishment and growth of a new world, the world in which God and *his* morality reign.[53]

Elaborating this position further in the first edition of *The Epistle to the Romans* (published in 1919), Barth is able to support a radical political practice. On the one hand, the type of support which his liberal teachers had given to the state is negated. "As Christians you have nothing to do with the power state." "That Christians have nothing to do with monarchy, capitalism, militarism, patriotism, free-thinking, is so self-evident that I do not even need to mention it."[54] The state stands under the judgment of God and is seen as evil. Hence, Christians must distance themselves from it. "Thou shalt starve the state of religion. Thou shalt not have your heart in your politics. Your souls are and remain alien to the ideals of the state."[55] The concern of Christians is only with the coming kingdom, with "the *absolute* revolution which comes from God so that he leaves the whole realm of the penultimate to the process of dissolution."[56]

On the other hand, Barth's theological position makes possible a socialist practice. One political option cannot be directly justified theologically over another. There can be no "Christian politics" and no "religious socialism." Nevertheless, this does not mean political withdrawal. The Christian lets "the healing unrest that is set in his heart by God deepen, grow stronger, and augment the generally rising flood of the divine which one day will of itself break through the dams."[57] For Barth this meant that Christians should stand "on the extreme left"[58] He saw in the bolshevist revolution in Russia, the revolution in Germany and the national strike in Switzerland a correspondence with the absolute revolution of God.[59] Like God's kingdom, these movements fought the existing state fundamentally. Barth looked with anticipation toward the time "when the now expiring glow of Marxist dogma will blaze forth anew as a world-truth, when the socialist church will experience its resurrection in a world that has become socialist."[60]

Barth, however, did not remain satisfied with the position of the *Romans* of 1919, and by 1920 he had begun a thorough revision.[61] The oft-cited reasons for this revision are given by Barth in the preface to the second edition. They include further study of Paul, the theology of Franz Overbeck, "closer acquaintance with Plato and Kant," greater consideration of Kierkegaard and Dostoevsky and the reviews (particularly the favorable ones) of the first edition of *Romans*.[62] In addition to these theoretical influences, however, it is also quite clear that Barth's revision cannot be understood apart from practice, from what is going on "in the street"[63] and from "the present state of the world."[64] The second edition of *Romans* is written in the practical context of the failure of the socialist-revolutionary movements in which Barth had placed much hope.[65] The failure of this praxis called for a theological revision. It convinced Barth

that his theology must be even more dialectical. The deity and sovereignty of God and the crisis it brings to all human activity had to be
thought through more thoroughly. God is the "minus sign outside the
bracket."[66] This means that the revolutionary as well as the conservative
and the state are brought under the judgment of God. There can be
therefore no divine sanction for revolution. Revolution cannot be "justified before the judgment-seat of God."[67]

Barth does not intend here to render all forms of practice indistinguishable in light of God's judgment on all human activity. The
distinction between God's revolution and human revolution must be
given special consideration precisely "because it is most improbable that
any one will be won over to the cause of reaction — as a result of reading
the Epistle to the Romans!"[68] The revolutionary is more dangerous than
the reactionary because "he is so much nearer the truth."[69] It can be
argued that Barth is still attempting to ground socialist praxis, but is also
curbing "revolutionary hubris."[70]

Nevertheless, the danger of Barth's position in the 1921 edition of
Romans is that it can be read as a leveling of political options and,
therefore, as an argument for political passivity and for the status quo.
Indeed, Barth states that in light of God's kingdom a political career is
possible "only when it is seen to be essentially a game."[71] Due to his
chastened attitude in the face of the failed revolutions, as well as to the
demands of his new position as a professor, Barth himself became less
politically active in the years following 1921.[72]

Once again, however, the need for a better theoretical support for
his social practice issued in a theological revision. This change moved
Barth from dialectical to analogical theology, from a negative theology
to the discovery of the positive side of the deity of God made clear in the
trinitarian formulation. Barth's encounter with Anselm gave him the
conceptual framework that enabled this change.[73] However, the practical context of this revision (and of the reading of Anselm) was Barth's
response to the German nationalists and Nazis. The first episode of this
involvement was Barth's support of Günter Dehn, a pastor and professor who was harassed by supporters of National Socialism because of his
stand against militarism and war.[74] Barth discovered that he needed a
theology which more clearly articulated a positive practice, instead of the
crisis of all human activity. He found the basis for this in the analogy of
faith, by which he spoke of human worldly reality on the basis of the
nature and deity of God seen in God's revelation in Jesus Christ, i.e., on
the basis of the triune conception of God.

We have already seen that this method enabled Barth to maintain
the sovereignty of God, which stands over against humanity, as well as

to speak positively of humanity in light of the humanity of God. Similarly, it gave him a positive theological basis which supported his practice against National Socialism. First, as indicated in the change of his *Christian Dogmatics* to *Church Dogmatics*, Barth affirmed the positive position of the Church which he had criticized so sharply in his dialectical phase.[75] The Church is grounded christocentrically on the Lordship of Christ. Therefore, the intrusion of the National Socialist state into church affairs and the German Christians' acceptance of this other lord must be rejected.[76] Second, the analogy of faith provided the basis for a revised conception of the state. It is no longer an evil reality with which the Christian should have little to do. The state also is grounded christocentrically, and on this basis it is judged and given its true character. In his 1937 essay "Church and State" Barth asserts that there must be a "correspondence" between the "heavenly *polis*" and the "earthly *polis*." The State should be "an image of him whose Kingdom will be a kingdom of peace . . . ."[77] Barth is able therefore to speak of the "just state."[78] National Socialism must be rejected because it is

> . . . a dictatorship which is *totalitarian* and *radical*, which not only surrounds and determines mankind and men in utter totality, in body and soul, but abolishes their human nature, and does not merely limit human freedom, but annihilates it.[79]

This means that Nazism has overstepped the true nature of the state and attempted to become "*a religious institution of salvation.*"[80] It is, however, "tyranny tempered by anarchy, but it is certainly *no* State."[81]

It ought to be pointed out here that in his 1946 essay "The Christian Community and the Civil Community" Barth worked out in some detail his theory of correspondence.[82] By drawing analogies from the nature of God, Barth develops concrete suggestions for the form of the just state. We will mention several of these suggestions in the next chapter. Here it will suffice to point out that since who God is is known only in his revelation in Christ, Barth's theory of correspondence is grounded in the doctrine of the Trinity, in the relationships among the persons of the triune God. Indeed, the *Church Dogmatics* in which Barth elaborates his trinitarian position originated in the early nineteen-thirties in the midst of his practical involvement in the German Church controversy and rejection of National Socialism. The *Church Dogmatics* also cannot be understood apart from Barth's social action. He makes this clear in the forward to the first volume of the *Church Dogmatics:*

> Because I am firmly convinced that we cannot reach the clarifications, especially in the broad field of politics, which

> are necessary today and to which theology today might have
> a word to say (as indeed it ought to have a word to say to
> them!), without having previously reached those com-
> prehensive clarifications, in theology and about theology
> itself, with which we should be concerned here . . . .
> Because I believe as a matter of fact that a better Church
> dogmatics (even apart from all utilitarian ethical applica-
> tions) might be an ultimately weightier and more solid
> contribution even to questions and tasks like that of
> German liberation, than most of the well meant stuff . . . .[83]

It must be concluded that Barth's turn to theology was not an
attempt to escape from praxis into a realm of abstract thinking. The
opposite is true. Barth wanted a theological basis for praxis. The theological energy poured into the *Church Dogmatics*, as John Deschner
correctly points out, "is not an unpolitical action."[84] Rather, for Barth
"political existence" is related to "theological existence" and this must
be understood when reading his theology, as Barth says, "to comprehend how the whole thing was meant all along."[85] There is "no
abstract God free from politics."[86]

Barth has fulfilled the first demand of the theory-praxis relationship suggested by Marx. His theological work is rooted in sensuous
human activity. It followed the course from a failure of praxis to a
critique of theology supporting that praxis, to an attempt at a new
theology that would give a more adequate basis for a praxis of transformation. This does not mean, however, that Barth draws the content of
his new theology from autonomous human praxis. It was the autonomous, nonrevolutionary practice of his teachers that Barth rejected.
Rather, his critique of their praxis and the theistic theology connected
with it led him to find a more adequate Christian praxis and basis for it
in a new reading of the Bible, so that the church could "consider
carefully what the real needs of the day are, by which she has to direct
her programme."[87] The new basis discovered by Barth in this way is
"God's deity."[88] But this discovery is not somehow independent of
praxis, even human praxis. God's deity is seen precisely in his practical,
material activity as the human Jesus. The new basis of Barth's theology
and ethics, therefore, is the practice of the God revealed in Jesus. "It's
theory" [i.e., theology and ethics], Barth says, "is simply the theory of
this practice."[89] Barth's theology, then, arises in the context of a collision
of competing practices — the praxis related to the theism of his day
opposed by the practice related to the deity of God seen in the concrete
activity of the man Jesus.

The role of the doctrine of the Trinity that is presupposed in this should not be missed. It is the place of the doctrine of the Trinity that signals Barth's break with the theistic tradition. Furthermore, because the doctrine of the Trinity claims that the activity of Jesus is the activity of God, it is trinitarian thinking that keeps theology tied to the praxis of God revealed in Jesus and which therefore contradicts the practice of theistic theology.

Inherent in this trinitarian thinking is the inclusion of the other aspect of the theory-praxis relationship called for by Marx. If a theory arises from human practice, the truth of the theory must also be verified in practice. For Barth, theology not only derives out of the practical context, but the truth of theology is proved in practice. God's deity, which Barth discovered as the basis for his social action and which is made comprehensible through the doctrine of the Trinity, means that God is the Lord of all life. God not only remains in control of our knowledge of him but commands action and expects obedience. However, in commanding, the triune God does not act heteronomously, introducing a theory of ethics from beyond the practical human context.[90] Rather, God's command is given in the context of, indeed is his, praxis, God's practical activity of becoming a man in Jesus. Barth makes this clear in a discussion of theological ethics in *CD* II/2:

> The first thing that theological ethics has to show, and to develop as a basic and all-comprehensive truth, is the fact and extent that this command of God is an event. . . . We cannot emphasize too strongly the fact that by the ruling principle of theological ethics, by the sanctifying command of God — corresponding to the fact that we do not know God Himself otherwise than as an acting God — we have to understand a divine action, and therefore an event — not a reality which is, but a reality which occurs. Not to see it this way is not to see it at all. It is not seen when we try to see it from the safe shelter of a general theory. It is not seen when we think we see a being and then ask whether and to what extent we can derive from this being this or that obligation. The proposition: "There is a command of God," is quite inadequate as a description of what concerns us. For we should naturally have to weigh against it the denial: No, "there is" no command of God. What "there is" is not as such the command of God. But the core of the matter is that God gives His command, that he gives Himself to be our Commander. God's command, God Himself, gives Himself to be known. And as He does so, He is heard. Man is made responsible . . . . The command

> of God is the decision about the goodness of human
> action. . . . It is only on the basis of this reality, which is not
> in any sense static but active, not in any sense general but
> supremely particular, that theological ethics has to make
> answer to the ethical question. Its theory is simply the
> theory of this practice. It is because this practice occurs,
> because theological ethics cannot escape noticing this prac-
> tice, in the contemplation of this practice, that theological
> ethics fashions its concepts.[91]

There can be, therefore, no separation between theology and ethical activity, for they both have the same basis. "The same practice of the Word of God," that is the foundation of Christian praxis, "forms the basis of the Church. It is in view of it that there is *faith* and *obedience* in the church."[92] The basis of both is the event, the practice of the triune God becoming man in Jesus. For if this Word where God gives himself to be known is identical with God's concrete practice in Jesus, then God is only to be known in this practice. There must be obedience to the practice of God. Knowing God includes already following God in praxis. "Therefore the theme of dogmatics is always the Word of God and nothing else," Barth says. "But the theme of the Word of God is human existence, human life and volition and action."[93] So for Barth knowing and doing, theory and practice, theology and action are one and inseparable. This means

> . . . that neither theology nor dogmatics can be true to itself
> if it is not genuinely ready at the same time to be ethics. . . .
> Dogmatics is ethics; and ethics is dogmatics.[94]

This eliminates any merely theoretical discussion of the truth of the Christian faith. For "a theoretical reality cannot possibly be the reality of the Word of God, no matter how great may be the richness of its content or the profundity of its conception."[95] Any theology that attempts to exclude practical truth is in "grave suspicion of being no more than an idle frivolity".[96] Rather, for Barth, the truth of theology and faith includes and is proved in practice.

> We are only repeating what we have often said before when
> we state again that only the doer of the Word is its real
> hearer, for it is the Word of the living God addressed to the
> living man absorbed in the work and action of his life.[97]

Two more points need to be made about the relationship of theory and practice in Barth's theology. First, it is not possible to first be in obedient relationship with this God and then in a second moment decide for concrete practice. Rather, God is known and therefore obeyed in the same event and therefore at the same moment. As Barth says, "In obedience we are not about to leap. We are already leaping."[98] Finally, as theology cannot be only theoretical, the practice of this faith cannot be only internal. An obedience that is only internal "is disobedience, disguised as obedience." For God's command, which is nothing other than God's triune self-giving, takes place in external, practical existence, in human activity. Therefore, obedience means "a concrete step out into the open country of decision and act."[99]

To summarize, Barth can accept Marx's assertions about the relationship between theory and practice. Trinitarian theology allows the concrete object of faith to control our thinking about it as Feuerbach demanded. But this object is no static object but, as Marx demanded, an event of transforming praxis. Furthermore, the truth of trinitarian thinking is found by meeting this object in the practical context where it is located. Therefore, the one who follows this truth is already involved in practice.

Further aspects of the trinitarian basis for the inseparability of truth and practice and the direction this practice takes will be developed in following sections. But now we will see how Jürgen Moltmann also sees theology integrally bound up with practice.

Jürgen Moltmann

The relationship between theory and praxis, which is for the most part implicit in the theology of Karl Barth, is advanced explicitly in and becomes a central focus of the theology of Jürgen Moltmann. Moltmann is in the forefront of theological dialogue with Marx and contemporary Marxist-humanists. He gains inspiration in this from Barth, in recognizing that both Barth's break with theism's natural theology and his development of the doctrine of the Trinity take place in the context of practical, political issues.

> The liberal rejection of trinitarian doctrine was the signal for the dissolving of the Christian faith into a political religion "for the Christian world." Therefore, Karl Barth consciously began his church dogmatics with the doctrine of the Trinity without a prolegomena on natural theology. This is not the Church withdrawing from the world of politics but the Church offering a radical critique of any political theology.[100]

For Moltmann theology cannot be interested in merely a theory about God, but must always focus on the relationship of theology to practice. "To follow Christ means to have faith, and faith is in fact an existential unity of theory and practice, as can be seen in the life of the apostles . . ."[101] Theology, then, can no longer be only a matter of orthodoxy, but is best described as "orthopraxy."[102] It must no longer be mainly "contemplative" but must become "operational."[103]

In analyzing this orthopraxy, we will see that Moltmann appropriates both poles of Marx's theory-praxis relationship and that the trinitarian formulation makes this possible. In the first instance this theology arises out of reflection on concrete practice. This means that theology in the contemporary world must develop a political hermeneutic. According to Moltmann, behind all theological investigation stands the question of theodicy — the attempt to uncover the righteousness of God in the face of human misery.[104] Although this attempt is constant, it has taken various forms. In pre-Enlightenment theism the question was raised in a cosmological context and answered in terms of "freedom to the agony of transiency."[105] God was conceived as "the ground of all transient things."[106] In modern times, as the Enlightenment progressed in understanding and control of the powers of nature, the context of the question shifted from the cosmological to the anthropological. "If man has become the master of his world, then he no longer finds grandeur and misery in the powers of nature, but in himself."[107] The question of the misery of existence became the question of human identity, humanity's search for itself, for true self-consciousness or authentic existence. The answer then was God conceived of as "the ground of the primal situation of human existence."[108] Today, Moltmann claims, another shift of context has taken place in the theodicy question. The locus now has become the social, political, the historical, *Sitz im Leben* of humanity. It has been discovered — by Marx and others — that the question of human identity and therefore of human misery cannot be separated from the concrete, historical condition. Persons "find their identity in history — not apart from history." The identity of humanity and the response to theodicy then have to do with overcoming the concrete misery of humanity, "in concrete historical identification with projects involved in overcoming affliction and enslavement."[109]

To be relevant to the present situation theology must develop a political hermeneutic, it must become political theology. This does not mean that theology is to become political in a narrow sense. "It does not want to make political questions the central theme of theology or to give political systems and movements religious support."[110]   Moltmann wishes to use politics "in the Aristotelian sense of the word, as the inclusive horizon of the life of mankind."[111] Therefore, political theology is not just one area of theology, but must move to the hermeneutical level. Theology must be done in the consciousness of its consequences for the practical political sphere. It must constantly be asking the question of for whom it is being done. It must no longer attempt to remain abstract, above the political realm, but "become the theory of practice."[112]

> Responsible theology must therefore engage in institutional criticism as it reflects on the "place" of the churches "in the life" of modern society and in ideological criticism as it reflects on itself. It can no longer self-forgetfully screen out its own social and political reality as the old metaphysical and personalistic theologies did. So in public, responsible theology itself stands consciously between the Christian, eschatological message of freedom and the socio-political reality. Thus, through an interrogation of institutions, words, and symbols, it must ascertain whether a religious opium is being mediated to the people or a real ferment of freedom; whether faith or superstition is being spread; whether the crucified one is made present or the idols of the nation are served.[113]

Theological thinking, if it is to be relevant to the present situation of humanity, must be based on this reflection on practice. But what was said about Barth must also be said about Moltmann. That is, the content of theology and the direction of the practice of faith do not arise out of independent practice. Rather, as is evident in the quotation above, these are given by the identity of the Christian faith itself. "Content and manner of proclaimed and lived freedom must be legitimized by reflections on their ground in the Crucified Christ."[114] The point, though, is that theology based on the identity of the Christian faith does not mean leaving the realm of practice. As a matter of fact, staying with the center of the Christian faith is precisely what makes it politically relevant.[115] For Moltmann, theological reflection on the center of Christian identity involves one in the concrete, human practice of God in the crucified Christ for the liberation of humankind.[116] As with Barth, it is clear that Christian identity is inseparable from this trinitarian action of God. Theology must become practical, then, because the focus of the activity of the triune God of the Christian faith is earth. The Christian must take social-political reality and its transformation through revolutionary practice seriously because the practice of the triune God takes place in the full earthly, political context.

The conclusion of this analysis is not only that theology is a reflection on the praxis of God in the history of Jesus for human liberation, which must also be critical reflection on its own praxis as it attempts to correspond to this triune praxis of God. It also means that the end of theology cannot be the reflection in itself, but must be the practice it supports. The truth of theology is proved in practice, in its correspondence in the present situation to the activity of God in his triune history, in its striving "for the practical congruence between the biblical tradition's horizon of concern and the present circumstances . . . of present social reality."[117]

It is for this reason that Moltmann rejects the existentialist interpretation of faith offered by Bultmann. It does not stand the test of either pole of the theory-praxis relation and therefore Moltmann's critique of Bultmann parallels Marx's critique of Feuerbach. Bultmann, while he perceives clearly the human questions behind the mythological form of the early Christian kerygma, reads these questions only in terms of individual self-understanding. He does not see that these thoughts are related to the concrete practice in which humans were involved. He fails to locate the origins of these questions in the real, practical afflictions of human beings in their social and historical context.

> For the quest for the sense and purpose of world history,
> Bultmann substitutes the search for the meaning of the
> history of existence, i.e., the search in the individual case for
> one's own being.[118]

As Marx claimed against Feuerbach, then, it can be said that Bultmann does not perceive clearly enough that thought is inseparable from the concrete social situation.

But this means, according to Moltmann, that Bultmann fails on the other side of the theory-practice relation too. His theology fails in practice. For Bultmann, the kernel of truth offered by the demythologized kerygma is a transformed self-understanding. But for Paul and other early Christians, the proclamation of the faith occurs within the context of, and includes the call for, concrete mission.

> The common ground and the common direction of the
> different proclamations and theologies in differing situations
> is therefore the social initiative which we most correctly
> describe as *mission*.[119]

This missionary initiative embedded in the kerygma is the result of "the initiative of God" for the overcoming of human misery in the trinitarian activity of the cross and resurrection, as in the proclamation of this

initiative, one "anticipates God's future at the front of real misery."[120]
The New Testament conceives the misery of humanity as "servitude
under the powers of sin and death."[121] Paul announces concrete human
liberation "for his time [when religion and idols repressed mankind]
with the gospel of free justification."[122] Now the question of human
misery has lost its cosmological context and in the modern world "has
become more of a political and social question."[123] Nevertheless, what is
clear is that the proclamation is not exhausted by the individual transformation of the self-understanding. "The content and forms of kerygmatic
language are not understandable without consideration of this concrete,
missionary initiative."[124] Rather, only one engaged in this concrete
mission can understand these texts.[125] To "grasp freedom in faith," one
"must serve through bodily, social, and political obedience the liberation
of the suffering creation out of real affliction."[126] Theology and faith that
care only for self-understanding and are not involved in practical liberation miss the truth of the faith, as they also fail in the face of the critique
of Marx.

> If one grasps only the promise of the freedom in faith and
> forgets the realistic demand for the liberation of this world,
> the gospel becomes the religious basis for the justification of
> society as it is and a mystification of the suffering reality.[127]

Moltmann paraphrases Marx when, in various contexts, he states,

> The theologian is not concerned merely to supply a different
> interpretation of the world, of history and of human nature,
> but to *transform* them in expectation of a divine
> transformation.[128]

Conclusion

So far we have established that in the theology of both Barth and
Moltmann there is — as the latter says — "a parallel with the Marxist
coordination of theory and practice . . . ."[129] Their theologies, that is
their theories, are reflections on praxis, reflections on the human praxis of
God in Jesus for the overcoming of human pain and suffering and,
therefore, reflections on the practice of faith in the contemporary situation. This means, furthermore, that the truth of these theologies, these
theories of God, is not found in the theory alone, but must be proved in
the practice of this faith. On its own terms the Christian faith, when
properly understood, includes in itself already what Marx perceived as
the praxological basis of truth.

But it is also clear that the understanding of the Christian faith that consciously includes this relation of theory and practice is found in the trinitarian formulation. For the doctrine of the Trinity comprehends the event of Jesus as an event of God. Therefore, the doctrine of the Trinity is the doctrine of God, the theology, developed on the basis of concrete, human practice — that of Jesus of Nazareth — in the socio-political sphere, rather than on the human attempt to understand God and liberation by projecting earthly abstractions into the heavens, without regard to the concrete earthly situation. The doctrine of the Trinity therefore keeps theology's focus on the concrete, down-to-earth practice of faith. Karl Marx's charge against theology, that it does not take the practical situation seriously, is substantiated against the tradition of theism that does not take the practice of God in Jesus seriously enough. Trinitarian theology, on the other hand, can respond to Marx at this point because it includes the praxological nature of truth and opposes any theology that does not as false. Trinitarian theology, then, can claim and demonstrate that on this issue Marx misidentified the true form of the Christian faith.

The questions remaining in the Marxist critique have to do with the form of practice supported by religion. It is not enough to consciously accept the theory-practice dialectic. Marx claims that all systems of thought operate in this relation even when they do so unconsciously. The more important question is the form of practice the theory supports. This has already been indicated to some degree but needs some further elaboration. The questions addressed to theology then are: Does it maintain the status quo? Does it support the transformation of the earthly situation? If it does support transformation, what direction does this follow? Reaction or revolution? The answers to these questions involve the issues of the eschatological nature of God and the form of the practice of God. Both of these issues will be developed in the next chapter.

NOTES

[1] See Chapter II above.
[2] Feuerbach, *Lectures on the Essence of Religion,* p. 22.
[3] *Ibid.,* p. 285.
[4] *Ibid.*
[5] *Ibid.,* pp. 284f.

⁶ See Küng, p. 213, where he quotes from an address praising Feuerbach by a spokesman for the Heidelberg Workers' Education Association.

⁷ *Ibid.*, p. 244. Küng writes, "It was not the wretchedness of the proletariat but left wing Hegelian philosophy which was responsible for his atheism."

⁸ Karl Marx, "Toward the Critique of Hegel's Philosophy of Right" (Hereafter cited as "Critique of Hegel") excerpted in *Marx and Engels — Basic Writings on Politics and Philosophy*, ed. Lewis S. Feuer (New York, 1959), p. 262.

⁹ See Küng, p. 244. Marx's acceptance of Feuerbach's basic direction does not justify Küng's claim that "Marx as a critic of religion does not really get beyond Feuerbach as critic of religion, in his substantiation of atheism." Because Marx was an atheist before he was a socialist does not mean that in his work his atheism remains in this relationship to praxis. This analysis will demonstrate that Marx does go beyond Feuerbach as a critic of religion. For in his epistemology he unifies the question of the truth of religion and, conversely, the truth of atheism with the question of revolutionary praxis.

¹⁰ Marx, "Critique of Hegel," p. 262.

¹¹ See Küng, pp. 245, 254.

¹² See *Ibid.*, p. 221. See also Arend Th. van Leeuwen, *Critique of Heaven* (New York, 1972), pp. 184ff.

¹³ Karl Marx, "Theses on Feuerbach," I, in Feuer, p. 243. (Hereafter cited as "Theses.") See also "Thesis," V, p. 244.

¹⁴ Ludwig Feuerbach, *The Essence of Christianity*, p. xl.

¹⁵ See Erich Fromm, *Marx's Concept of Man* (New York, 1966), pp. 16, 40ff.

¹⁶ Karl Marx, *A Contribution to the Critique of Political Economy*, trans. N.I. Stone, excerpted in Feuer, p. 43. See also *German Ideology*, trans. T. B. Bottomore, in Fromm, p. 20, where Marx writes,

"The production of ideas, of conceptions, of consciousness, is at first directly interwoven with the material activity and the material intercourse of men, the real language of life. . . . The same applies to mental production as expressed in the language of politics, laws, morality, religion, metaphysics of a people. Men are producers of their conceptions, ideas, etc. — real, active men, as they are conditioned by the definite development of their productive forces . . . ."

¹⁷ van Leeuwen, p. 186.

[18] Marx, "Critique of Hegel," p. 262.

[19] Marx, "Theses," VI, p. 244.

[20] *Ibid.*, p. 245. See also *Ibid.*, VIII, p. 245.

[21] *Ibid.*, VII, p. 245.

[22] Marx, "Critique of Hegel," p. 262.

[23] See Fromm, pp. 47ff.

[24] In *Capital I*, Marx wrote about the laborer in capitalism: "The laborer exists for the process of production, and not the process of production for the laborer." (Quoted in *Ibid.*, p. 48.)

[25] Marx, "Critique of Hegel," pp. 262ff. ·

[26] *Ibid.*, p. 263.

[27] *Ibid.*

[28] Marx, "Theses," II, p. 241.

[29] Marx, "Critique of Hegel," p. 263. See also "Theses," IV, p. 244.

[30] Marx saw in Feuerbach the beginning of a theoretical basis for socialism. See van Leeuwen, p. 186.

[31] Marx, "Theses," XI, p. 245.

[32] Marx, "Critique of Hegel," p. 263.

[33] *CD* II/1, 258.

[34] See Joseph Bettis, "Political Theology and Social Ethics: The Socialist Humanism of Karl Barth," *Scottish Journal of Theology*, XXVII, no. 3 (August, 1974), 288, for agreement with this point. This essay also appears in George Hunsinger, ed., *Karl Barth and Radical Politics* (Philadelphia, 1976), pp. 159-179. See also Joseph Bettis, "Theology and Politics — Karl Barth and Reinhold Niebuhr on Social Ethics after Liberalism," *Religion in Life*, XLVIII (September, 1979), 55.

[35] Reinhold Niebuhr, "Barth's East German Letter," *Christian Century*, LXXVI, no. 6 (Feb. 11, 1959), 168. See also the articles in Reinhold Niebuhr, *Applied Christianity* (New York, 1959), pp. 141-96; particularly the articles "Barth — the Apostle of the Absolute," pp. 141-47, and "Why is Barth Silent on Hungary?", p. 195. See also Niebuhr, "The Quality of our Lives," *Christian Century* (May 11, 1960), p. 571. In all of these references Niebuhr makes the point that Barth's theology is "irrelevant" or "defective for wise political decisions."

[36] Will Herberg, "The Social Philosophy of Karl Barth" in Karl Barth, *Community, State and Church* (Gloucester, Mass., 1968), pp. 11-67.

[37] Charles West, *Communism and the Theologians* (New York, 1958).

[38] See Frederick Herzog, "politische Theologie und die Christliche Hoffung," in *Diskussion zur politischen Theologie* (München, 1969), pp. 135, 123.

[39] See James H. Cone, *God of the Oppressed* (New York, 1975), p. 145; and James H. Cone, *A Black Theology of Liberation* (New York, 1970), pp 51f.

[40] See Reinhold Niebuhr, "Toward New Intra-Christian Endeavors," *Christian Century*, LXXXVI (Dec. 31, 1969), 1662-67. Discussing Barth's position on the East-West struggle Niebuhr, in the context of U.S. involvement in Vietnam, wrote, "I must ruefully change that decade-ago opinion of mine in regard to Barth's neutralism . . . . I misjudged both Karl Barth and Catholicism" (pp. 1662 f).

[41] Paul L. Lehmann, "Karl Barth, Theologian of Permanent Revolution" *Union Seminary Quarterly Review*, XXVIII (1972-73), 76.

[42] *Ibid.*, p. 77.

[43] See *Ibid.*, pp. 73-77. Robert McAffee Brown, in *Theology in a New Key* (Philadelphia, 1978), pp. 142f, indicates how Barth anticipates some themes of Liberation Theology.

[44] See Friedrich-Wilhelm Marquardt, *Theologie und Sozialismus: Das Beispiel Karl Barth* (Munich, 1972) and "Socialism in the Theology of Karl Barth" in Hunsinger, *Karl Barth and Radical Politics,* pp. 47-76. Karl Barth's son, Markus, in "Current Discussions on the Political Character of Karl Barth's Theology" in *Footnotes to a Theology — The Karl Barth Colloquium of 1972,* ed. Martin Rumscheidt (Canada, 1974), p. 82, has called Marquardt's book "remarkable" and suggests that he has "put his finger upon an essential element of Karl Barth's theology," even though he is critical of "the methods and arguments chosen by Marquardt" (p. 94).

[45] See the articles by these men in Hunsinger, *Karl Barth and Radical Politics.*

[46] Barth's 1911 address, "Jesus Christ and the Movement for Social Justice," in *Ibid.*, pp. 19-37, is representative of this period. See also Helmut Gollwitzer, "Kingdom of God and Socialism in the Theology of Karl Barth," in *Ibid.*, p. 78, and Markus Barth, *op. cit.*, pp. 77-78, for accounts of his Safenwil work.

[47] See Markus Barth, p. 78; Marquardt, "Socialism in the Theology of Karl Barth," pp. 47-48; Gollwitzer, pp. 78-79. These writers notice correctly that Barth's joining the Social Democratic Party was not a theoretical or ideological commitment but a matter of praxis. In a letter to an East German in 1968, Barth explains his membership in the Social Democratic Party:

"It sounds very fine and good that as a Christian one should
not belong to any political party, but this is true only when
it is a matter of belonging in principle. . . . In specific cases
in relation to specific points, they can and should join up
with a party which stands for the right thing." [*Karl
Barth — Letters 1961-1968*, trans. and ed. Geoffrey W.
Bromiley (Grand Rapids, 1981), p. 303.]

This praxological basis for decision making puts Barth in relationship to Marx whom he cites favorably in this same letter. It also helps
explain why — unlike Tillich whose socialism Barth identifies as being
ideologically based — Barth refused to resign from the party when
pressured to do so, and as Tillich did, in 1933. (See Barth's letter to
Tillich in Hunsinger, pp. 116-17.) Here again Barth stresses praxis:

"Membership in the SPD does not mean for me a confession to the idea and world view of socialism . . . . Membership in the SPD means for me simply a practical political
decision" (p. 116).

[48] Marquardt, in an afterword to "Socialism in the Theology of
Karl Barth" in Hunsinger's volume, says that "many of the more
provocative conclusions . . . may come to be modified or set aside" (p.
69). Markus Barth makes the same point about Marquardt's book
(Markus Barth, pp. 83f). Bettis (in Hunsinger, *Karl Barth and Radical
Politics*, p. 161) also believes that Marquardt has overstated his case .
And Helmut Gollwitzer (in *Ibid.*, pp. 101f) recognizes some
problematic areas remaining in the relationship of theory and praxis in
Barth's life and thought. For instance, when Barth became a professor,
for long periods of time his political interest was "down played" in his
theology.

[49] Barth, *The Humanity of God*, p. 14.

[50] *Ibid.*, p. 40.

[51] Quoted by John Deschner, "Karl Barth as Political Activist,"
Union Seminary Quarterly Review, XXVIII, No. 1 (Fall, 1972), 56. See
also Hunsinger, *Karl Barth and Radical Politics*, p. 203.

[52] For Barth's articulation of this position in 1916, see, for instance,
The Word of God and the Word of Man, trans. Douglas Horton (New
York, 1957), p. 43:

"It is not the right human thoughts about God which form
the content of the Bible, but the right divine thoughts about
men. The Bible tells us not how we should talk with God
but what he says to us; not how we find the way to him, but

how he has sought and found the way to us; . . . . The word of God is within the Bible."

53 *Ibid.*, p. 40.

54 Quoted in James D. Smart, *The Divided Mind of Modern Theology* (Philadelphia, 1967), p. 85.

55 Quoted in Hunsinger, *Karl Barth and Radical Politics*, p. 208.

56 Quoted in Smart, p. 85.

57 Quoted in *Ibid.*, p. 86.

58 Quoted in Hunsinger, *Karl Barth and Radical Politics*, p. 207.

59 See *Ibid.*, p. 210.

60 Quoted in Smart, p. 86.

61 See Smart, p. 87, and Hunsinger, *Karl Barth and Radical Politics*, p. 210.

62 See Karl Barth, *The Epistle to the Romans*, trans. Edwyn C. Hoskyns (Sixth edition, London, 1933), pp. 3ff. (Hereafter cited as *Romans.*)

63 *Ibid.*, p. 4.

64 *Ibid.*, p. 5.

65 See Hunsinger, *Karl Barth and Radical Politics*, pp. 210, 212.

66 Barth, *Romans,* p. 482.

67 *Ibid.* See also p. 483.

68 *Ibid.*, p. 478.

69 *Ibid.* See also p. 480.

70 Thus Hunsinger, *Karl Barth and Radical Politics*, p. 213. See also Barth, *Romans*, pp. 478-484.

71 Barth, *Romans*, p. 489. It is a game for Barth in the sense that "absolute political right" has vanished.

72 See Hunsinger, *Karl Barth and Radical Politics*, p. 217.

73 See *Ibid.*, pp. 220ff.

74 See *Ibid.*, p. 75, n. 2.

75 On this see Barth, *Romans*, pp. 332ff, 368, 373f, 247f, 252f, 266ff, 269.

76 On Barth's position on this from 1933 through 1939, see Karl Barth, *The German Church Conflict*, trans. P.T.A. Parker (Richmond, 1965). Also *see Karl Barth, The Church and the Political Problem of Our Day (New York, 1939) and Karl Barth, Theological Existence To-Day!, trans. R. Birch Hogle (Lexington, Kentucky, 1962).*

77 Included in Barth, *Community, State, and Church*, pp. 135, 148.

78 See Barth, *The Church and the Political Problem of Our Day*, pp. 52, 55, 71, 74, 77. See also Will Herberg, "The Social Philosophy of Karl Barth" in Barth, *Community, State, and Church*, p. 30.

[79] Barth, *The Church and Political Problem of Our Day*, p. 38.

[80] *Ibid.*, p. 41.

[81] *Ibid.*, p. 55. This work was written in 1939. On pp. 32ff, Barth explains why he did not explicitly reject the Nazi state sooner.

[82] Included in Barth, *Community, State, and Church*, pp. 149-189.

[83] *CD* I/1, xiii.

[84] Deschner, p. 59.

[85] Barth, *How I Changed My Mind* (Richmond, 1966), p. 54.

[86] *Ibid.*, p. 49. This discussion calls into question analyses like that of Gerald Butler in "Karl Barth and Political Theology", *Scottish Journal of theology*, XXVII, No. 4 (November, 1974), 441-458, which concludes that "it is inappropriate to speak of Barth as either a political theologian or of Barth as having a political theology" (p. 458). Butler claims this because, as he sees it, Barth, unlike Metz, Moltmann or Herzog, does not give to socio-political reality a hermeneutical status (pp. 456-458). But our analysis has demonstrated that Barth's political praxis did serve as a fundamental element in his interpretation of the Christian faith.

[87] *CD* I/1, xiii.

[88] See Barth, *Humanity of God*, p. 4l.

[89] *CD* II/2, p. 548.

[90] See Bettis' discussion of the distinction between "extrinsic heteronomy" rejected by Barth and "intrinsic heteronomy" proposed by Barth (in Hunsinger, *Karl Barth and Radical Politics*, pp 162-169).

[91] *CD* II/2, 548.

[92] *Ibid.*, Emphasis mine.

[93] *CD* I/2, 793.

[94] *Ibid.*

[95] *Ibid.* See also p. 787.

[96] *Ibid.*, p. 787.

[97] *Ibid.*, p. 792.

[98] *CD* IV/2, 542.

[99] *Ibid.*, p. 544.

[100] Jürgen Moltmann, "The Cross and Civil Religion," trans. Thomas Hughson and Paul Rigby, in *Religion and Political Society*, ed. The Institute of Christian Thought (New York, 1974), p. 26. See also p. 32 and p. 28 where Moltmann places Barth's discussion with Brunner over nature and grace in the practical political context. It should be noted that Moltmann employs "political theology" in two different ways. Here it is used negatively to refer to a theology that supports the established society. We will see that positively it designates a theology that has become politically self-conscious.

[101] Moltmann, *CG*, p. 60.

[102] *Ibid.*, p. 11.

[103] See Jürgen Moltmann, "Theology as Eschatology" in *The Future of Hope*, ed. Frederick Herzog (New York, 1970), p. 3.

[104] See *Ibid.*, p. 3ff; also Jürgen Moltmann, "Toward a Political Hermeneutic of the Gospel" in *RRF*, pp. 90ff, 100f. This essay also appears in *New Theology No. 6*, ed. by Martin E. Marty and Dean G. Peerman (London, 1968), pp. 66-90.

[105] Moltmann, *RRF*, p. 100.

[106] Moltmann, "Theology as Eschatology," p. 3.

[107] Moltmann, *RRF*, p. 100.

[108] Moltmann, "Theology as Eschatology," p. 5.

[109] Moltmann, *RRF*, p. 101.

[110] Jürgen Moltmann, "Political Theology" in *The Experiment Hope*, trans. Douglas Meeks (Philadelphia, 1975), p. 102. (Hereafter cited as *EH*.)

[111] Moltmann, *RRF*, p. 98.

[112] See *Ibid.*

[113] Moltmann, *EH*, p. 102.

[114] Moltmann, *RRF*, p. 102.

[115] Moltmann, *CG*, pp. 24f.

[116] Moltmann, *RRF*, p. 102f. This point will be discussed further in Chapter VI.

[117] *Ibid.*, p. 96f.

[118] *Ibid.*, p. 91.

[119] *Ibid.*, p. 99.

[120] Moltmann, "Theology as Eschatology", pp. 8, 43.

[121] *Ibid.*, p. 43.

[122] Moltmann, *RRF*, p. 96.

[123] *Ibid.*, p. 100. See also Moltmann, "Theology as Eschatology," p. 47.

[124] Moltmann, *RRF*, p. 99.

[125] Moltmann, "Theology as Eschatology," p. 44. See also *RRF*, p. 99.

[126] Moltmann, *RRF*, p. 95.

[127] *Ibid.*

[128] Moltmann, *TH*, p. 84. See also "Theology as Eschatology," p. 39; *CG*, p. 11; *RRF*, p. 95.

[129] Moltmann, *RRF*, p. 98.

CHAPTER VI

THE ESCHATOLOGICAL TRINITY — PROTEST AND LIBERATION

In this chapter we will continue the development of trinitarian responses to atheism's questions about praxis and theodicy. Since we have already established the fact that trinitarian theology is always related to praxis, we need now to show the direction and content of that praxis. We will accomplish this by developing two aspects of trinitarian theology. First, we will see that the doctrine of the Trinity speaks of a God who is an eschatological reality. The triune God has a future and from that future calls present reality into question. This means that in following this God human beings are freed from the status quo and for a praxis in the direction of God's future. Second, we will discover that God's future is not indeterminate but is given content by its concrete appearance in Jesus who identified with and proclaimed the liberation of the poor, the oppressed and the outcast. Christian praxis therefore is always in solidarity with these suffering ones and aims at correspondence to God's future in which the transformation of all things is promised.

It is precisely at this point that the further trinitarian response to the question of human suffering becomes perceptible. It is not only the case that the triune God is with us in our suffering, or takes that suffering into his own inner being, although the importance of this should not be underestimated. Rather, because the doctrine of the Trinity is a reflection of the God who is constituted as an eschatological reality whose future includes the overcoming of all agony, it also conceives of God as existing in protest against the present structures of oppression and the conditions of suffering. From his future, God challenges them and calls them into question. This means that the triune God is one with atheism in the protest against suffering. He makes this protest ingredient in his own being by his self-limitation on the way to his future. The triune God will not be who he will be without the transformation of all human misery and the situations that cause it.

Moreover, we will see that trinitarian theology does not only speak of God's protest. It also asserts that in the Spirit this protest becomes concrete in believers as well. As the Spirit brings folk into the history of

God which is constituted by protest and movement toward his future, they must become protesters against the conditions of suffering and practitioners of God's future.

The reason that the trinitarian response to Marx and to atheism based on human suffering have been brought together should now be apparent. Both forms of atheism have to do with a protest against the present situation and with the hope and praxis of transforming it. The response to both, therefore, can be developed in the context of the eschatological nature of the triune God.

The Future of the Triune God

According to Karl Marx, religion with its belief in a transcendent God is an opiate. That is, it is always an ideological system that is related to the practice of the status quo. Many interpreters of Marx indicate that the central issue in this criticism is the relationship between a transcendent God and human freedom to bring about change.[1] If God is the omnipotent, immutable ruler of all things, then the conditions on earth are willed or permitted by this ruler. Moreover, since God has the power and freedom to rule as he chooses, humans have no power or freedom over against God to change these conditions. Ernst Bloch declares,

> Where the great world-ruler holds sway, there is no room for freedom, not even the freedom of the children of God or the mystical-democratic figure of the kingdom that is found in the chiliastic hope.[2]

Roger Garaudy asks,

> If God exists, is my liberty decreased? Is God alienating where my liberty is concerned? And Marxist atheism answers: "Yes, God is alienating insofar as he is regarded as a Moral Law existing before the creation of Man, as a heteronomy, opposed to the autonomy of man.[3]

According to this view, religion holds a conception of God who is responsible for the present condition of suffering and who offers no possibility of human freedom to transform present conditions. It attempts to abandon the realm of concrete practice and offers fulfillment in the inner transformation of the individual and in the hope of heaven above the conditions of real history. Religion, however, does not escape a relationship to practice but ends up ideologically supporting the status quo.

Can this criticism justifiably be directed against faith in a trinitarian context? Certainly there have been forms of the doctrine of the Trinity that have been esoteric and the possession of a few theologians and church officials. There have also been trinitarian formulations that have become speculative, detached from the concrete revelation of God in Jesus and, therefore, essentially marks of God's mystery and eternity abstractly defined. In both cases the doctrine of the Trinity could be destructive of human freedom for action and supportive of the status quo. Our concern, however, is not with all trinitarian perspectives but with those offered by Barth and Moltmann. In this context responses can be given to this Marxist critique.[4] On the one hand it can be affirmed, for it exposes the questionable character of the conception of God that is commonly found in theism. On the other hand, this critique can be transcended, for the doctrine of the Trinity of Barth and Moltmann speaks of God as an eschatological being who challenges the present conditions of suffering and in his self-limitation allows, indeed calls for, free human activity in the direction of his liberating future. Therefore, the eschatological element in the doctrine of the Trinity is important in distinguishing a liberating conception of God from oppressive ones.

Making eschatology a key for the interpretation of the doctrine of God is associated for obvious reasons with Moltmann. But Barth is instructive here also. For both theologians the doctrine of the Trinity requires serious attention to eschatology on account of the eschatological history of Jesus. Every point of this history points to a transformed future.

Barth and Moltmann isolate at least three moments on which to base their eschatological emphasis. First, Jesus appears in the context of the eschatological promisory history of the Old Testament. In light of his resurrection, Jesus is revealed to be the fulfillment of the promises pronounced in the Old Testament. As Barth says,

> And in Him they saw all come to life again. The promise made to the Fathers had not been annulled, but fulfilled. The history of Israel recorded in the Old Testament was not in vain, but destined for this goal. The words of the Law and the Prophets, uttered so long ago, had not faded away, but now rang out as never before . . . . Who was it, then, who had come? The One who was to come in all that time before. The One who was prefigured and expected in it.[5]

Moltmann states it:

> If on the other hand theology takes seriously the fact that Jesus was a Jew, then this means that he is not to be

> understood as a particular case of human being in general
> but only in connection with the Old Testament history of
> promise and in conflict with it.[6]

Therefore,

> The Gospel has its inabrogable presupposition in the Old
> Testament history of promise. In the Gospel the Old Testa-
> ment history of promise finds more than a fulfillment which
> does away with it; it finds its future.[7]

The most appropriate question about Jesus, then, is "Are you he who is
to come?"[8]

For Barth this sense of the expectation and straining towards the
future extends back further than the covenant to the creation itself. He
says,

> The apostolic community understood creation itself only as
> the external basis of the covenant attested in the Old Testa-
> ment, and therefore the covenant as the internal basis of
> creation. It thus saw in the man Jesus, prophetically
> prefigured and expected in Israel, and finally appearing in
> His own time, the real object of God's foresight and fore-
> ordination in creation and ordering of reality distinct from
> Himself.[9]

Therefore, as Barth concludes, it was "primarily the Old Testament
background to the New Testament message which gave to the first
Christian consciousness of time its forward direction and eschatological
orientation."[10]

Second, the preaching of Jesus himself that was vindicated by his
resurrection is the basis for the eschatological reading of transcendence
within the trinitarian context. Jesus appears proclaiming the hope of the
kingdom of God in the imminent future. Barth declares,

> The reader of the Gospels is bound to look to the future, if
> only because the Jesus attested by them was not waiting for
> nothing but positively living and speaking and acting
> towards his future revelation . . . . It is the kingdom with
> veil removed, manifest, and visible in glory. Everything
> Jesus said revolved implicitly, and in the parables explicitly,
> around the coming kingdom in this sense.[11]

Moltmann concurs,

> Jesus identified the eschatological kingdom of God with his
> Word, activity, and his suffering and thus his person.[12]

. . . the message and acts, miracles and parables of Jesus
before Easter are described as "the kingdom of God."[13]

Third, and most importantly, it is the resurrection of Jesus that is
the foundation for belief that the being of God includes the future. It is
the resurrection that demonstrates that Jesus is the fulfillment of the Old
Testament promises and integrates them into the future of Jesus. It is the
resurrection that vindicates Jesus' preaching of the imminent, eschatological kingdom of God that is coming to suffering humanity. And,
because resurrection is itself an eschatological term, when it is applied to
what happened to the crucified Jesus on Easter day, it indicates that
Jesus is the first to enter the future kingdom to which now, on this basis,
the whole creation looks forward. It identifies Jesus as the eschatological
agent of God, as the coming Son of Man, as the One who is to come
again.[14] "What came upon the world and man in the resurrection of the
man Jesus . . . ," Barth writes, "was this presence of its future salvation . . . ."[15] And Moltmann says,

> The Christian hope for the future comes of observing a
> specific, unique event — that of the resurrection and
> appearing of Jesus Christ. The hopeful theological mind,
> however, can observe this event only in seeking to span the
> future horizon projected by this event. Hence to recognize
> the resurrection of Christ means to recognize in this event
> the future of God for the world and the future which man
> finds in this God and his acts.[16]

We will now see in more detail how these concrete elements in the
history of Jesus become the basis for Barth's and Moltmann's claim that
the triune God is an eschatological reality.

Karl Barth: The Future in God's Being

Critics of the theology of Karl Barth often point to a certain
ambiguity in his eschatological emphasis.[17] In the *Epistle to the Romans*,
Barth remarked, "If Christianity be not altogether eschatology, there
remains in it no relationship whatever with Christ."[18] But then in his
early works Barth went on to interpret the *eschaton* uneschatologically as
the possible presence of God to every moment of time. In *The Resurrection of the Dead*, he writes, "Of the *real* end of history it may be said at
any time: The end is near!"[19] This apparent problem with eschatology is
found in the *Church Dogmatics* also. Moltmann directs criticism towards
Barth's conception of revelation. In Barth's conception of the revelation
of God, when God reveals himself he reveals nothing else than himself.

This means that as God is in his revelation he is "before hand in himself."[20] Barth develops this view in the context of the doctrine of the Trinity where the immanent Trinity is the ground of the economic Trinity. God's revelation in Jesus is a repetition of God's eternal decision to distinguish himself from himself, to be triune. Moltmann charges that if this is the case, however, everything has already taken place in eternity, and there is no ground for eschatological thinking. The results of this are disastrous for an eschatological view of transcendence. One can speak of God non-eschatologically: "Only of God Himself, which means at this point the Holy Spirit as such, can one speak non-eschatologically, i.e. without this reference to something other, beyond and future."[21] Revelation is conceived of as the presence of God's eternal decision, a "'pure presence of God', an 'eternal presence of God in time', a 'present without any future.'"[22] Eschatological can mean then only the relationship of eternity to time: "what accrues to us from the side of God,"[23] or the "unveiling" to human beings of what has already taken place in eternity for God.[24] As Colin Gunton put it,

> ... Barth sometimes appears to hold that the eschatological future is future only in being so for 'our experience and thought', that it is a matter of ignorance rather than time. The corollary would be that *objectively*, so far as God is concerned, there is no divine futurity, and all has been already decided in a timeless past.[25]

If these positions were all Barth had to say about eschatology, then he would be open to the Marxist critique and to the critique based on the theodicy question. For the concept of transcendence seen thus far is ahistorical. Nothing new in history can be expected other than a noetic unveiling of what has already occurred. Religion, then, would function as an opiate as attention is turned away from the earth where the status quo would rule and toward eternity where God's eternal activity has already taken place. Suffering humanity could expect nothing further from God, for in spite of the remaining agony God has completed his work.

However, Barth's unbalanced emphasis on the "already" of the eternal decision of God is only one side of his theology, and it is confined mainly to his early theology and the first volume of the *Church Dogmatics*. And yet even in *Church Dogmatics* I/1 Barth can say of redemption that it does not coincide with revelation or reconciliation, but is "God's act still outstanding, future, consummating." And further, "reconciliation, or revelation, is not creation or a continuation of creation, but an inconceivably new work of God above and beyond creation" that "gives

rise to the expectation of this future . . . ."[26] As early as *Church Dogmatics* II/1, written in 1940, Barth begins to find a way to take eschatology
and the temporal future it indicates more seriously. In a discussion on the
knowledge of God as Redeemer, Barth insists that no analogy for this
hope avails.

> If there is real hope, hope which has content and substance,
> a confident, joyful, active looking to the future, then this
> future is the future of God the Redeemer.[27]

And if God the Redeemer is to be known, it "is only through the
revelation of His future."[28] Also, in the discussion of the event character
of God's being that was mentioned in Chapter III, Barth says that the
event "has not merely happened and is now a past fact of history." Nor
is it only present or both past and present. The event that characterizes
God's being "is also future — the event which lies completely and
wholly in front of us, which has not yet happened . . . ."[29] Again in this
context, the doctrine of the Trinity is necessary because it identifies the
event of Jesus Christ, which has a past and present but also a future, as
the revelation of the being of God.[30] "God is He who in this event is
subject, predicate, object; the revealer, the act of revelation, the revealed;
Father, Son and Holy Spirit."[31] Finally, in *Church Dogmatics* II/1,
Barth explicitly rejects his earlier interpretation of eschatology:

> That we had only an uncertain grip of the matter became
> apparent, strangely enough in those passages of exposition
> in which I had to speak positively about the divine future
> and hope as such. It emerged in the fact that although I was
> confident to treat the far-sidedness of the coming kingdom
> of God with absolute seriousness, I had no such confidence
> in relation to its coming as such. So when I came to
> expound a passage like Rom.13:11f . . . , in spite of every
> precaution I interpreted it as if it referred only to the
> moment which confronts all moments in time as the eternal
> "transcendental meaning" of all moments in time.[32]

Although Barth claims that he said things that were essential to a proper
understanding of Rom. 13:11f, he concludes that he "missed the distinctive feature of the passage, the teleology which it ascribes to time as it
moves towards a real end."[33] Because Barth's thinking is so christologically based, he is led to move beyond his earlier conceptions to a concrete
eschatology.

    In light of this re-evaluation of eschatology, based on the concrete
revelation in Jesus, which begins in *Church Dogmatics* II/1 and continues in the later volumes of the *Church Dogmatics*, Barth takes issue

with his critics for not dealing adequately with his views on eschatology. In a gracious but critical letter to Moltmann after having read his *Theology of Hope*, Barth responded, "Have my concepts of the threefold time (*Church Dogmatics* III, 2, 47.1) and threefold parousia of Jesus Christ (*Church Dogmatics* IV, 3, 69.4) made so little impact on you that you do not even give them critical consideration?"[34] There are three important contexts in which to examine the revision that Barth made to do justice to the future and eschatological side of the Christian God. To the two mentioned by Barth, the section on the three forms of the temporality of God (*CD* II/1, 31.3) can be added.

In these places Barth explicitly attempts to develop a concept of transcendence which will not render temporality meaningless. Barth claims that God's eternity is not to be conceived as "timelessness" or in contradiction to time. "God's eternity does not invalidate past, present and future, and therefore time; it legitimates them."[35] This claim is made on the basis of the by now familiar line of argument. The eternity of God is not known abstractly, it is not eternity derived from abstracting from the world, but solely from God's concrete revelation in Jesus. As God appears in his act of revelation he is in himself. This means that Barth is speaking of eternity only in the context of the doctrine of the Trinity:

> A correct understanding of the positive side of the concept
> of eternity, free from all false conclusions, is gained only
> when we are clear that we are speaking about the eternity of
> the triune God.[36]

The eternity of the triune God has a "positive relation to time," because in Jesus this God makes time for us, "enters time," and "takes time to Himself." In Jesus the eternal one "becomes temporal."[37] And, because the revelation of Jesus "has a 'before' and an 'after'," it is certain that the eternity of God is "genuinely temporal."[38]

Barth does not find the temporality of God to be only past or present. It includes them, but also includes the future. Through an analysis of revelation he claims that the eternity of the triune God is threefold: The "temporality of eternity may be described in detail as the pre-temporality, supra-temporality and post-temporality of eternity."[39] God's eternity includes a past, a present and a future. In both the section on the eternity of God and the section on the threefold time of Christ, we see Barth developing this claim in the trinitarian context of God's concrete self-communication in Jesus. On this basis one must say that the being of Jesus is past.[40] He entered time as a human in the first century. And yet his past goes back beyond this; for he was the one who was the promised goal of the Old Testament expectation, where he was "objectively prefigured" in such a way "and with such reality that we cannot say of the man Jesus that He was "not yet" in this time before His time . . . ."[41] However, his past goes back beyond this also. For the covenant that Jesus fulfilled was the internal basis for creation itself. Therefore, the past of Jesus extends back to and before creation.[42] Because in Jesus we have to do with the God who created all things and was before all things, it is clear that the eternity of God must be conceived so as to include the past, to be post-temporal.

But God is not only in the past. He is with us through all time. "In all its inaccessible distance the divine 'before' does not separate us from God's love."[43] Again this is based on the concrete history of Jesus. Jesus continues to be concretely present in the Holy Spirit. Barth writes,

> And to His own on their further journey into time, in and with the witness continually to be proclaimed and heard by them, He has given them His Spirit, the Holy Spirit. But where the Spirit is, there is more than a mere tradition or recollection of Jesus . . . . But the message of His past is proclaimed, heard and believed in order that it should no longer be past but present.[44]

It is this that Barth means when he says that God's eternity is also supra-temporal. It does not mean God is above time in a timeless eternity, but that every time and all of time, "its whole extension from beginning to end, each single part of it, every epoch, every lifetime, every new and closing year, every passing hour; they are all in eternity like a child in the arms of its mother."[45]

That God's eternity is past and present, pre-temporal and supra-temporal, does not mean that it is exhausted or completed in these. It also includes the future; it is also post-temporal. Again, the concrete history of Jesus has a future. His past and presence do not conclude his work, but are "full of import for the future."[46] Jesus' life of future expectation, his proclamation of the coming kingdom, has been vindicated. In the resurrection it is revealed that this future kingdom is present in this one man.[47] Moreover, this future glory has been also promised but not yet given, except in anticipation and in a hidden way, to the rest of humanity.

> In this promise there was enclosed the glory of Jesus for His own, the inheritance which was to be theirs, the new creation. This promise entitled them to believe and love, but for the time being they could not see or hear or feel anything more. What was now before the eyes and ears of the

> apostles and their communities was the fact that they not
> only had faith and love, but that even they too, not to speak
> of the world outside, were subject to sin and error, sighing
> and tears, suffering and death. What they now saw and
> heard and felt was certainly the word of proclamation, the
> sacraments . . . , the fellowship and gifts of the Spirit . . . ,
> but also the great "not yet" . . . .[48]

The history of Jesus, therefore, includes the future, the fulfillment of this
"not yet," promised in the resurrection, in the parousia of Jesus Christ.
For Barth, then, the Christian faith should be "not only faith in Him
who was, and love for Him who is, but also hope in Him who comes."[49]

The discussion thus far has drawn from Barth's analysis of the three
forms of the temporality of God (*CD* II/1) and the threefold time of
Christ (*CD* III/2). It is in a discussion of "Him who comes", that is, the
parousia, that Barth emphasizes again the temporal and future element
of the Christian understanding of God. In *Church Dogmatics* IV/3, First
Half, Barth speaks of the threefold parousia of Christ. Here he once
again demonstrates that the resurrection of Jesus and his presence in the
Spirit are not the completion of the history of Jesus, but the foundation
for his future work. According to Barth's analysis the first form of the
parousia of Jesus is his resurrection. Even though in the resurrection the
future salvation is really present in the world — "not reconciliation
alone, but [also] the ensuing redemption and consummation"[50] — it
has to do with the "commencement of the revelation, reconciliation and
its fruits . . . , but not with this revelation in its full development."[51]
That is, salvation is fully present in the event of the resurrection of Jesus,
but still future for us, although it can be hoped for precisely because it is
fully present there.[52]   Thus Barth claims that the resurrection is the
parousia, the return of Jesus, but only in "its first but not its final and
conclusive form."[53]

There is also a form of the parousia that takes its place between
Easter and the universal manifestation of the Kingdom of God. This is
Jesus' coming in the promise of the Spirit.[54] But the analysis of this is
similar to that of the first form of the parousia. For, although the Spirit
brings the past being of Jesus into our present so that persons may
participate in it and although the Spirit is no less God than the Son, the
presence of the Spirit points to the future and Jesus Christ's coming as
Redeemer in the third and final form and to "the new cosmic form to be
inaugurated by him as the future of the world and their own ultimate
future."[55]

If it is true that from the concrete basis of his revelation, it can be
determined that the work, the revelation, of Jesus Christ is not yet

concluded, that it is "'still' in process and 'not yet' completed,"[56] and that it will not be until he comes again in a "universally perceived," "evident Lordship" which will usher in a "new age" and a new heaven and new earth, then following the logic associated with the doctrine of the Trinity, God's eternity is post-temporal and holds the future of all things and all times.

> Eternity is also the goal and end beyond which and over which another goal and end cannot exist. All roads necessarily lead to it. It is the sum of that to which anyone or anything can move. Any roads leading away from it can lead only to utter nothingness, and therefore cannot be roads at all.[57]

In this future of eternity, when God has completed his works, when the redemption of the world is accomplished and the kingdom established, God will be "all in all."[58]

In these passages, and in contrast to his earlier theology, Barth is attempting to take seriously the outstanding future that is contained in the eschatological elements of Christian faith. Barth has opened the doctrine of God for the future. Here is not a transcendence that is tied exclusively to the past and present, although it includes them. To the critics who claim that, because in Barth's theology everything is accomplished already in the immanent Trinity, in God's decision to be triune, the response can be made that it is precisely the doctrine of the Trinity which enables an understanding of the God who is related to the past in his full deity and to the present in his full deity, but also includes a real, non-illusory future.

Already it has been seen that it is trinitarian thinking that controls the discussion about God's eternity. Because the concrete history of Jesus is past, present and future, the eternity of God is pre-temporal, supra-temporal and post-temporal. But Barth also claims that the unity and the distinction of these three forms in eternity are based in the Trinity. God's eternity is fully present in each form, yet without cancelling or making meaningless the other two.

> There is just as little place for this rivalry here as between the three persons of the Trinity, whose distinction is really in the last resort the basis of these three forms. In this connection, too, there is in God both distinction and peace.[59]

Barth does not work this out in detail, but his position seems to be as follows: The triune God is characterized by the unity and *perichoresis* of the Father, Son and Holy Spirit. In the different works and different times of God all three persons are involved. Each of the triune modes of existence are "undividedly beginning, succession and end, all at once in His own essence."[60] This unity is established "by the inner movement of the begetting of the Father, the being begotten of the Son and the procession of the Spirit from both."[61] And yet this unity is not static, but dynamic event. In it "there is order and succession. The unity is in movement. There is a before and an after. God is once and again and a third time, without dissolving the once-for-allness, without destroying the persons . . . ."[62] This establishes a trinitarian basis for the unity but also the distinction among the past, present and future of God. Paralleling the unity and *perichoresis* among the persons of the Trinity, is the unity of the past, present and future of God. Barth speaks of a *perichoresis* of the past, present and future of God's eternity.[63] Paralleling the real distinctions among the persons of the Trinity and the appropriation of certain works to the different triune modes of being are the real distinctions among the past, present and future of God and the appropriation of these times to the various triune persons.[64] In each work in a different time — past, present, future, respectively — the same God is at work with the same intention but in a different mode of being. Therefore, the various times of God are not in conflict with one another, nor do they cancel each other out. And yet, as among the triune persons (and indeed grounded in the distinction of these persons), there are real distinctions.

> Once we are clear that eternity is the living God Himself, it
> is impossible to look on eternity as a uniform grey sea
> before, above, and after time, or to smooth out the distinc
> tions between before, now and after.[65]

For our purposes the important aspect is that according to this analysis the transcendence of the Christian God is not tied to the past or to the present status quo, but rather has a real, distinct future. When Barth speaks of the future in terms of "unveiling" the already of God, it is perhaps, then, misleading. It is an "unveiling" in the sense that the future redemption has already arrived in Jesus. There is a *perichoresis* of God's past and future here. But it has only arrived for Jesus and "not yet" for us. This "unveiling" then brings something new to us, our redemption, the transformation of the world, God's future. It is something new for God too, a new, distinct work.[66]

> There really is in it [God's eternity], then, direction, and a
> direction which is irreversible. There really is in it an origin
> and goal and a way from the one to the other. There is no

uniformity in it. Its forms are not to be exchanged or confused.[67]

Because this future which is the kingdom is "not yet," followers of the triune God know that God is still at work in overcoming human pain, that his being is not a reality in which all is accomplished. The triune God is an event in movement toward a transformed future. In light of this future persons are freed from the past and present, freed from every fate[68] to follow God's direction from the past to the future, because they know there are new things left to happen.[69]

How this view of God enables further response to the Marxist challenge and the problem of suffering voiced by protest atheism must wait explicit explication until we have examined Jürgen Moltmann's view of the relationship between the divine and the future.

Jürgen Moltmann: The Future as the Mode of God's Being

Jürgen Moltmann begins his theology with Barth's revised thinking about eschatology and goes beyond him in emphasizing its importance for Christian theology. Accepting Ernst Käsemann's exegetical conclusion — "Apocalypticism is the mother of all Christian theology"[70] — Moltmann asserts that Christianity is essentially eschatological and is misunderstood without this key. In an oft-quoted passage from the opening of the *Theology of Hope*, he writes,

> From first to last, and not merely in the epilogue, Christianity is eschatology, is hope, forward looking and forward moving, and therefore also revolutionizing and transforming the present. The eschatological is not one element of Christianity, but it is the medium of Christian faith as such, the key in which everything in it is set, the glow that suffuses everything here in the dawn of an expected new day.[71]

From this position Moltmann develops a view of transcendence that is open for the new, the future. In fact, for Moltmann the future is not to be considered only as a mode of God's being but is "*the* mode of God's being."[72] It is the "New Paradigm of Transcendence."[73] The Christian God is not a transcendent reality related to the past or an eternal deity above the world, who at any moment may enter the present and fulfill time. Rather, according to Moltmann, God is related to every past and present only from the future where his full power and deity are realized and which he promises. There is nothing in present experience that yet corresponds to God's full deity and eternal presence.[74] Moltmann associates the deity and eternal presence of God with his unmediated, complete, unambiguous reign over all things. "God is Lord in carrying out his reign . . . . The divinity of God will become manifest and real only in the coming of his unlimited reign."[75] Because this reign is not yet present, God's being must be thought of as "not yet," "in front of us," as in the future.

The basis for this position Moltmann finds in the revelation of Jesus which takes place in the horizon of the Old Testament God whose epiphanies were always marked by his promise for the future. The resurrection of Jesus reveals him to be the fulfillment of this Old Testament history of promise. But he does not fulfill it in such a way that this history is ended. Rather, the Old Testament history of promise is vindicated and given a new future in the promised future of Jesus. The resurrection, in that it vindicates Jesus' preaching of the kingdom, identifies him as the "one who is to come" and belongs itself to the imagery of the coming kingdom, also does not end the history and work of Jesus, but reveals their future. "Jesus is recognized in the Easter appearances as what he really *will be*."[76] Jesus is known in faith and promise as the Lord, as having brought the kingdom into the present. Yet this Lordship and kingdom are "not yet," not only "hidden" but also "unfinished."[77] Therefore, the resurrected Jesus is "the Lord on the way to his coming lordship."[78] Nevertheless, the resurrection of this one is the promise and guarantee of his lordship, through which comes the new creation of all things and the full reign of God as he becomes "all in all."[79] On the other hand, the resurrection demonstrates that Jesus is the "incarnation" of the future kingdom, the Son of the God who will then be all in all. Therefore, this God and this kingdom are really present in him.[80]

The God who is present in this incarnation and yet whose mode of being is future becomes comprehensible for Moltmann in the doctrine of the Trinity.[81] In Chapter IV we saw that Moltmann developed the doctrine of the Trinity from the presence of God in the event of the cross of Jesus. But the God who is present there, whose being is identified in the event of the cross, has a future, comes from the future and is in process toward that future. For in the midst of the separation at the cross between the Father and Son, there is a unity of will that is the Spirit — the Spirit of the suffering love of the Father and the Son for humankind — who proceeds from the cross into the world to bring this love to all creation, and this creation to the future kingdom.

For Moltmann, then, the triune God is an open reality, an open event that will only be completed in the future. This God is an open history that seeks to bring all things into the "trinitarian history of

God." Accordingly, he suggests that the doctrine of the Trinity must not only be understood in terms of the "sending" of Christ, but must also be understood eschatologically.[82] The "Trinity in the sending" is the traditional way of interpreting the doctrine of the Trinity. It asks about the origin of the appearance of Christ, finds it in God and perceives in this the Father who sends and the Son who is sent, both of whom send the Holy Spirit. In terms of sending the Father is always active, the Son both active and passive and the Spirit always passive.[83] This is the form of the Trinity which we have seen thus far in this essay. Barth's trinitarian doctrine derives from the correspondence of revelation with God himself. Therefore, God is Father, the revealer or one who sends, and Son, the revelation or one who is sent, and Spirit, the revealedness or one who is sent by the Father and Son. The origin of this sending is the immanent Trinity, for as God appears in history he is beforehand in himself. Moltmann, far from rejecting this understanding of the Trinity in sending and origin,[84] makes use of it in his discussion of the suffering involved in the sending of the Son by the Father. Nevertheless, the doctrine of the Trinity must be taken further and understood eschatologically from the perspective of the future history of Christ and its culmination. The central focus here is not the origin of Christ in the trinitarian history of Father's sending the Son, but the Son's future with the Father that is the culmination of the trinitarian history in the eschatological unity and glory of God. Moltmann writes,

> Protologically we talk about the Father's sending of Christ into the world. Eschatologically we talk about his being raised from the dead to the Father. Protologically his being sent points to his origin with the Father. Eschatologically his resurrection points to his future with the Father. His messianic mission in the world corresponds to his eschatological gathering of the world . . . . When we relate a *historical narrative* we always begin at the beginning, and ultimately come to the end. But when we think *eschatologically* we begin with the end and from there arrive at the beginning.[85]

In following this eschatological interpretation Moltmann is able to comprehend the future of God and the process that leads to it by speaking in trinitarian terms. The term in the New Testament that describes God's future, the divine power and beauty, is *doxa*.[86] Moltmann sees God's future, then, summarized as his glorification and, therefore, the trinitarian history of the work of the Son and Holy Spirit as the process by which God the Father is glorified.[87]

Why did Christ come, and die, and why was he raised? For
the forgiveness of sins, for righteousness, in order to be Lord
of the dead and living, for the sake of the salvation of the
world — but ultimately for the glorification of God the
Father.[88]

In thinking about the trinitarian history from this perspective, the
direction of generation and spiration related to the Trinity in origin is
reversed: "All activity proceeds from the Holy Spirit."

The Holy Spirit is the one who glorifies; he glorifies both the
Son and the Father. The Son can be glorified but only
through the Spirit; whereas the Son for his part can also
glorify, but only the Father; the Father is glorified both
through the Spirit and through the Son.[89]

This process of glorification is brought about by the Holy Spirit
who unites believers and all creation to Christ. That is, the Holy Spirit
glorifies human beings and creation by uniting them in fellowship with
the glory of the Son, who "in" and "with" this glorification "arrives at
his own glorification."[90]   But the future of the Son is union with the
Father and therefore the unification of all things with the Son and to his
glory serves ultimately the glorification of God the Father as all things
are brought to him.

The Holy Spirit glorifies Christ in us and us in Christ for the
glory of God the Father. By bringing this about, he unites
us and creation with the Son and the Father, as he unites the
Son himself with the Father. The Spirit is the bond of
fellowship and the power of unification. Together with God
the Father and through God the Son, he is the unifying
God.[91]

We see here in Moltmann a trinitarian notion of transcendence that
is essentially eschatological. God's full deity and glory are future, are
now in process and are not yet fully realized. All things have not yet been
brought to Christ and handed over to the Father. Within this conception
it is also true that the future of God is the future of all things. God's
glorification and unification will not be complete without the transformation of all things, without the Spirit uniting all things to the Father
through the Son. We find here Moltmann again employing what must
be termed the self-limitation of God on behalf of humanity, which in
truth, turns out to be the expansion of God to unite with all creation.

God does not desire glory without his glorification through
man and creation in the Spirit. God does not desire to find

> rest without the new creation of man and the world through the Holy Spirit. God does not desire to be united with himself without the uniting of all things with him.[92]

Therefore, God's future, his eschatological unity and glory, "contains in itself the whole union of the world with God and in God" and is inextricably "bound up with the salvation of creation."[93]

> Just as his glory is offered to him out of the world by the Holy Spirit, so his unity too is presented to him through the unification of the world with himself in the Holy Spirit. The history of the Spirit, which unites man and creation with the Son and the Father, is hence directed toward the perfect unity of the Son with the Father.[94]

This trinitarian conception of God, then, means something for the world. It does include the future of God where through the Spirit the Son delivers all things to the Father and God becomes "all in all." But the creation is not left behind. Rather, it is an obedient, transformed creation that is delivered to the Father. According to Moltmann's analysis, the future transcendence of the triune God is realized as the creation is transformed; the trinitarian history of God is completed, God becomes "all in all", in that all things have been glorified.

> The transference of the Kingdom from the Son to the Father at the End-time is to be understood both as a world-embracing event which completes history, and as an event within the Trinity itself. Analogously, the glorification of God at the End-time in the Spirit and through the Spirit is to be understood as a world-embracing, world-renewing event, and at the same time as an event within the Trinity. God comes to his glory in that creation arrives at its consummation. Creation arrives at its consummation in that God comes to his glorification.[95]

The Eschatological Trinity and Atheism

We are now in a position to indicate how the doctrine of the Trinity developed along the lines suggested by Barth and Moltmann can serve as an apologetic basis in response to the Marxist critique of the Christian conception of transcendence and the atheistic protest against suffering. Once again it appears that these critiques are based on the misidentification of God — conceived of as the omnipotent, timeless power who as such supports the existing status quo by limiting human freedom and promising fulfillment in the heavenly realm above the earth and history.

In this conception God can give only an abstract answer to human suffering because the situation of earth is unchanged. This is not, however, the conception of God that emerges when the doctrine of the Trinity controls Christian thinking. Both Barth and Moltmann show that the trinitarian notion of transcendence involves the category of the future. For Barth God's eternity cannot be understood apart from God's future and his movement in the direction of the future. For Moltmann the future is the paradigm for the transcendence of the triune God. That is, God's being is not yet a finished reality that exists above time, offering fulfillment to any present moment. God's being and transcendence are future. This future, furthermore, includes the transformation of all creation and all history and is therefore not complete until all things, human beings included, are transformed. Thus, in contradistinction to the charges of Marx and his followers, trinitarian transcendence does not validate, and is not to be associated with, present reality. As Barth wrote in a letter to an engineer in East Germany in 1968: "Faith in God's revelation has nothing whatever to do with an ideology which glorifies the status quo."[96] Rather, because nothing is yet as God intends, but all things are promised a new future as they are integrated into God's trinitarian history, this form of transcendence presents a radical critique of present reality which calls into question every existing situation. Moltmann writes that the promised future of God "contradicts existing reality . . . ."[97]

> Hence every view which sees the world as a self-contained cosmos, or history as a universal whole that contains and manifests the divine truth, is broken down and transposed into the eschatological key of "not yet."[98]

Likewise, in *Church Dogmatics* IV/2, Barth identifies the appearance of Christ with the revelation of the future kingdom of God which is made present in him. The kingdom of God is "among the kingdoms of this world" but it "confronts and contradicts and opposes them."[99] It represents "God's destruction . . . . of all the so-called 'given factors,' all the supposed natural orders, all the historical forces, which with the claim of absolute validity and worth have obtruded themselves as authorities . . . ."[100] In light of the kingdom of God, which Barth designates "the *coup d'etat* of God" and "God's revolution,"[101] we

> are awakened by Him from the dream that these forces are divine or divinely given actualities, eternal orders. We can no longer believe, and therefore we can no longer think or accept, that men, including ourselves, are indissolubly bound and unconditionally committed to them.[102]

God's future, therefore, "really is a turning" which must be understood "as the overcoming and dissolution of the past by the future, not as an equilibrium . . . ."[103]

This conception of God offers a response not only to Marxist atheism, but also to atheism which is a protest against human suffering. For we see here that God also protests present suffering and the structures that produce it. In being constituted as future, in the self-limitation of his deity which will not be fully realized without the overturning of all conditions of suffering and, ultimately, in his promised eschatological transformation itself, the triune God in his own being joins the atheist in protesting against human agony and against any conception of a God who does not.

Moreover, this protest against present reality does not remain hidden in the life of God. Rather trinitarian thinking allows a further response to the two related forms of atheism under discussion here: The doctrine of the Trinity speaks of the God who frees persons and engages them in this protest against present conditions and in praxis toward God's liberated future. The triune God does not support the status quo by robbing human beings of their freedom for action as the Marxist critique charges against Christian notions of transcendence. Rather the triune God brings freedom to them. It brings the knowledge, as Barth says, "that there are other possibilities," that things "can and should be different,"[104] because in the promised future kingdom of God things are going to be different. When persons realize that the triune God stands as a contradiction to present realities, they "are freed by Him from their rule."[105] Because — as Moltmann continues this theme — "it prepares the way for it in historical criticism, in ideological criticism and, finally, in criticism of institutions," this theology "serves the future freedom."[106] Between the appearance of God's future in Jesus and its culmination in the kingdom, an interval is opened for free human action. If this is correct, then, as Moltmann says, our freedom comes "from God, not against him." "The Christian faith understands itself authentically as the beginning of freedom that was, hitherto, unseen to the world."[107]

It is important to realize that this freedom from the past and present is received by faith in God's future. Therefore, this is not only "freedom from" present structures but is also "freedom for" God's future and in the direction of that future. A dialectic is at work here that prevents God's future from merely relativising every worldly institution. This future does liberate persons from present structures and provide a basis for constant critique. But if this were its only function, God would alienate humans from every earthly structure and praxis — socialist as well as capitalist for instance — and the Marxist critique would be verified. However, as we will see, the direction and content of God's future is defined by the concrete history of Jesus. This means that in obedience to this liberating future, believers are to be committed to those institutions and forces which in practice proximate it. Once again the unity of theory and practice in the trinitarian context is sustained. Barth writes about Christian freedom from the present authorities: "This does not mean that we are made superior, or set in a position of practical neutrality. It means that we must exercise our freedom in relation to them."[108]   The freedom given by faith in God's future entails the practice of that freedom as it moves from the present toward God's future, which promises to bring freedom to the whole creation. And, it is again the difference between the freedom experienced in faith now and the future freedom of all things that motivates the "work of realizing freedom in history."[109]   As Moltmann puts it, "The *pro-missio* of the kingdom is the ground of the *missio* of love to the world."[110] Followers of the triune God, therefore, are called to practice their freedom, to anticipate in obedience to it God's future as best they can. In a discussion about the kingdom of God, Barth concludes,

> The man whom Jesus calls to Himself has to stand firm by the revelation of it [the kingdom of God]. Indeed, he has to correspond to it in what he himself does and does not do. His own action, if it is obedient, will always attest and indicate it.[111]

> And it is for this reason that His disciples cannot be content with a mere theory about the relativisation of those false absolutes; a mere attitude of mind in which these gods no longer exist for them: an inward freedom in relation to them. It is for this reason that in different ways they are called out in practice from these attachments, and it is denial of the call to discipleship if they evade the achievement of acts and attitudes in which even externally and visibly they break free from these attachments.[112]

Moltmann, too, asserts that the trinitarian conception of God involves Christians in concrete practice in anticipation of God's future:

> We are construction workers and not only interpreters of the future whose power in hope as well as in fulfillment is God. This means that Christian hope is a creative and militant hope in history. The horizon of eschatological expectation produces here a horizon of ethical intentions which, in turn, gives meaning to the concrete historical initiatives. If one hopes for the sake of Christ in the future of God and

ultimate liberation of the world, he cannot passively wait
for this future and, like the apocalyptic believers, withdraw
from the world. Rather, he must seek this future, strive for
it, and already here be in correspondence to it in the active
renewal of life and of the conditions of life and therefore
realize it here according to the measure of possibilities.[113]

In summary, trinitarian thinking has thus far made possible the
following additional responses to the Marxist critique that religious
conceptions of transcendence are necessarily tied to the status quo and
the atheistic protest against suffering. First, because a trinitarian notion
of transcendence is defined by relation to the future of God's concrete
revelation, which promises the transformation of all things, it does not
support things as they are. The triune God protests against present
reality and calls it into question. Second, following this God has a
practical consequence. Transcendence in this form does not destroy
human freedom, but frees persons from the past and present by revealing that the present situation can and will be different in the future.
Thus, believing in the future of this triune God engages persons in
practice in the direction of this future.

However, one further question arises. Even if the trinitarian conception of transcendence challenges the present, opens up the realm of
free human activity and directs it toward the future, one must ask what
this means concretely for the direction of practice. Can this form of
transcendence be attached to any practice of change? Is it possible that
this God could be used to support activity in the direction of a future in
which hierarchical social ordering is even more rigidly established or
where some are even more oppressed? Could the trinitarian notion of
God support a revolution that moves in the opposite direction from that
liberation of which Marx dreamed? The questions here have to do with
the content of God's future. What does God's redemption look like?
Therefore, when one follows the trinitarian history of God in what praxis
is he or she engaged? Answers to these questions have already been
indicated but now will be analyzed specifically.

The Doctrine of the Trinity
and the Direction of Christian Practice

If the future of God were vague transcendence, an undefined
"absolute future" (Rahner) which challenges the status quo, then it
could be correlative with any practice of change, even one that is directed
towards greater injustice. Or it could alienate persons from all forms of
practice thereby once again functioning as a support for the status quo.

However, this is not the case with the triune God and his history and future. Already we have seen that God includes all creation in his triune history, thereby bringing it to redemption in his future. We have also shown that implicit in this process of salvation is the promise of the transformation of the suffering of humankind and all creation. This future of God, this promised salvation, therefore, is not vaguely defined, but is given specific content. Once again the doctrine of the Trinity is the basis for this content. For it is the doctrine of the Trinity that carries the Christian theological claim that the future of God and his promised transformation have occurred proleptically in a concrete manner in the history of Jesus. God's future, therefore, is given positive content by the triune God's revelation in Jesus. Obedience to the triune God means praxis in the direction of his future. And this direction is discovered by following in theory and practice the praxis of God in the life, death and resurrection of Jesus.

Both Barth and Moltmann follow this line of thinking and arrive at the practical consequences for Christians. In his analysis of God's mercy and righteousness revealed in the trinitarian history of God, Barth discovers that God acts on behalf of the suffering victims of the present structures:

> . . . in the relations and events in the life of his people, God always takes His stand unconditionally and passionately on this side and on this side alone; against the lofty and on behalf of the lowly; against those who already enjoy right and privilege and on behalf of those who are denied it and deprived of it.[114]

> . . . God's righteousness, the faithfulness in which He is true to himself, is disclosed as help and salvation, as a saving divine intervention for man directed only to the poor, the wretched and the helpless as such, while with the rich and the full and the secure as such, according to His very nature He can have nothing to do.[115]

The practical consequences of this, Barth argues, are clear and unavoidable. Because God's righteousness

> . . . does in fact have this character . . . we cannot hear it and believe it without feeling a sense of responsibility in the direction indicated.

> As a matter of fact, from the belief in God's righteousness there follows logically a very definite political problem and task. . . . a political attitude, decisively determined by the fact that man is made responsible to all those who are poor

and wretched in his eyes, that he is summoned on his part to espouse the cause of those who suffer wrong.[116]

For, Barth argues,

> . . . the human righteousness required by God and established in obedience . . . has necessarily the character of a vindication of right in favour of the threatened innocent, the oppressed poor, widows, orphans and aliens.[117]

Thus the one who follows a God of this sort "cannot avoid the question of human rights" and "can only will and affirm a state which is based on justice."[118] For Barth, then, following the the triune giving of God entails human practice — the service of liberation for the oppressed. Practice in any other direction is a rejection of God's righteousness.[119]

Moltmann gives a much more explicit and detailed analysis of the praxis related to the doctrine of the Trinity. Because Moltmann's whole theology is aimed at "orthopraxis," we cannot give a complete account of his arguments here. Rather, we will discuss his central themes.

For Moltmann, as for Barth, the transcendence of the triune God of the Christian faith is not vaguely defined. Rather it is given specific, translucent content by the appearance of Jesus, the Son. We have already seen Moltmann's method of reading history backwards as well as forwards. By his resurrection Jesus is vindicated. He is shown to be the true Son of the God he called father. He is therefore known to be the "anticipation" and "incarnation of the coming God."[120] If this is the case, it is important to "ask who this one man was"[121] in his concrete human life, for the coming God and his future have appeared in and are therefore defined by this man Jesus. Moltmann, therefore, closely examines the concrete human history of Jesus — his whole life, but particularly his cross. Chapter IV focused on the suffering of Jesus as the Godforsaken one. There it was seen that the triune God identifies with and includes in himself all human suffering and abandonment and promises their transformation.

But more can be added to this. For in the history of Jesus, God reveals himself in solidarity with and as working for the liberation of the economically poor, the politically oppressed and the socially outcast. In his ministry Jesus is the one who goes to these. He proclaims the kingdom of God as hope for sinners, the poor, the outcasts.[122] This does not mean that God is not interested in the salvation of the rich and powerful too. He is; but he brings the promise of salvation to all by identifying with the lowest.

> Jesus' proclamation and deeds were valid for all men
> precisely because he took sides with the meek, the poor, and
> the victims of discrimination. Jesus grasped human society,
> so to speak, at the lowest extreme, where he found the
> miserable and the disdained.[123]

The point in his history, however, at which Jesus most radically identifies
with the poor, the oppressed and outcast is in his passion. Jesus is
crucified, rejected and condemned by the leaders of his religion, as a
blasphemer against the law.[124]   It was not in itself the apocalyptic
proclamation of the coming kingdom that brought him into conflict
with the religious leaders. Rather his preaching of it "as prevenient and
unconditional grace to those who according to the law were rightly
rejected and could have no hope"[125] shattered the conception of the
righteousness of God and the whole legalistic system based upon it
prevailing at the time. Jesus dies therefore as an outcast, one cut off from
religious sanction and social acceptability in the community of Judaism.

Jesus, however, not only dies as a blasphemer but also suffers the
death of a rebel against the political order. His condemnation by the
religious authorities — who executed blasphemers by stoning — cannot
explain his crucifixion, which was used exclusively by the Roman
authorities as the punishment for threatening or breaking the political
and social order of the Roman empire, against revolting slaves and
rebels.[126]   Pilate in condemning Jesus to crucifixion misidentified him as
a Zealot agitator. Moltmann shows what Jesus had in common with the
Zealots, but also how he differed from them fundamentally.[127]   But in
the context of a culture where there was no separation of politics and
religion — where the state had its own gods — it can also be said that
Pilate understood Jesus very well. There is in Jesus' message a more
radical attack on the *Pax Romana* than even that of the Zealots.
Moltmann asks,

> But is there not implicit in his eschatological message of
> freedom for sinners and of his coming kingdom for the poor
> a much greater attack against the religiously deified state?
> Did he not cause with this message an "agitation" in the
> political situation of Rome which was more radical than the
> ones cause by the Jewish Zealots?[128]
>
> . . . Jesus' eschatological message of freedom was implicitly
> a total attack on the very existence of the religious state.[129]

This means that Jesus' crucifixion by Pilate was not a mere mistake.
Jesus is the one who is executed by the Roman state as a threat against it.

Because Jesus defines what Christians mean when they speak about transcendence, because Jesus gives content to the future of God, God is seen to be the God of the lowly, the poor, the outcast, the oppressed victims of injustice.[130] His future holds hope for them. "With the cross, the future of God allies itself with those whom a self-satisfied and conformist society has reduced to nothing."[131]

> According to the scale of social values of the time, crucifixion was dishonor and shame. If this crucified man has been raised from the dead and exalted to be the Christ of God, then what public opinion holds to be the lowliest, what the state has determined to be disgraceful, is changed into what is supreme. In that case, the glory of God does not shine on the crowns of the mighty, but on the face of the crucified Christ. The authority of God is then no longer represented directly by those in high positions, the powerful and the rich, but by the outcast Son of Man . . . .[132]

The Christian conception of the triune God, therefore, does not call the status quo into question merely by being defined as future. God's transcendent future is given concrete critical, revolutionary content and direction in its identity with the crucified Jesus. God's transcendence is defined in social and political as well as religious terms.

Commitment to this God and his future, therefore, means that Christian practice has a certain direction. It always sides with the poor and the oppressed against the structures of wealth and power. The Church, as a "manifestation of the future kingdom,"[133] has the task of "struggling against not only religious alienation of man but also his political, social and racial alienation in order to serve the liberation of man to his likeness to God in all areas where he suffers from humanity."[134]   Because Jesus, crucified by the ruling religious and political authorities, was vindicated as God's incarnation, any divine sanction for these authorities must be challenged. The Church must stand for "social critical freedom in institutions." As such, it must uncover not only religious idolatry, but political idolatry — "representations of the divine in politics" — as well and stand for justice and freedom in both systems for all human beings.[135]

For both Moltmann and Barth the direction of Christian praxis given by the triune God in the history (practice) of Jesus leads to certain social-political forms. Commitment to these is not ideologically based, but is determined by what are believed to be the best practical choices available in the contemporary world in which to anticipate God's future.

Barth and Moltmann both speak for democratic socialism, that is for political democracy and economic socialism.

In his essay, "The Christian Community and the Civil Community," Barth, by employing the analogy of faith, concludes that even though the Christian "will beware of playing off one political concept — even the 'democratic' concept — as *the* Christian concept," "the Christian line that follows from the gospel betrays a striking tendency to the side of what is generally called the 'democratic' State."[136] Moltmann sees the essence of democracy as political iconoclasm and therefore as serving the "freedom of God" and every man in the political sphere.[137]

> If and to the degree that the democratic movement means the abolition of privilege and the establishment of political human rights, *democracy is the symbol for the liberation of men from the vicious circle of force.*[138]

Both theologians consider socialism as the best way in the economic sphere to stand in solidarity with the poor and to break through the privilege and power connected with the ownership of capital. Because the command of God is "in all circumstances a call for countermovements on behalf of humanity and against its denial in any form," Barth argues that Christianity in the West must recognize the exploitation implicit in capitalism and "keep to the 'left' in opposition to its champions, i.e., to confess that it is fundamentally on the side of the victims of this disorder and espouse their cause."[139] This means that even though the church's central word is "the revolution of God" against "all ungodliness and unrighteousness of man" and cannot be absolutely linked with any particular economic form the

> . . . Christian community both can and should espouse the cause of this or that branch of social progress or even socialism in the form most helpful at a specific time and place and in a specific situation.[140]

Moltmann echoes Barth:

> If and in so far as socialism in this sense means the satisfaction of material need and social justice in a material democracy, *socialism is the symbol for the liberation of men from the vicious cycle of poverty.*[141]

We can now add this to the Christian response to an atheism based upon religion's failure of practice: Not only does trinitarian thinking find theory and practice inseparable, not only does it conceive of transcendence in terms of the future that calls the status quo into question and leads to concrete change, it also indicates that the necessary transformation called for in the political, economic, social and religious spheres of life must be on behalf of the poor, the outcast, the victims of injustice. It is the doctrine of the Trinity which provides the framework for this content. It is based upon the history of Jesus which the trinitarian conception identifies with God. In the trinitarian context God's activity in Jesus demonstrates his intention and praxis in the concrete social sphere. This means that the doctrine of the Trinity has political consequences.

Moltmann sees these political consequences as implicit in the original development of trinitarian formulation:

> In the doctrine of the Trinity Christian theology describes the essential unity of God the Father with the incarnate, crucified Son in the Holy Spirit. So this concept of God cannot be used to develop the religious background to a divine emperor.[142]

With the development of this doctrine, therefore, "Christian theology made a fundamental break with all political religion and its ideology in political theology." Because of the doctrine of the Trinity the "Christian faith can no longer be misused to justify a political situation."[143] We saw earlier that, according to Moltmann, it was its political implications that led Barth also to begin with the doctrine of the Trinity in his *Dogmatics*.[144]

Because the doctrine of the Trinity comprehends the socio-political praxis implied in the Christian faith, it is therefore the basis for this prong of the Christian apologetic in the face of Marxist atheism and atheism based on the theodicy question. Furthermore, because these two forms of atheism and the responses to them become one in relation to the protest against the present structures of suffering and the human praxis of transformation, the final section of this chapter can be written as a response to Marx.

The Trinitarian Practical Rejection of Traditional Theism and Response to Marx

Theology which is grounded in the doctrine of the Trinity and developed along the lines of Barth and Moltmann has given directions for responding to the basic issues of the Marxist critique. Trinitarian theology, as well as Marx, holds that truth is found in the union of theory and praxis. It comprehends a form of transcendence that is future and effects the transformation of the status quo. And, it directs that revolutionary practice to stand in solidarity with oppressed, alienated human beings.

Consequently, there is again a two-sided response on the part of trinitarian theology to Marxist forms of atheism. There is a yes and a no, an acceptance of his critique but a move beyond it as well. First, the doctrine of the Trinity, because it implies the transformation of the status quo on behalf of the oppressed, enables agreement with and the acceptance and use of the Marxist theory and practice of liberation. Although Moltmann has criticisms of Marx — his tendency to make humanity into God, to attribute to humanity all the theistic notions taken back from God, and Marxism's failure in practice to bring human emancipation where it has been applied in socialist states, for instance — [145] his use of Marx and his call to stand in solidarity with movements of liberation are so extensive that they do not need explication here.[146] And in this Moltmann is already anticipated by Barth. While Christianity cannot identify its message with Marxist programs, Marxism is one of the "countermovements on behalf of humanity" that Christians may espouse. In an analysis of the social injustice inherent in capitalism, Barth speaks of "the great and radical analysis . . . particularly associated with the name of Karl Marx" which has been instrumental in

> . . . the awakening of the working class to consciousness of
> its power when properly organized . . . both politically and
> in the form of trade unions and cooperative societies.[147]

Agreement with Marx on the need for the practice of liberation leads to another point of correspondence. Trinitarian theology, determined in practice by God's practice in Jesus, agrees with Marx in rejecting any ideology or theology that in practice supports unjust systems. This means that traditional theism, which defines God abstractly as the perfection of, and therefore as the opposite of, everything human and worldly, must be rejected for several reasons. In the first place the eternal, omnipotent, omnipresent, immutable God, which characterizes much of traditional theism, tends to render human practice meaningless by offering happiness and fulfillment in heaven above the earth and by bringing human history to a close prematurely by giving believers an "inner," "spiritual" transformation and completion regardless of external, physical suffering. Traditional theism parallels, therefore, what Moltmann has described as epiphany religion — the form of the religions that surrounded, and was rejected by, Israel and early Christianity. In this form of religion, as in theism, the impassible, immutable, secure world of the divine, defined as everything human life is not, is seen as the answer to the suffering, transient, chaotic conditions of earth. This earthly life gains significance and meaning, is overcome and fulfilled, then, through epiphanies of the divine.

> For where they come about, there comes the hallowing of place, of time and of men in that act in which man's ever-threatened culture is granted correspondence with, and participation in, the eternal divine cosmos. The threat to human existence from the forces of chaos and of annihilation is overcome through the epiphany of the eternal present. Man's being comes into congruence with eternal being, understands itself in correspondence and participation as protected by the presence of the eternal.[148]

In theism and epiphany religion this appearance of the divine in all its impassibility, immutability and eternity can occur at any moment of time, fulfilling and completing history and human existence from beyond history, and therefore rendering historical human activity unimportant. For in the moment of the epiphany, history, regardless of the concrete conditions of earth, is completed and therefore destroyed, and human life, regardless of situations of suffering and oppression, finds fulfillment. The availability of the divine in all its glory at any time, regardless of earthly conditions, implies that these conditions are immaterial and need not be changed. This theology, therefore, serves to justify the status quo[149] and gives an empty response to human suffering.

Another reason for trinitarian theology's rejection of traditional theism is the latter's malleability. While the epiphany structure of traditional theism means that it can be used to support the status quo, actually both its methodology and doctrine of God can be manipulated to serve almost any practice. Because it accepts natural revelation, traditional theism is able to combine the knowledge of God in Christ with knowledge of God obtained from other spheres. The results of this procedure for practice can be catastrophic. Barth points out that the German Christians were only following this well-established method in supporting their position.

> If it was admissible and right and perhaps even orthodox to combine the knowability of God in Jesus Christ with his knowability in nature, reason and history, . . . it is hard to see why the German Church should not be allowed to make its own particular use of the procedure.[150]

The German Christians, then, used this method to combine revelation through Jesus with the reflection of God — however dim — in the government and policies of Adolf Hitler. The result was the religious support for German nationalism based on racial purity and the "new totalitarian state of 1933."[151]

Theism's God can also be used to support change. Because this God is defined in contradistinction from everything earthly — because it possesses earthly attributes taken to perfection — because it is eternal as opposed to everything temporal, absolute over against all things relative, it can challenge every earthly reality and structure. However, even this absolute critique of every earthly thing generally tends to support the status quo. For why make a change if the change too is in no closer correlation with the divine than the status quo? Nevertheless, the absolute quality of theism's God can lead to continuous revolution. But if theism's God can signal a practice of critique and transformation, in what direction should the practice move? The formal attributes of this God — omnipotence, impassibility, immutability, etc. — are vague and abstract and, therefore, like theism's natural theology, can be used to support any practice of change. Because the God comprehended by the doctrine of the Trinity supports not just any practice, but only the practice for the liberation of the poor, it opposes the neutrality of the God of theism. Barth goes so far as to criticize his own early "dialectical theology" because of its insufficient break with the vague God of theism. In speaking mainly in terms of the "wholly other" it was impossible "to make it clear that we actually meant to speak of God and not a general idea of limit and crisis."[152] An undefined "general limit and crisis" could be used to support movement toward fascism as well as toward liberation of the oppressed.

Finally, while it may be possible to use the God of theism to criticize political power that claims to be absolute, Moltmann argues that "metaphysical monotheism" usually supports the practice of political monarchy and absolutism. He traces the history of this political implication of theism from Aristotle and the early Christian apologists, where it supported the emperor and unified empire, to the modern period, where it has undergirded modern absolutism.[153] The one omnipotent ruler of heaven suggests the one almighty ruler of the earthly kingdom.

> The one God, the one heavenly king and the one sovereign nomos and logos corresponds to the one king on earth. The idea of unity in God therefore provokes both the idea of the universal, unified church, and the idea of the universal, unified state: one God-one emperor-one church-one empire.[154]

Because trinitarian based theology does not support the rulers of the political establishment, but, by perceiving God in the Christ who was crucified by the state, identifies with the oppressed, weak, and lowly ones, it must reject traditional theism, in as much as it does legitimate the powerful. As Moltmann says,

> The expansion of the doctrine of the Trinity in the concept of God can only really overcome this transposition of religious into political monotheism, and the further translation of political monotheism into absolutism . . . .[155]

Trinitarian thinking, therefore, makes possible an apologetic response to Marx that does not merely reject him outright. The doctrine of the Trinity's function of identifying for the Christian faith its God — a God who demands that Christian truth be proved in the practice of the concrete liberation of oppressed humanity — and, therefore, its theological function of rejecting interpretations of God — including traditional theism — which do not support this practice, gives a basis for this first and positive dimension of a response — agreement with Marx. There is between trinitarian theology and Marx a praxological solidarity.

But as in other chapters there is a second aspect to the trinitarian based apologetic. Precisely because it is able to correspond to Marx, the doctrine of the Trinity also demands a "no" to him. For it shows that Marx's critique functions fully and only within the context of traditional theism. Marx, not without good reason from the religion of his time, uncritically equated traditional theism and Christianity and therefore based his atheism on a misidentification of the true Christian conception of God. Hence, trinitarian theology calls into question not the praxological foundation of Marx's critique, but its conclusion. If the Marxist rejection of God is based on praxis, and is not merely an abstract denial, the triune God, who calls for concrete practice of liberation and rejects ideologies supportive of the status quo, cannot be negated along with the God of traditional theism.

Moreover, because of the nature of the triune God, the trinitarian "no" to Marx also must take the form of a critique of the failure of the Marxist state which has established its own status quo and failed to realize political liberation while attempting liberation in the economic sphere. Thus, it appears that trinitarian praxis is better able than Marxism itself to keep the process of transformation open and without premature closure.

Once again the triune conception of God takes up into itself the atheistic protest, this time based on practice, and thereby demonstrates that the triune God will not rest until this protest is answered in the liberation of all things.

NOTES

[1] See Thomas W. Ogletree, ed., *Openings for Marxist-Christian Dialogue* (Nashville, 1969), pp. 29ff. See Roger Garaudy, "Creative Freedom" in *The Christian Marxist Dialogue,* ed. Paul Oestreicher (London, 1969), p. 144; also Roger Garaudy, "Communists and Christians in Dialogue" in Marty and Peerman, *New Theology, No. 5,* pp. 212ff; also Roger Garaudy, *From Anathema to Dialogue,* trans. Luke O'Neill (New York, 1966), pp. 75ff, 92ff.

[2] Cited in Wolfhart Pannenberg, *Basic Questions in Theology,* II, trans. George H Kehm (Philadelphia, 1971), 238. At this point a self-contradiction in protest atheism becomes manifest. On the one hand God is rejected because in his omnipotence he does nothing to overcome suffering. Thus, atheism rejects God because he does not use his omnipotence. On the other hand in this quotation Bloch rejects God because he is omnipotent and, as such, limits human freedom. Protest atheism seems to both desire and reject an omnipotent deity.

[3] Garaudy, "Creative Freedom," p. 144.

[4] Responses to this Marxist charge are already available from previous sections. First, this Marxist critique once again presupposes the theistic concept of God which by abstraction defines God as the omnipotent, immutable ruler who has all the qualities humans lack. This means that if God possesses infinite liberty humans have none. If he has omnipotence, humans do not have the power to change anything. But this concept again is based on a misidentification of the Christian God. The transcendent God of the Christian faith cannot be identified with just any form of transcendence. It is not determined by abstracting from the world or in opposition to humanity. Rather, as we saw in Chapter II, this transcendence is comprehended by the doctrine of the Trinity. That is, the triune God defines himself concretely not as a transcendence over against the world, but in the world, in the history of Jesus. There is no need therefore to rob qualities from humankind as they are given to God. Because God is free to act as God does not mean that humans lose their freedom.

Second, we saw in Chapters III and IV that because it arises from an analysis of God's concrete revelation in Jesus, the doctrine of the Trinity indicates a revolution in the concept of God. The transcendence of the triune God cannot be abstractly defined as a static, omnipotent, immutable reality above the earth in heaven. Rather, the transcendence of this God is seen in his concrete activity in the cross of Jesus — transcendence involved there in opposing and transforming the present situation, both individual and social, of the suffering of humanity. The

God delineated by the doctrine of the Trinity is engaged in revolutionary praxis of freeing humanity from its misery. And, furthermore, in doing this, the means this God employs do not contradict his end, which is human liberation. God does not act in a way that ends human freedom. Rather, in love he encourages it. He does not force or coerce his will. Rather, in his willingness to act through the human suffering of the cross, his self-limitation in the name of love and human freedom is seen. The desire for human freedom is so great that God allows humans, in the exercise of their freedom, to force him out, to crucify him.

Third, in Chapter V we saw that the doctrine of the Trinity cannot be merely a theory of God but is inseparable from the life of practice. The triune God's concrete revelation in the history of Jesus is also his command for practical activity. Jesus commands "love of neighbor" and solidarity with the "least of these." But more than this, because the doctrine of the Trinity comprehends the God who is known in his practical activity to liberate humanity in the history of Jesus, the triune God cannot be known outside the context of the practice of human liberation; the truth of faith in the triune God is proved in practice. Because the man Jesus has been revealed as the second person of the Trinity, because the command of the triune God comes in this human form, far from this transcendence serving as an opiate that inhibits human practice, "far from being a heteronomy, opposed to the autonomy of man," the transcendence of the triune God includes a yes to practice. "The Command of God," as Barth says, "is the decision about the goodness of human action" (*CD* II/2, 548).

⁵ *CD* III/2, 476.

⁶ Moltmann, *TH*, p. 142.

⁷ *Ibid.*, p. 147. See also "Theology as Eschatology", pp. 15ff.

⁸ Moltmann, *CG*, pp. 98ff.

⁹ *CD* III/2, 476f.

¹⁰ *Ibid.*, p. 497.

¹¹ *Ibid.*, p. 498.

¹² Moltmann, "Theology as Eschatology," p. 23.

¹³ Moltmann, *TH*, p. 217. See also *CG*, pp. 121ff.

¹⁴ On this see Moltmann, *TH*, pp. 197ff, and *CG*, pp. 160ff.

¹⁵ *CD* IV/3, First Half, 316.

¹⁶ Moltmann, *TH*, p. 194.

¹⁷See *Ibid.*, pp. 50-58; Gunton, pp. 164-66, 181ff; G.C. Berkouwer, *A Half Century of Theology*, trans. Lewis B. Smedes (Grand Rapids, 1977), pp. 197-208.

¹⁸ Barth, *Romans*, p. 314.

[19] Karl Barth, *The Resurrection of the Dead*, trans. H. J. Stenning (New York, 1933), p. 112.

[20] See Moltmann, *TH*, p. 56.

[21] *CD* I/1, 464. See *TH*, p. 57, where Moltmann says, "The immanent form of the doctrine of the Trinity is always in danger of obscuring the historical and eschatological character of the Holy Spirit . . . ." See also *CG*, p. 240. It should be noted that in later works Moltmann follows Barth's method of moving from the economic Trinity to the immanent Trinity and of seeing the latter as the eternal foundation of the former. See Chapter IV, note 96.

[22] Moltmann, *TH*, p. 57ff. Quotations from *CD* I/2, 114f.

[23] *CD* I/1, 530. See Moltmann, *TH*, p. 58, n. 1.

[24] Barth uses the notion of "unveiling" in discussions about the eschaton which will not be a different reality from God in his revelation in Jesus. In *CD* IV/3 Second Half, 489, Barth writes,

> "On the contrary it is already the one reality which here and now still encounters us in concealment, but there and then will make itself known, and will be knowable and known without concealment."

See also *CD* IV/3, First Half, 498; *CD* II/1, 630, and the discussion in Berkouwer, *A Half Century of Theology*, pp. 201ff.

[25] Gunton, p. 164. While Gunton's meaning here is clear, his choice of words renders his statement false. The absence of futurity is correlative to the absence of "past." A "timeless past" is as self-contradictory as a "timeless future."

[26] *CD* I/1, 468, 469. Here Barth implicitly connects the Trinity to these new moments — the Father to creation, the Son to the "new work" of revelation or reconciliation, and the Holy Spirit to the outstanding future act of redemption. Needless to say, for Barth, even though these different works are appropriated to the various modes of God's existence, and therefore call for distinction among them, Father, Son and Spirit do not work separately from one another (pp. 424f). *Opera trinitatis ad extra sunt indivivisa.*

[27] *CD* II/1, 78.

[28] *Ibid.*, p. 79.

[29] *Ibid.*, p. 262.

[30] See *Ibid.*: In the analysis of this event, Barth says, "What is concerned is always the birth, death and resurrection of Jesus Christ, always His justification of faith, . . . always his coming again . . . ."

[31] *Ibid.*, p. 262f.

[32] *Ibid.*, p. 635.

[33] *Ibid.*

[34] Barth, *Letters: 1961-1968*, p. 176.

[35] *CD* III/2, 484.

[36] *CD* II/1, 615.

[37] *Ibid.*, p. 616.

[38] *Ibid.*, p. 617.

[39] *Ibid.*, p. 619.

[40] *CD* III/2, 474.

[41] *Ibid.*, p. 475.

[42] See *Ibid.*, pp. 477f, for this; also *CD* II/1, 622.

[43] *CD* II/1, 625.

[44] *CD* III/2, 467.

[45] *CD* II/1, 623.

[46] *CD* III/2, 468.

[47] See *Ibid.*, p. 489.

[48] *Ibid.*, p. 488.

[49] *Ibid.*, p. 489.

[50] *CD* IV/3, First Half, 317.

[51] *Ibid.*, p. 318.

[52] See *Ibid.*, p. 327.

[53] *Ibid.*, p. 318. See also p. 334.

[54] *Ibid.*, p. 350.

[55] *Ibid.*, p. 351.

[56] See *Ibid.*, p. 334.

[57] *CD* II/1, 629.

[58] See *Ibid.*, pp. 630, 631; *CD* IV/3, First Half, 319.

[59] *CD* II/1, 639.

[60] *Ibid.*, p. 615.

[61] *Ibid.*

[62] *Ibid.*

[63] See *Ibid.*, p. 640.

[64] See *CD* I/1, 468f., for the discussion of how these various works are associated with the respective triune persons.

[65] *CD* II/1, 639.

[66] See *CD* III/2, 486; "Nor is the future merely the result of what Jesus Christ was yesterday and is today. It is again He Himself, His own person and work, in a new mode and form."

[67] *CD* II/1, 639.

[68] *Ibid.*, p. 627.

[69] See *CD* III/2, 494.

[70] Quoted in Moltmann, "Theology as Eschatology", p. 6, and in *RRF*, p. 206.

[71] Moltmann, *TH*, p. 16.

[72] See Moltmann, "Theology as Eschatology", p. 9; *RRF*, p. 208 and *TH*, p. 139.

[73] See Moltmann, "The Future as New Paradigm of Transcendence" in *RRF*, pp. 177-199. Here Moltmann argues that because the context of the questions of humanity has shifted from the cosmological to the existential and now to the socio-political, answers to these questions are seen in temporal terms as a future transcending of the present socio-political situation. Moltmann asserts therefore that the future now serves as the paradigm of transcendence. This makes the Christian faith with its stress on eschatology particularly relevant to today's questions.

[74] See Moltmann, "Theology as Eschatology", p. 11; *RRF*, p. 209.

[75] Moltmann, *RRF*, p. 208. See also "Theology as Eschatology," p. 10.

[76] Moltmann, *TH*, p. 85.

[77] *Ibid.*, p. 88.

[78] *Ibid.*, p. 87.

[79] See *Ibid.*, p. 88; "Theology as Eschatology," p. 10; *RRF*, p. 213.

[80] See Moltmann, *RRF*, pp. 213f.

[81] See *Ibid.*, p. 214: "The real anticipation of God through Christ attains its abiding significance through the trinitarian relationship of the Father to the Son and the Son to the Father."

[82] See Moltmann, *FC*, pp. 80-96, and *CPS*, pp. 50-65, for what follows.

[83] See Moltmann, *FC*, p. 88.

[84] See *Ibid.*, pp. 87f.: Moltmann says that in interpreting the doctrine of the Trinity eschatologically "we are not criticizing or rejecting the previous doctrine of the Trinity.... but are simply taking them further."

[85] *Ibid.*, pp. 86f.

[86] *Ibid.*, pp. 88f.

[87] Moltmann, at least partially, derives the theme of the eschatological glorification of God and all things from Hans Joachim Iwand. See Meeks, *Origins of the Theology of Hope*, pp. 30-41.

[88] Moltmann, *FC*, p. 90.

[89] *Ibid.*, p. 88.

[90] *Ibid.*, p. 90.

[91] *Ibid.*, p. 91.

[92] *Ibid.*, p. 94.

[93] *Ibid.*, p. 91.

[94] *Ibid.*, p. 92.

[95] *Ibid.*, p. 94.

[96] Barth, *Letters 1961-1968*, p. 303. Barth adds parenthetically, "Here again we should be bold to read Marx attentively."

[97] Moltmann, *TH*, p. 86.

[98] *Ibid.*, p. 92.

[99] *CD* IV/2, 543.

[100] *Ibid.*

[101] *Ibid.*, pp. 543 and 545 respectively.

[102] *Ibid.*, p. 544.

[103] *CD* II/1, 627. Barth points out in this context that even though persons live in the present, between the past and future, these times, all of which have their basis in God, do not have equal claim on the Christian. The Christian is always turning in the direction of God's future. Barth goes on to interpret Luther's notion of the Christian as simultaneously saint and sinner in the same way. Barth declares,

> "Luther's *simul justus et peccator* cannot and should not, in Luther's sense, be taken to mean that the totality with which we are righteous and sinners involves an equal and equally serious determination of our existence . . . . It is not as legitimate for us to sin as to practise our righteousness. . . . The two things which are 'at the same time' are our past and our future. Our sin has been, and our righteousness comes. God affirms our righteousness as He negates our sin."

[104] *CD* IV/2, 721, 722.

[105] *Ibid.*, p. 544.

[106] Moltmann, *RRF*, p. 81.

[107] Moltmann, "The Revolution of Freedom" in *Openings for Christian-Marxist Dialogue*, pp. 53, 51.

[108] *CD* IV/2, 544.

[109] See Moltmann, "The Revolution of Freedom," in *Openings for Christian-Marxist Dialogue*, p. 51: "The difference between freedom in faith and the realm of freedom is the motor and motive power for our work of realizing freedom in history."

[110] Moltmann, *TH*, p. 224.

[111] *CD* IV/2, 543.

[112] *Ibid.*, p. 544.

[113] Moltmann, *RRF*, pp. 217f.

[114] *CD* II/1, 386.

[115] *Ibid.*, p. 387.

[116] *Ibid.*, pp. 386-387.

[117] *Ibid.*, p. 386.
[118] *Ibid.*, p. 387.
[119] See *Ibid.*
[120] See Moltmann, *CG*, p. 184.
[121] See *Ibid.*, p. 175.
[122] See Moltmann, "The Cross and Civil Religion", pp. 42f, and *EH*, p. 111.
[123] Moltmann, *EH*, p. 115.
[124] See Moltmann, *CG*, pp. 128-135, for this and for what follows. See also *EH*, pp. 110ff.
[125] Moltmann, *CG*, p. 130.
[126] See Moltmann, *EH*, pp. 110f; also pp. 136ff; and "The Cross and Civil Religion," pp. 33f.
[127] Moltmann, *CG*, pp. 138-142. Jesus' agreement with the Zealots, according to Moltmann, has to do with his focus on the imminent arrival of the kingdom of God. He also was critical of Herod and the practices at the Temple, while apparently silent about Zealot activity. There were also Zealots among his followers. However Jesus' proclamation that the kingdom was for sinners broke through the legalism on which the Zealots' conception was based. He included in his closest followers enemies of the Zealots, tax collectors. Therefore, Jesus broke through the cycles of violence and retribution, for the kingdom was not one of revenge, but forgiveness for all, whether Zealot, Gentile, tax collector, etc.
[128] Moltmann, *EH*, p. 111.
[129] Moltmann, "The Cross and Civil Religion," p. 34.
[130] See Moltmann, *CG*, p. 329.
[131] Moltmann, "The Cross and Civil Religion," p. 43.
[132] Moltmann, *CG*, p. 327.
[133] *CD* IV/2, 721.
[134] Moltmann, *EH*, p. 115.
[135] See *Ibid.* pp. 114-115 and *CG*, p. 328.
[136] Barth, *Community, State, and Church*, pp. 161, 181. In this article Barth suggests correlations with the Christian faith other than democracy and socialism. Some of these, such as concentrating "on the lower and lowest levels of human society" and standing "for social justice in the political sphere" (p. 173), have been seen previously. Among other things he also suggests opposition to any totalitarian state (pp. 173-174), to secret diplomacy and policies (p. 176) and support for the separation of power in the political sphere (p. 175) and for freedom of speech and the press (p. 177).

Will Herberg ("The Social Philosophy of Karl Barth," pp. 35-36) follows Emil Brunner in charging that Barth's method of correspondence, drawing analogies between the history of Jesus and the political sphere, is arbitrary. Herberg asks, "Is it possible to doubt that what Barth is really doing is adjusting his "christological" arguments to conclusions *already* reached *on other grounds*" (p. 35)? Certainly one would not wish to maintain that Barth overcame all cultural influences in his theology or even that he might not have had an attachment to "the values of a pluralistic constitutional democracy." Nevertheless, Barth affirms these positions on theological grounds. Therefore, instead of merely asserting that they are abstracted from culture, one would do well to argue theologically. Herberg gives only two brief, unconvincing theological arguments. First, his suggestion that Barth's method of correspondence between "above" and "below" has no biblical warrant (p. 36) is far from a settled issue. It seems to me that throughout the Bible (in the Prophets for instance) there is a call to bring social forms into correspondence to the nature of God. As we will see in the next chapter, patristic writers also drew analogies between God and the political and economic spheres.

Second, in relation to the charge of arbitrariness itself, Herberg cites Brunner:

> "... anything and everything can be derived from the same principle of analogy: a monarchy just as well as a republic (Christ the King), a totalitarian state just as much as a state with civil liberties (Christ the Lord of all, man a servant, indeed a slave, of Jesus Christ)" (p. 35).

On the basis of the analysis of Barth in this essay, we can reply that such interpretations would be wrong and only possible on the basis of an abstract reading of Christ's Kingship and Lordship. To interpret his Kingship and Lordship, which are given content by his concrete proclamation and practice of liberation for the poor and oppressed, as supporting a totalitarian state or a denial of human rights would be arbitrary indeed and, in fact, not an interpretation at all.

What I believe Herberg misses is that behind Barth's article lies his continuing theological work in the *Church Dogmatics*. Perhaps Barth can be faulted for a lack of theological support for the claims he makes for the social sphere in "The Christian Community and the Civil Community." But when this article is read in the context of Barth's work in the *Church Dogmatics* his "correspondences" appear to be much more firmly grounded and less arbitrary than Herberg supposes.

[My claim finds support in the analysis of Hans Urs von Balthazar:

> "To the extent that certain of Barth's political positions can
> stand at the origins of a dogmatic pursuit, to that extent
> such a pursuit is in a position to lead back once again to
> practical and political consequences. The more deeply one
> enters into Barth's thought, the more evident such connec-
> tions become . . . ."

This is quoted in Hunsinger, *Karl Barth and Radical Politics*, p. 230, n.
51.]

Herberg's charge that Barth's method of analogy is arbitrary takes
another form. Herberg (See pp. 55-64) follows Emil Brunner, Reinhold
Niebuhr, Charles West and others in complaining that Barth did not
show the same rigor in rejecting communist totalitarianism in the
nineteen-forties and fifties as he had fighting Nazism. Robert McAfee
Brown [See "Introductory Essay" in Karl Barth and Johannes Hamel,
How to Serve God in a Marxist Land, trans. Thomas Wieser (New York,
1959), pp. 11-45] and George Hunsinger (*Karl Barth and Radical
Politics*, pp. 226f) have responded to this criticism. Here a few observations are in order.

Barth did not support Soviet communism. In 1948, he reiterated
his position which had been clear since the second edition of *The Epistle
to the Romans*:

> "Are we not all convinced . . . that we cannot consider the
> way of life of the people in Soviet territory and in Soviet-
> controlled 'People's democracies' to be worthy, acceptable,
> or of advantage to us, because it does not conform to our
> standards of justice and freedom? . . . It has rightly been
> said that 'totalitarianism' is a dreadful thing." [Karl Barth,
> "The Christian Community in the Midst of Political
> Change," in *Against the Stream: Shorter Post-War Writ-
> ings 1946-52*, pp. 116f.]

Furthermore, we must remember that Barth attempted to make
political decisions based on practical considerations rather than on
"principles" (See *Ibid.*, p. 114.). In this matter he did not believe that
the church could merely denounce communism, for that would practically support the West. On the one hand, Barth saw in the East at least
the attempt to address economic justice. On the other hand, no matter
how bad the East was, the West was not much better. The West
supported Franco. And, the West neglected the social problem:

"As long as there is still a "freedom" in the West to organize economic crises, a "freedom" to dump our corn into the sea here while people are starving there, so long as these things can happen, we Christians, at any rate, must refuse to hurl an absolute 'no' at the East" (Karl Barth, "The Church Between East and West" in *Ibid.*, p. 140).

Barth's refusal to denounce the communists, therefore, was not merely capricious. Nor did it signify political disinterest. Rather, it was a practical decision in light of the failures and dangers of both the East and the West. At that particular time the church could support neither side.

Whether or not Barth's position was correct or not can be debated. We have already seen, however, that during the Viet Nam War, Reinhold Niebuhr retracted his criticism of Barth's "neutrality" (See Chapter V, n. 40). In light of that war "against communism" and the United States' policy of support for "anti-communist" regimes (in Central America for instance), regardless of how oppressive and brutal they might be, perhaps Barth's position will not seem as arbitrary and misguided today as it did to earlier critics.

[137] Moltmann, *EH*, p. 114. Moltmann, in "On Latin American Liberation Theology: An Open Letter to Jose Miquez Bonino," *Christianity and Crisis* (March 29, 1976), p. 61, explicitly uses the term "democratic socialism." In this context Moltmann chides Marxists and other for thinking that to gain justice in the economic sphere, humans would be willing to give up the freedoms and justice they have won in the political sphere (pp. 61-62).

[138] Moltmann, *CG*, p. 333.

[139] *CD* III/4, p. 544.

[140] *Ibid.*, p. 545. See also *Community, State, and Church*, p. 173, for Barth's support of socialism.

[141] Moltmann, *CG*, p. 332.

[142] *Ibid.*, p. 326.

[143] *Ibid.*,

[144] Moltmann, "The Cross and Civil Religion", p. 26.

[145] Moltmann, *CG*, pp. 251f.

[146] See *Ibid.*, pp. 332-338, for instance.

[147] *CD* III/4, 543. See also *CD* III/2, 387-390, where Barth analyzes positively Marx's historical materialism and claims that, because it has sided with "ruling classes," the Christian Church need not be surprised . . . that it has come under fire of Marxist polemic . . . ."

[148] Moltmann, *TH*, p. 99.

[149] Moltmann uses this critique also against theologians who have attempted to break with traditional theism, but whose break has not

been sufficient to escape this critique of the praxis related to theism. Bultmann is the primary example here. According to Bultmann's existentialist interpretation, the Christian eschaton occurs, the eternal enters time, in the life of the individual in the transformation of the self-understanding with the coming of faith. But Moltmann asks whether Bultmann has not given up on history and reduced Christian hope to an individualistic matter. Does not the transformation of the self-understanding, which can take place at any moment of time, parallel epiphany religion, and against the intentions of Bultmann, render history and practical activity unimportant? On this see particularly *RRF*, pp. 72-77. See also "Theology as Eschatology", pp. 42-43, where Moltmann makes a criticism of Bultmann similar to Marx's criticism of Feuerbach. Bultmann fails to realize that human self-understanding is concretely and historically conditioned. There can be, therefore, no transformation of the self-understanding without a change in concrete, material reality. See also *TH*, pp. 65-69.

[150] *CD* II/1, 174.

[151] See *Ibid.*, pp. 172-178.

[152] *Ibid.*, p. 635. See Hunsinger, *Karl Barth and Radical Politics*, p. 216, for a similar argument.

[153] See Moltmann, *TK* pp. 193-197. See also pp. 106ff. Moltmann's rejection of the term "monotheism" to describe Christianity is unnecessarily provocative. The following quotation is typical: "Christianity is not a 'monotheistic kind of belief,' as Schleiermacher insisted, and not a 'radical monotheism,' as H. Richard Niebuhr said, but trinitarian faith" (*EH*, p. 107). Is Moltmann proposing that Christianity believes in more than one God? Does the doctrine of the Trinity refer to more than one? Moltmann's statement is true only if he is speaking of an abstract, metaphysical traditional monotheism. This is really what he is attacking. There is therefore no reason to reject the term outright, for we need not keep its abstract meaning. The doctrine of the Trinity speaks of God as one, but in a concrete way revolutionizes the concept. Opposed to traditional monotheism is trinitarian monotheism. For a similar criticism see Richard John Neuhaus, "Moltmann vs. Monotheism," *Dialog*, XX (Summer, 1981), 239-243. However, Neuhaus' criticism of Moltmann's trinitarian position must be rejected. He criticizes Moltmann for not bringing clarity to the word 'God' before introducing trinitarian conceptions (p. 240). In this sense Neuhaus remains a theist. I will discuss the problems with suggestions like Neuhaus' in the next chapter.

[154] Moltmann, *TK*, p. 195. Here Moltmann quotes Erik Peterson, "Monotheismus als politisches Problem", in *Theologische traktate*

(Munich, 1951), p. 91. Notice also that Moltmann is engaged in a trinitarian critique of ecclesial structures as well as political systems (See pp. 200-202).

[155] *Ibid.*, p. 197.

CHAPTER VII

CONCLUSION:
APOLOGETICS AND TRINITARIAN THEOLOGY —
THEISM AND BEYOND

In light of contemporary atheism and the crisis that it brings to traditional theism, Christian theology is faced with various apologetic choices. The five preceding chapters have shown how the tradition of protest atheism has directed its critique and how the doctrine of the Trinity, as employed by Barth and Moltmann, offers the basis for a cogent response. The aim of this concluding chapter is to evaluate this trinitarian option in relation to other apologetic attempts, suggesting ways in which it has succeeded in giving answers where they remain problematic. No full analysis of the issues involved in answering the atheistic protests is possible here. But it is possible to indicate directions for responses to the issues discussed in previous chapters. Moreover, no complete analysis of the attempts of theism to respond to these challenges can be given here either. But we can focus leading questions which suggest inadequacies in typical theistic responses. Thus, this chapter constitutes an argument that trinitarian thinking offers a promising method for the construction of a more adequate response than is available in other apologetic options. We will first examine and raise critical questions about other apologetic options. Second, we will discuss the relative strength of trinitarian responses. In a final section we will ask why much of contemporary theology has failed to see the apologetic usefulness of the doctrine of the Trinity and argue for its validity by finding precedents in patristic theology.

Options in Contemporary Apologetics

We mentioned earlier in this work that, for the most part, the doctrine of the Trinity has been given minimal attention in recent theology. Likewise, the role it might have in apologetics has generally not been recognized. Contemporary apologetics has, rather, taken quite a different course. The strategies that we will consider here, to be sure, all take into account both atheistic critiques in particular and the continuing process of secularization in general. That they take these as serious challenges to faith and the Christian conception of God is attested by their determination not to circumvent secularism and atheism but to pass through them. In each case these apologists attempt to reformulate the Christian faith without the "mistakes" of traditional theism that they — in agreement with the position of this essay — see as the object of atheism's critique. Nevertheless, despite their efforts these "reformulations" serve as, at best, only partial responses, for ultimately — as signaled by the absence of the doctrine of the Trinity — they remain much more closely tied to traditional theism than their proponents imagine. For this reason, they do not see, and therefore cannot respond to, the real thrust of much of the atheistic tradition.[1]

Christianity Without God

One way to respond to atheism and the secularism of contemporary culture is to no longer insist that God or religion are necessary prerequisites for the Christian faith and, therefore, to theologize only within secular, empirical or positivistic categories. Paul M. van Buren proposes this alternative in his *The Secular Meaning of the Gospel.*[2] In this work van Buren asks about the possibility of Christianity's intelligibility to secular human beings. If it is to be intelligible, it must be meaningful within the empirical categories of our "scientific" and "technological" age, which van Buren sees expressed philosophically in contemporary linguistic analysis.[3] Because secular culture recognizes no world beyond this one and therefore finds God a meaningless concept, Christianity and Christian theology, if it is to be intelligible in this secular context, must be accomplished without 'God'. As van Buren declares,

> The empiricist in us finds the heart of the difficulty not in what is said about God, but in the very talking about God at all. We do not know what God is, and we cannot understand how the word 'God' is being used.[4]

The problem is not as Nietzsche cried that "God is dead!" For, as van Buren points out, "if it were so, how could we know." Rather, "the problem now is that the *word* 'God' is dead."[5]

But if Christianity no longer has God as a referent then has it not also died? Van Buren declares "no," for Christianity still has the historical man Jesus and his story. There can certainly no longer be repetition of the Chalcedonian formulation of the divinity as well as the humanity of Jesus. This would again introduce meaningless god-language into Christian discourse, rendering it once again unintelligible to secular persons. But, van Buren argues, what Chalcedon really intended to say in any case was that, for the Christian, Jesus was the point of reference for his or her "perspective" on the world and form of life.[6] He explains that "to say Jesus is divine, very God of very God," means "that his perspective is my ultimate."[7] In Jesus Christians perceive "a man of remarkable and particular freedom"[8] who, as such, possesses "the power to awaken freedom also in them."[9] This freedom that flows from Jesus and is "contagious" for the Christian transforms life, marks it as authentic and leads it, as it did for Jesus, into concern and service for others.

The force of van Buren's case cannot be denied. He has seen that for many traditional Christianity and its god-language have become an obstacle. Nevertheless, as an apologetic strategy this position is replete with problems. First there is the matter of his presupposition about the position of secularism in contemporary society. This does not only have to do with van Buren's uncritical appropriation of the empiricism of linguistic analysis,[10] but with his claim of the pervasiveness of secularism itself. It appears, in light of developments since his proposal was made — at least in the United States — that van Buren overdrew the extent of secularism and the consequent meaninglessness of the word 'God'. Religion and God seem to be living and operative categories for a large portion of the population, in spite of the achievements of the natural and social sciences and philosophy. If this is the case, then apologetics based on proposals like van Buren's finds itself in a rather odd position. Instead of using the prior religiosity of persons — their willingness to use god-language, for example — in encountering them with the Christian faith, the strategy becomes first to convince them of the meaninglessness of all god-language and only then introduce the Christian message. In this case one must convert to secularism before becoming Christian.[11]

The second problem with van Buren's thesis has to do with the nature of Christianity itself. Is Christianity without God really Christianity at all? Does van Buren's apologetic preserve or destroy the essentials of the Christian faith? Langdon Gilkey claims that van Buren's assertion that his interpretations are true to the intentions of the New Testament and patristic writers will not hold. At the end of his critique Gilkey writes,

> And what *is* this logic of the New Testament and of
> patristic literature except the use *they* made of their words, a
> use that included speaking of God as well as of Jesus and

> mankind? . . . The logic of their ancient God-centered
> language is surely not identical to that of a modern natural-
> istic system which refers nothing to God — for they did in
> fact speak of God.[12]

Gilkey suggests that it would have been better for van Buren to admit that his is not, after all, an interpretation of historic Christianity, but a new and different proposal.[13] Or, as Schubert Ogden writes in criticizing van Buren, "If theology is possible today only on secularistic terms, the more candid way to say this is to admit that theology is not possible today at all."[14]

One must ask then if the secular interpretation that van Buren gives to the Gospel is intelligible without reference to God. For it is clear in the New Testament that the freedom of Jesus, so prized by Van Buren and which is to be received by Christians today, flowed only from Jesus' relation with, and indeed was carried out in obedience to, the God whom he called Father. Without this ground Jesus' freedom would not have been what it was, nor can this freedom be appropriated by Christians today. In any case, unless there is stronger theological warrant, unless "Jesus somehow discloses transcendent structures of reality," the question must be raised as to why he is any more relevant for secular persons than any other human hero,[15] why the freedom lived by him has any greater claim than that lived by another. Van Buren has lost the trinitarian claim that the Son is of equal status with and reveals the Father, and therefore he reduces Christianity to a Jesuology without ontological foundation. The conclusion of Ogden seems affirmed: "However absurd talking about God might be, it could never be so obviously absurd as talking of Christian faith without God."[16]

Finally, the fundamental reason for the weakness of van Buren's apologetic is that despite his intentions his position in *The Secular Meaning of the Gospel* remains within the context of traditional theism. Van Buren was a pupil of Barth and his reduction of god-language to Jesus-language can be seen as a Feuerbachian reduction of Barth's Christology. But van Buren's reduction, like Feuerbach's, arises in response to a theistic understanding of God. He cannot get beyond the theistic duality that defines God in opposition to the world. He has also lost the other side of the claim of the doctrine of the Trinity — that in Jesus God shows his identification with and involvement in the concrete, sensuous, secular world. Therefore, according to van Buren, God and the secular are completely separate categories. Any relation to God is non-secular and any secular activity can have no relation to God. "Either 'being a Christian' is something 'religious' and quite distinct from secular affairs, or Christian faith is a human posture conceivable for a man who is a part of his secular culture."[17] It is no wonder, in the context of this theistic antithesis, that in the name of secular existence "the *word* 'God' is dead." And van Buren says that this is true regardless of "what is said about God."

But does this not again demonstrate his bondage to traditional theism in which the existence of God, supposedly without regard to what God is being spoken of, is the primary issue? For van Buren it is not the existence of God that is the issue, but the meaningfulness of the word God. This issue is addressed in the theistic manner, supposedly without regard to the specific content of the concept. And yet, like traditional theism, van Buren's concept of God, God's "whatness," is in fact filled out. God is defined as opposed to everything secular. Van Buren cannot see that it is precisely this concept of God, this "whatness," that has given rise to the crisis in god-language, that has determined the reaction against Christianity. On the other hand, has he not also failed to see that there is a conception of God that claims that God is not the opposite of the secular world, but is found in its center? To discover a conception of God like this might better complete the apologetic task. This "God" has meaning in a secularized world, for that is precisely where he is found.

The Reconstruction of Theism

For the most part contemporary theologians have rejected formulations like van Buren's. Theologians as diverse as Schubert Ogden, Gordon Kaufman, John Macquarrie, Langdon Gilkey and John Cobb also take seriously the challenge of modern atheism and secular mentality. However, this does not lead them to give up god-language. Rather, in agreement with the position presented in this essay, they see atheism directed against the conception of God found in traditional theism. According to Macquarrie, it is primarily "the God of much traditional theism,"[18] of "supernaturalistic theism, a God conceived in subtle metaphysical categories . . . but nonetheless a God 'up there' or 'out there', separate from and independent of the world,"[19] that has given rise to the distinction between theism and atheism. Or as Schubert Ogden writes,

> Historically regarded, modern secularism is the most extreme expression of a centuries-long reaction against the classical metaphysical-theological tradition of the Western World. Although its denials typically take an unqualified

form — for example, "All talk of God is meaningless" —
what makes them seem far from arbitrary is their effective-
ness against *this* particular tradition and its ways of thinking
and talking about God.[20]

Because most of us assume that the reality of God stands or
falls with the classical theistic scheme for conceiving it, our
rejection of that scheme in the name of secularity seems to
leave us with nothing but complete secularism.[21]

The identification of the intelligibility of "God" with traditional
theism, according to these theologians, is illegitimate, "an illusion."
For, as Ogden concludes, while we are justified in abandoning this
"system of thought" — "the supernaturalistic conception of his [God's]
reality" — we are not justified in "rejecting God as such."[22]

Therefore, theologians of this persuasion answer atheism and secularism by attempting to reconstruct theism on a new basis.[23]   This
reconstruction requires several steps that are fairly similar among different theologians. First, while there is generally no longer an attempt to
prove God's existence, theologians argue for the intelligibility and meaningfulness of god-language.[24] On the one hand, the claim is made that
this is necessary because faith stands or falls with the acceptability or
rejection of God. God is the central focus, therefore, of all theology.
Gilkey speaks for most when he declares that "these questions of the
reality of God and the possibility of language about him are still our
most pressing current theological problems, prior to all other theological
issues."[25]

For only if we can legitimately discourse about the dimension and category of deity, about God and his works, can
we speak of other theological issues and problems of which
those divine works are the presupposition: . . . Our theological question about God precedes the hermeneutical, the
christological, and the ecclesiological questions.[26]

On the other hand, because the traditional basis of god-language has
broken down, the "primary problem is to find where we can begin in this
effort"[27] to speak god-language meaningfully. Because a world beyond
this one is no longer intelligible, this new theism attempts to find its
starting point for meaningful discourse about god in secular human
experience.

With various emphases and nuances the theologians of reconstructed theism time and again argue that the human experience "in this
world" which provides the context where the word "God" is used

meaningfully has to do with human limitation and questions of the value of existence. As Kaufman asserts,

> Such speech appears within the context of man's senses of limitation, finitude, guilt and sin, on the one hand, and his question about the meaning or value or significance of himself, his life and his word, on the other.[28]

In various ways humans experience, as Kaufman argues, the "basic fact" of limits or boundary situations in their "actual situation." The concept of God "functions as a *limiting concept*" as the "ultimate limit of all our experience."[29] Without this experience of the limit of our world, of our finitude, "there would be no justification whatsoever for the use of 'god-language.'"[30]

Similarly, making use of the theory of religious language set forth by Stephen Toulmin, Ogden agrees that god-language is ultimately unavoidable for secularized human beings because it answers what he refers to as the "limiting question."[31] He claims that neither scientific explanations nor moral reasoning can be completely self-contained.[32] These endeavors reach boundary situations where questions arise which they are unable to answer on their own terms.

> Sometimes in a chain of moral reasoning, for example, we reach the point where the question demanding an answer looks like a moral question, and yet clearly is not, since no strictly moral statement or argument could ever answer it. Thus someone may ask, "But why ought I to keep my promise anyway?"[33]

God-language finds its context of intelligibility in this setting. It gives "answers to questions that naturally arise at the limits of man's activities as moral actor and scientific knower."[34]

Likewise, Macquarrie argues that the meaningfulness of the term "God" is related to these limiting questions. "For any question that we ask leads to further questions and if we push our questioning far enough, we come to the question of God, even if god-language is not explicitly used."[35] Macquarrie then indicates several questions that lead to the question of God. In addition to his appeal to the moral question,[36] he gives the unanswerable, boundary question of all the sciences: "Why is there something rather than nothing?"[37] He also points to the question of human being itself.[38] He then claims that we can meaningfully employ god-language in response to each of the questions. Humans, for instance, experience the 'shock of being.' Both the whence and the whither of human existence constitute questions about humanity to which all scientific answers are only partial answers. "Thus we may say," Macquarrie concludes, "that the question of God is concealed in man himself. For to use the word 'God' is one possible way of answering the question of man."[39]

The other context mentioned above in which these theologians claim that meaningful god-language can arise involves the question of the significance and meaning of human existence. Even though some discuss this also as a question at the limit of human experience, because of its implications it needs a separate, though brief, analysis. According to Ogden the reason that the other limiting questions arise "naturally" in human life is that they are all ultimately pointing to and subsumed under the more profound question of the meaningfulness of human existence in the face of human minuteness in time and space, of a human being's brief life and death.[40] In this situation god-language can arise to answer the question of (as Macquarrie puts it) "whether there is an ultimate context of meaning, embracing all the others, gathering up the many different activities, giving sense and worth to history and to human striving as a whole."[41] For these theologians of the new theism, the use of god-language in this context implies an affirmation of the meaningfulness of human existence. As the last quotation makes clear, Macquarrie believes that faith in God "is equivalent to 'faith in being'" —

> an attitude of acceptance and commitment in the face not
> only of my own being or even that of the society in which I
> find myself, but ultimately of the wider being within which
> human society and history have themselves their setting . . .
> [Faith] would mean that 'reality is trustworthy at its deepest
> level.'[42]

Ogden speaks of this affirmation of existence in terms of the "reassurance" religious discourse brings. He quotes Stephen Toulmin approvingly:

> Over those matters of fact which are not to be 'explained'
> scientifically [like the death on their birthdays of three
> children in one family], the function of religion is to help us
> resign ourselves to them — and so feel like accepting them.
> Likewise, over matters of duty which are not justified
> further in ethical terms, it is for religion to help us embrace
> them — and so feel like accepting them.[43]

The apologetic challenge of this line of argument for the secularist is the claim that regardless of whether or not there is any ultimate truth to god-language, its meaningfulness, in the context of the secular experiences discussed above, cannot be denied. All human beings, unless they exist only on the surface of life, face situations of limitation and the question of meaning. But this means, then, that this apologetic has another point: Because modern atheism and secularism focus their entire attention on the meaning of this world, and because existence in this world and the question of the meaning of this world raise the limiting questions that imply the question of God, which, in turn, is the language of the affirmation of the meaning of human existence and this world, the argument is advanced that secularists and atheists can deny the intelligibility of god-language only at the risk of self-contradiction. As Ogden declares,

> . . . I now wish to claim that for the secular man of today, as surely as for any other man, faith in God cannot but be real because it is in the final analysis unavoidable . . . . To hold that even these persons [those who "seem to get along quite well with no belief in God" and those "who expressly deny any such belief"] cannot finally avoid faith in God is to imply that men may be wholly mistaken about the real scope or direction of their own beliefs.[44]

The secularist may believe that scientific or moral questions can stand on their own. But in this they are mistaken, for they always ultimately reach a limiting question. "Always presupposed by even the most commonplace of moral decisions," Ogden states as an example, "is the confidence that these decisions have an unconditional significance."[45] He continues,

> No matter what the content of our choices may be, whether for this course of action or for that, we can make them at all only because of our invincible faith that they somehow make a difference which no turn of events in the future has the power to annul . . . . In sum, to be moral at all is always to beg the basic question to which the religions of mankind are more or less adequate attempts to express the answer.[46]

Therefore, the secularist, if he or she takes the world seriously and is consistent, cannot ultimately escape god-language.[47]

However, convincing the secularist about the intelligibility of god-language does not end the apologetic attempt of the new theists. One must move beyond mere demonstration that god-language has a context where it might function meaningfully to the task of showing how this might be done, of actually speaking about God in a meaningful way. Because traditional metaphysical language has collapsed, a new conceptual framework for god-language must be found, a framework rooted in secular experience. Macquarrie finds what he believes the most adequate language for discourse about God in the philosophy of Martin Heidegger.[48] He consequently suggests translating the word "God" with the phrase, "Being which lets be."[49] On the other hand, Ogden, who began his theological efforts also with an orientation towards existentialism in the Bultmannian camp,[50] moved on to propose the process philosophy of Alfred North Whitehead and Charles Hartshorne as providing the most appropriate language for speaking about God.[51] God comes to be conceived of here as "the unique and in all ways perfect instance of creative becoming."[52]

One must appreciate the attempts of these new theists to reformulate the doctrine of God in a way meaningful in the modern world. However, the odd apologetic position of the new theism must be noticed also.[53] For according to their argument at least two presuppositions must first be accepted if the concept "God" is to be understood. First, as with van Buren's proposal, a person must "convert" to secularism. That is, one must be convinced that traditional theism has collapsed, but that (unlike van Buren) secular, human experience can provide a basis for speech about God. Second, one must be a "convert" to a Heideggerian, a Whiteheadian or some other philosophical system before god-language can be meaningful. It cannot be denied that this approach might be successful and meaningful among secular Heideggerians and Whiteheadians. But in the first place it must be asked, as it was in the discussion of van Buren, if secularism is really that pervasive. In the second place it must be questioned whether the new god-language based on Heidegger or Whitehead is more intelligible to non-Heideggerians or non-Whiteheadians than the more traditional language.[54] Certainly theology places itself in a tenuous position and takes on an added burden if, in order to speak about God, it must first seek conversions to this or that philosophy.

This criticism of the new theism is related to a larger problem. It shows that this theism is finally much more in line with traditional theism than its proponents suppose. First, like traditional theism, this new theism, for apologetic reasons, is grounded in a philosophical position external to the Christian faith. This means that finally the acceptability of Christianity in these systems is dependent on the acceptability of this prior philosophy. As Thomas' theology is incomprehensible unless one accepts Aristotle, the theology of the new theists is unintelligible unless one presupposes secularism and/or a Heideggerian or a Whiteheadian philosophy, for example.

Second, like traditional theism, the focus of attention of the new theists is primarily on a general discussion of the one God, unrelated to the specifically Christian conception of God. For it is argued that unless one can speak about God in general, there can be no ground for speech of God the Father of Jesus. This means that there is often little mention of the doctrine of the Trinity and only after the general discussion of God, or it is analyzed as an ancient formulation that failed.[55] The general discussion of God, as in traditional theism, centers first around a proof. Instead of, for instance, Thomas using Aristotelean modes of thought to prove that God exists, the new theism uses existentialist, linguistic or process philosophy to prove the intelligibility of god-language in the secular world. Again it must be pointed out that, if the former is rejected, the latter collapses, and all before any mention of the specifically Christian conception of God.

Third, this means that again like traditional theism, the new theism's talk about God is abstracted from human experience. The new theist's quest for a concrete basis in secular life for intelligible god-language is accomplished in the human experience of limits or boundary situations. God is the expression for a possible answer to the unanswerable questions encountered in secular living. God-language is abstracted from these experiences and becomes intelligible when translated as, for example, "ultimate limit" or "the affirmation of Being."

Now we are in a position to see the central problem for apologetics of this reconstituted theism's relationship to traditional theism. It might be successful in dealing with certain forms of secularism and atheism. In establishing the intelligibility of god-language the new theists tend to see secularism expressed philosophically in logical positivism or other forms of linguistic analysis, and therefore respond to questions raised in this context. Whether or not their response is convincing and whether or not a more adequate response from a trinitarian perspective might be available, can remain in this essay an open question. However, what is clear is that the new theism, because of its similarity to traditional theism, does not provide a satisfactory response to the tradition of protest atheism analyzed in this work and — even if it answered atheism in other forms — would be rejected by it. In the first place, its response does not take into account Feuerbach's epistemological critique. The problem for Feuerbach is not whether or not the notion of God is meaningful. For him it certainly is. The issue is how to read theology so that you know what its referent really is. To say that god-language functions meaningfully at the human experience of limit, that God can be thought of as the "ultimate limit" of human experience, is nothing of which Feuerbach would have to be convinced. But Feuerbach would demand that this theology acknowledge that it is speaking of human experience only, that it is in reality anthropology only. According to his sensuous epistemology, the new theism, like the old theism, has no concrete basis from which to suggest that its god-language refers to anything other than human experience.

Protest atheism, furthermore, is not interested in epistemology for its own sake, but primarily in how it affects the human situation of alienation, suffering and oppression. This means that again — for Marx, Horkheimer, Adorno and others, as well as for Feuerbach — there is not a central concern with the intelligibility of god-language in any abstract sense, unrelated to the concrete human situation of pain. Again, the question for these atheists is never — as it is for the new theism — whether or not god-language can be spoken to meet the requirements of linguistic analysis or secularism in general. They know too well that god-languages function quite meaningfully in the social, political, suffering existence of human beings. The question for them is rather *how* god-language functions in these concrete contexts. These protest atheists claim god-language must be rejected because it gives a false answer to and/or helps support this human situation. To be sure, the new theists deal with the issues of human suffering and praxis.[56] Nevertheless, in their discussions of the intelligibility of god-language, which they insist must come first and which serve as their apologetic basis, they fail to respond to, and even give fuel for, the central thrust of this critique. For not only do the new theists discuss the intelligibility of god-language without reference to human suffering or economic and political injustice, but in one way or another they claim that the use of god-language implies the affirmation of existence and in a way that it helps us "resign ourselves" even to tragic deaths "and so feel like accepting them."[57] It is precisely this type of the affirmation of existence, this function of god-language, that both atheism grounded in the theodicy question and atheism grounded in a critique of practice reject in the name of the transformation of the present condition of human suffering and social, economic and political injustice. The danger, therefore, is that the discussion with atheism is foreclosed even before theology can address the issues of suffering and praxis specifically.

Moreover, similar problems become apparent when we do examine attempts by the new theists to deal specifically with the questions of theodicy and praxis. We will take Schubert Ogden as exemplifying the others. In the context of process thought, Ogden attempts to develop a concept of God that responds to the theodicy question and the question of praxis.[58] In answer to the former question, Ogden develops a concept of God who is a limited being,[59] who is passible in the sense that to him "everything makes a difference because it in part determines his actual being."[60] We are redeemed from transience, death and sin and our lives are given meaning since God creatively synthesizes "all of his creatures. . .

. into his everlasting life."[61] This has implications for praxis. For in freeing us from transience and death we are freed for creative action. Moreover, God is not only a being "to whom all things make a difference," he is also one "who himself makes a difference to all things." What he does for human beings in terms of practice is "to optimize the limits of their own free decisions."[62] By this Ogden means that God establishes "such fundamental limits of natural order as allow for a greater possibility of good than of evil to be realized through their exercise of freedom."[63]

In spite of these efforts problems remain that call into question the adequacy of Ogden's position as a response to atheism. First, his theology as a whole again fails to answer Feuerbach's epistemological critique. His conception of God and therefore also his responses to suffering and the praxis of liberation are abstracted from the world. The process that is observed in the world is predicated of God as well, only in the proportion due him, i.e., as the greatest process of which one can conceive while taking into account the process of every other thing.[64] The relative dependence and independence of all things in process and therefore the reciprocal determination of things by one another is likewise abstracted from the world and formulated as god-language. Thus, according to Feuerbach's critique, Ogden's conception of God finds its concrete basis only in human reflection on the world and is therefore only anthropology (or physiology).

In relation to the answer to human suffering it must be admitted that Ogden approaches the trinitarian response. In that humans partly determine and are synthesized into God's being, one can say that God suffers with humanity and that human suffering finds its way into God. Nevertheless, Ogden's process thought does not go as far as trinitarian theology. While in its view God is a "fellow-sufferer" who therefore "understands," he does not protest against suffering. God's passibility is not a freely chosen protest against human suffering, but arises because God is a thing and, like all things, is in part determined by other things.[65] God's limitation, therefore, is not a self-limitation in protest against the agony of the world, but is God's in that God is an actual thing at all. Even God's "liberating" determination of all other beings, defined as it is above as the establishment of "limits of natural order" that produce "a greater possibility of good than of evil," can scarcely be called a protest. In fact, in light of human suffering the protest can be made that God's "limits of natural order" have established a greater possibility of evil than of good.

Also problematic is Ogden's relation to the question of praxis. Despite his commitments to human freedom, his suggestions remain abstract and without concrete content and definite imperatives. First, Ogden's separation of liberation into redemption — the overcoming of death, transience and sin — and emancipation — the freedom to realize one's full potentialities[66] — implies an abstract understanding of human beings, separated from their social context. This conception can be used to support the status quo, for a human being can somehow be liberated (redeemed) individually without liberation (emancipation) in the social context. Furthermore, even though God's emancipating action of optimizing the limits of freedom means that humans should "labor for fundamental social and cultural change"[67] to bring this optimization of freedom about, Ogden gives little concrete direction here. One may ask in what direction this practice should move. He believes that it should be in solidarity with the oppressed, but gives us no way of determining who the oppressed are or how we should proceed. Because of the vagueness of this position, it could be maintained that the present situation offers the best optimization of freedom. In spite of Ogden's exemplary intentions, his theology may without contradiction also be used to justify the status quo.

In terms of its theological method in which it grounds itself in one philosophical position or another, its concentration on the general notion of the one God drawn in relation to human experience with at best secondary references to the triune God, the reconstructed theism finds itself in a position similar to its older manifestation. And consequently, like its traditional predecessor, the new theism does not give complete responses to protest atheism.

The Doctrine of the Trinity and Apologetics

The theologians who attempt to reconstitute theism advance beyond van Buren in understanding that it is not merely the word 'God' in an abstract sense that has been attacked by atheism. They correctly perceive that the unintelligibility of god-language is related to a particular conception of God, that of traditional theism. Nevertheless, in apparent contradiction to this insight, the new theists begin their theological reflections with an attempt to defend the meaningfulness of the word 'God' in a general, abstract sense, before explicating the specifically Christian conception of God. This procedure appears to be as unnecessary for apologetics as it is a failure in responding to the forms of atheism we have discussed in this essay. For if atheistic critiques arise and are formulated on the basis of a particular conception of God, it might be that a clear articulation of the specifically Christian doctrine of God, as opposed to the conception of God presupposed by atheism, already provides Christian theology with responses to atheistic protests without having to tie the success of its responses to a defense of a general concept of God.

This is precisely the different approach for apologetics that is possible on the basis of the doctrine of the Trinity as developed by Karl Barth and Jürgen Moltmann. It may be called an "indirect apologetics" for, as we have seen throughout this essay, apologetics grounded on this kind of trinitarian theology does not proceed by first attempting to defend the acceptability of religion or the intelligibility of 'God,' whether God's existence or the meaningfulness of god-language, in order to make room for the Christian faith. Nor does it assert that speech about God must be tied to any particular philosophical system, although it does not reject the use of philosophical categories. Rather, apologetics based on the doctrine of the Trinity begins by clarifying the Christian conception of God (which as we have seen is not separate from other Christian doctrines, like soteriology for instance), thereby distinguishing it from other and false understandings which might occur both inside and outside the church.

This means that trinitarian apologetics can prevent a premature rejection of the Christian conception of God. For one thing that the analysis of theism has shown is that any claim for the existence of God in general or for the intelligibility of speech about God in general, based on this or that human experience and/or tied to this or that philosophical system, always faces the possible counter-claim that this is not the case and, hence, the possible foreclosure of discussing the specifically Christian doctrine of God. In the trinitarian context the issue is no longer whether or not God exists or the intelligibility of god-language in any general sense, but whether or not the proper Christian conception of God is open to the charges made by atheism.

Only after its clarification of the Christian claim, and based on it, does trinitarian apologetics give its responses to attacks on Christian faith. It might be asked how it could be otherwise. How can a Christian response to an attack on faith in God be given before one knows what the Christian conception of God is? In any case, as we have seen in both Barth and Moltmann, the doctrine of the Trinity represents the insistence that the Christian conception of God stand on its own, unencumbered by philosophical conceptions of God, of God's existence or of the intelligibility of the very word. But on the other hand, it has been shown how this very clarification of the triune God of the Christian faith makes responses to atheism possible. Nevertheless, it has been charged that the move by trinitarian theologians to clarify first the specifically Christian conception of God signifies a retreat from the world, a failure of apologetic nerve, a theological *incurvatus se,* an unwillingness to dialogue. We have already seen this charge made against Barth in Chapter II. And the new theists make it likewise.[68] Certainly Barth with his polemic against "apologetic" theology is responsible at least for some of this attitude.[69] Whatever Barth meant by this polemic, however, it did not mean for him the withdrawal of theology from discussion with the world. One of the remarkable aspects of the *Church Dogmatics* is Barth's extensive treatments of the philosophical tradition. And we saw in Chapter II that there is a sense in which the doctrine of the Trinity is Barth's response to Feuerbach. Likewise for Moltmann, the doctrine of the Trinity does not signify theological isolation but provides a way to respond to Marx, Horkheimer and Adorno.

This essay has shown that the development of the doctrine of the Trinity along the lines of Barth and Moltmann, while it may at first glance appear as a move toward theological isolation (because of its focus on developing the Christian understanding of God), surprisingly represents a theological opening out to the world, to the sensuous, secular existence of humanity. For when the doctrine of the Trinity clarifies the Christian God — that is the God who is fully present in Jesus the Son and is therefore known as Father, Son and Spirit — we find a God who is not isolated in heaven or located only at the boundaries of human existence in the questions of limit, but who is open to the world, who reaches out into the world, who becomes human and who, therefore, is able to and does respond to the secular atheistic protests. When Feuerbach attacks the idealism of theology and philosophy by demanding an epistemology grounded in a concrete, sensuous object that controls human thinking, trinitarian theology does not respond like the old and new theism with a conception of God drawn from human experience of the self or the world. According to Feuerbach, because its sensuous basis is either the self or the world, such theology can only be an idealistic, projected "anthropology" or "physiology." Rather the doctrine of the Trinity comprehends the God who becomes a concrete, sensuous object that determines our thinking about him in Jesus.

Furthermore, Feuerbach's and later protest-atheism's charge that the God "out there" must be rejected because of the theological tendency to glorify God at the expense of humanity — to see God as omnipotent and humans therefore as weak, for instance — can also, on the basis of the sensuous epistemology guaranteed by the doctrine of the Trinity, be answered. Because God is known in a sensuous way in Jesus, his attributes no longer have to be abstracted or robbed from humanity; the conception of God is no longer developed through a *via negativa* as everything humanity is not or as humanity's "ultimate limit." Rather, this trinitarian thinking, which conceives of God as he appears in the concrete person of Jesus, speaks instead of a God who defines himself precisely by becoming human and, hence, by glorifying humankind.

Furthermore, this sensuous, trinitarian way of speaking about God can respond similarly to atheism that, because of the depth and persistence of human suffering, rejects the omnipotent, good God who nevertheless is neither touched by, nor acts against, suffering. Again, because the doctrine of the Trinity comprehends the God who is known and who acts in the sensuous, concrete event of Jesus, the triune God's omnipotence is not defined abstractly as his potential to do anything, but is seen concretely as acting through self-limitation, as the divine life enters the condition of human suffering and acts to overcome it by taking it into itself in divine protest.

Finally, when Marx claims that God must be rejected because a transcendent divinity supports the earthly status quo by offering a heavenly solace, trinitarian theology does not respond as does theism by claiming that some notion of God is logically required to give any moral action a basis. Rather, again because of its claim of the sensuous knowledge of God in Jesus, the doctrine of the Trinity exegetes the God who is in praxis against the suffering of humanity in its earthly political, social, economic context. This means that the knowledge of the triune God entails and cannot be separated from human praxis against these forms of oppression, because this is precisely where the triune God gives himself to be known concretely.

To summarize the issue here, while traditional theism and the new theism begin with general human experience and so at first appear truly open to the questions raised by atheism, we have seen that they first develop their conception of God abstractly, without concern for the central issues of protest atheism. What is an attempt to show how God or god-language relates to human experience ends up giving a conception of God that restricts God from doing just that. This indicates an apologetic failure. On the other hand, the doctrine of the Trinity, which looks at first like a theological withdrawal from the world, surprisingly ends up providing a basis for apologetics. For the triune God, according to Barth and Moltmann, cannot be conceived of without his concrete activity in Jesus, without his full involvement in human life where he gives himself to be known sensuously as involved in human suffering and in praxis against it and, therefore, as calling humans to meet him in the praxis of overcoming suffering in all its forms. This means that the doctrine of the Trinity can provide a promising apologetic basis, for it understands the God who is open for the world, who already is related to human experience to such a degree that the protests on which atheism is based are already ingredient in the divine life. In each case the apologetic strength of the doctrine of the Trinity is that, without traditional and new theism's habit of first introducing other concepts that may or may not be acceptable to the atheist and which do not touch upon or even fall under atheism's protest, precisely in clarifying the Christian understanding of God, it is simultaneously involved in, and giving answers to, the concerns voiced by protest atheism.

The doctrine of the Trinity as developed by Barth and Moltmann, therefore, offers the basis for a cogent response to protest atheism with two sides. First, the trinitarian response does not merely reject the atheists' claim. Rather, it recognizes in the atheistic protest something of itself. It sees that the triune God has already included in the divine life the protest of the atheists. The doctrine of the Trinity speaks of the God who rejects idealism by becoming a sensuous object. It conceptualizes the God who, on the basis of human suffering, protests against omnipotent, impassible deity, by limiting himself and entering fully into human suffering, by existing in suffering. The doctrine of the triune God protests against human suffering and oppression and the God who supports this status quo, by taking them on himself in order to transform them and, thereby, challenging the present conditions and leading humans into the praxis of liberation toward God's promised future. Therefore, trinitarian theology can affirm the critiques of protest atheism in that they serve to demonstrate the false elements in traditional theism.

Second, precisely by demonstrating its agreement with the grounds of the atheistic protest, theology based on this understanding of the doctrine of the Trinity represents a challenge to this atheism. While the doctrine of the Trinity permits theology to say yes to, and agree with, atheism's attack over against traditional theism, it also demonstrates that traditional theism is not to be identified as the distinctive Christian conception of God. As we have seen, the doctrine of the Trinity, as developed by Barth and Moltmann, represents a theological move beyond traditional theism, its methods and its consequent conception of God. This means that trinitarian based theology shows that atheism, by uncritically accepting traditional theism as correct, has misidentified the Christian God. It has, therefore, presupposed and rejected a false conception of God, one that Christian trinitarian theology also rejects. If this is the case, the protests of atheism must be considered in a new context, in relation to the triune God who contains these protests in his own being. In light of this, it must be asked if, in the context of the doctrine of the Trinity as developed by Barth and Moltmann, this atheism must reject the God who is triune. Unless it is somehow reformulated on new grounds, could such a rejection stand? Has not trinitarian theology in moving beyond theism moved beyond atheism as well?

Trinitarian Apologetics and Patristic Theology

We have seen that the trinitarian theologies of Barth and Moltmann offer the basis for responses to protest atheism which overcome the problems of the other apologetic choices examined here. A remaining legitimate question has to do with the appropriateness of using the doctrine of the Trinity as the basis for apologetics. This question can be framed in terms of the relationship of the doctrine of the Trinity as developed by Barth and Moltmann to that of patristic writers. Are Barth and Moltmann talking about the same doctrine or have they introduced intentions different from those of patristic theologians?

While a complete answer to this question cannot be given here, a look at this relationship might be suggestive for two important reasons. First, it might be that the new theists continue to ignore the doctrine of the Trinity not only because of Barth's use of it in the context of his polemic against "apologetic" theology, but also because they do not take full account of its use in patristic theology. Second, if it can be indicated that Barth and Moltmann are true to the intentions of the patristic use of the doctrine of the Trinity, then it would not be unreasonable to suggest that the same basis for apologetics we have seen in their trinitarian theologies should be present in any proper understanding of the doctrine of the Trinity.[70]

One reason many theologians do not perceive the apologetic usefulness of the doctrine of the Trinity is that they have a one-sided view of trinitarian theology. Illustrative of this is Langdon Gilkey who, in a chapter entitled "God" in *Christian Theology*, discusses briefly the doctrine of the Trinity.[71] His position is that in early patristic theology trinitarian thinking stood for the "absolute aspect of God" — "the utterly primordial, unoriginate, changeless, eternal, unrelated source of all else" — on the one hand and the "related aspect of God" on the other.[72] Gilkey writes,

> Thus at the outset of the philosophical career of the Christian God, the symbol of the Trinity served to provide conceptual expression for the dialectical polarity of the Christian God as at once the self-sufficient creator of all, transcendent to all finitude (Father), and as the active, revealing, loving redeemer (Son), present in grace and power to God's people (Holy Spirit).[73]

But, Gilkey argues, this understanding soon disintegrated under the pressure of the Arians who argued that, if God is the "transcendent absolute," the Son who is related to the temporal, creaturely realm cannot be fully God. Gilkey asserts that the arguments of Athanasius and the Councils of Nicea and Constantinople, by asserting the full divinity of Father, Son and Holy Spirit, "pushed the conception of the entire divine Trinity in an absolutist direction," thereby negating for the whole Trinity "temporality, potentiality, changeableness, relatedness, and dependence."[74] The result of this, according to Gilkey, is that "the Trinity ceased to be the central symbolic expression of the polarity of the divine relatedness."[75]

But is not this interpretation one-sided? It is true that declaring the Son *homoousia* with the Father meant, as Lonergan points out, "that what is said of the Father is to be said also of the Son, except that the Son is Son and not Father."[76] And this meant that the Son was, like the Father, not a creature, not temporal and not mutable.[77] As Athanasius declared, "He is the offspring of His Father's substance, so that none may doubt that in virtue of His likeness to His immutable Father the Word also is immutable."[78] On the surface it looks as if Gilkey is correct in claiming that in language like this the whole Trinity came to be conceived of as absolute. Moreover, it also seems as if Barth and Moltmann, with their talk of change and suffering in God, have altered the doctrine of the Trinity beyond recognition. But once Athanasius' intent becomes clear, so does the one-sidedness of this conclusion. For Athanasius' main concern was not philosophical, "his guiding thought was the conviction of redemption."[79] In claiming the equality of the Son with the Father, his intention was not the absolutizing of the Son, but ensuring a conception of God that adequately affirmed the Christian experience of revelation and salvation in Christ. J. N. D. Kelly points out that perhaps Athanasius' most impressive argument, the one that carried the most weight at the Council of Nicea, was that "only if the Mediator was Himself divine could man hope to re-establish fellowship with God."[80] Furthermore, Athanasius argues that if the Son reveals the Father he cannot be less than the Father, but must be like him.[81] The real intent, then, of Athanasius' claim of the Son's equality with the Father is, as Rowan Williams affirms, "the capacity of God to involve himself in the historical order."[82] The Son is claimed to be *homoousia* not to absolutize the entire Trinity and beg the question of God's relation to the world, but precisely to make it clear that in Jesus the Son it is really God who is relating himself to us.

The doctrine of the Trinity emerges then to safeguard and bring to speech God's openness for real relationship to, and involvement in, the created world and human life. As we have seen, this insight is at the heart of Barth's and Moltmann's trinitarian thought and also forms the basis of the apologetic function of the doctrine of the Trinity. At this point both appear to be in line with the original intention of the trinitarian formulation. On the other hand, Gilkey does not adequately take this intention into account, and so passes over the doctrine of the Trinity and seeks other language in which to speak of God's relation to the world and through which to develop his apologetics.

In this essay our analysis has suggested four aspects in which the doctrine of the Trinity as formed by Barth and Moltmann explicates God's relation to the world. They have to do with epistemology, the identity of God, God's relationship to suffering and God's relationship to earthly praxis. The question now is whether these specific elements can also be found in early trinitarian theology.

It appears that for Athanasius (and Lonergan suggests for the whole process of the development of the doctrine of the Trinity)[83] the doctrine of the Trinity contained a concrete epistemological principle from which to develop a conception of God in contrast to more abstract presuppositions about divinity. This epistemological principle appears to be at work in the Arian controversy. Arius begins with certain presuppositions about God's absoluteness and from them logically derives conclusions about what God could and could not do or be.[84] Because God is absolutely transcendent he cannot come into direct relation with the creation, he cannot be the Son who does relate to creatures. He also cannot be the Son, for that would contradict the divine unity and simplicity.[85] Athanasius, on the other hand, basing his knowledge about God on what God had done in Jesus the Son, denies that we can speak correctly about God based on a preconceived notion of divine transcendence.[86] This means that, while Athanasius sees God as a transcendent being and retains categories like immutability and eternity and applies them to the Son as well as the Father, these notions themselves are interpreted on the basis of what God has done in the Son. God's transcendence, therefore, cannot "be interpreted in such a way that God cannot enter into direct contact with his creatures."[87] Rowan Williams summarizes this issue:

> Nonetheless, Athanasius unambiguously affirms that we cannot deny in advance God's ability to be incarnate on the grounds of a preconceived notion of divine transcendence; nor can we deny God's ability to be Father and Son on the grounds of a preconceived definition of the divine simplicity . . . . The Athanasian God 'transcends his transcendence' to be encountered in human shape: his hiddenness

and unknowability are grasped in and through the weakness of the flesh of Christ . . . . We do not begin from innate
or intuitive ideas of the absolute or the transcendent; we are
drawn into a transformed life, speech and activity in which
the inexhaustible resource of the God who draws us is
gradually discovered. And the agent of that 'drawing' is the
historical figure of Jesus . . . .[88]

We see, therefore, in the trinitarian formulation of the early church
a move away from classical philosophy's method of defining the divine
in opposition to the human. The conception of the triune God's deity
does not ultimately depend upon conceiving humanity as unworthy,
transient and weak. In no sense is this God's deity constituted at human
expense. The triune God becomes human. And in this salvific act, early
trinitarian theologians perceived the glory that God brings to
humankind. The theme of "deification" is common. Athanasius says,
"For he was made man that we might be made God."[89]   It is not
necessary to analyze the notion of "deification" in order to understand
that for Athanasius the triune God stood for true worth and value of
humanity and not its diminution.[90]

It is perhaps worth noting again in this context how one-sided is
Gilkey's judgment that Athanasius pushed the doctrine of the Trinity in
an "absolutist direction." What our analysis again suggests is that
Athanasius, in claiming full divinity for the Son, did not so much
absolutize the Son as, by affirming God's activity in the Son, sought to
concretize the process of thinking about the divine transcendence and
attributes, opening them for relationship with, and the glorification of,
humankind. Thus Barth and Moltmann appear to be in line with, and
find support in, Athanasian trinitarian thought.

Here we can draw another conclusion about Barth's and
Moltmann's use of trinitarian theology. It can be safely affirmed that in
using the doctrine of the Trinity, not to prove some general conception of
God but to distinguish clearly the Christian doctrine of God, Barth and
Moltmann are following the intentions of the early Church in the
development of the doctrine of the Trinity. For the question of the
Trinity in patristic thought did not have to do with the existence of God
or with the meaningfulness of a general conception of God. Divine
reality was readily admitted by both Jewish and Hellenistic cultures.[91]
Judaism and the philosophical schools had different forms of monotheism; hellenistic religions recognized several deities. The doctrine of the
Trinity, then, arose out of a long process of the church's attempt to
distinguish the Christian conception of God, which had always been
bound to the salvific work of Christ, from these other options which were

constantly threatening to intrude and control Christian thinking.[92] This point is demonstrated precisely in the case of Arius, who attempted to force the Christian understanding of God into a previously determined "framework."[93] Because of his attachment to a philosophical definition of the "absolute uniqueness and transcendence of God, the unoriginate source . . . of all reality,"[94] he could not admit the Son's equality with the Father. Athanasius and the Nicene Council affirmed trinitarian language to distinguish the correct Christian conception of God from that of Arius.[95] On this point also it appears that trinitarian apologetics is in line with the patristic use of the doctrine of the Trinity.

The next point with which we are interested is more difficult to support. On the issue of the relation of suffering to God, from the New Testament on there was the claim that the suffering of Jesus was somehow the work of God. Ignatius refers to the death of Jesus as "the passion of my God."[96] We have already seen that according to Eberhard Jüngel the relation of this suffering to God is ultimately at the heart of the doctrine of the Trinity.[97] We have also just seen that Athanasius uses trinitarian language to give assurance of the longstanding Christian conviction that "God and Christ were to be held together, and that the work of Christ was in some sense the work of God,"[98] that in Jesus the Son salvation is real because here true God is relating himself to us to bring us to him. Athanasius is also aware that if humanity is to be transformed that God must relate himself to human pain and death or these would remain spheres of human existence unredeemed.[99] The problem is that Athanasius is still working in the context where the divine is given the attributes of immutability, impassibility and the like. How can such a divine which according to the doctrine of the Trinity includes both Father and Son be related to suffering? We have already seen that Athanasius does not allow preconceived notions like these finally to determine what God could or could not do. He, of course, already knew that Jesus, the immutable, impassible Son in his work of redemption had somehow suffered and died. "For," Athanasius declares, "our Saviour did not redeem us by inactivity, but by suffering for us, He abolished death."[100] And he also knew, as he asserted in his trinitarian debates with the Arians, that the Savior must be fully God, for only then is he "both able to recreate everything and worthy to suffer on behalf of all."[101] There can be no doubt, then, that it is the intention of Athanasius to claim that God in the work of the Son somehow took on human suffering and death.

In explicating how it is that the impassible, fully divine Son can suffer, Athanasius often employs the awkward but common scheme of attributing the impassibility to the divine Son while suffering and death

are his in his bodily nature.[102] Nevertheless, he makes it clear through
the use of a strong notion of "communication of properties"[103] that

> the properties of the flesh are said to be His, since He was in
> it, such as to hunger, to thirst, to suffer, to weary, and the
> like, of which the flesh is capable . . . .Whence it was that,
> when the flesh suffered, the Word was not external to it,
> and therefore is the passion said to be His . . . .[104]

We see here that, even under the burden of hellenistic philosophy, the
doctrine of the Trinity allows Athanasius to affirm God's relation to
creation even at the point of suffering and death by ascribing these things
to the earthly existence of the Son. It appears, therefore, that when Barth
and Moltmann offer a ground for apologetics by showing how the
doctrine of the Trinity indicates God's own suffering that they, no longer
encumbered by Greek philosophical categories, are carrying further the
intention of early trinitarian theology as represented by Athanasius.

The correspondence between Barth's and Moltmann's use of the
Trinity and patristic usage with respect to the relation of trinitarian
theology to social-political praxis is by far the most difficult to argue.
Certainly, claims like Moltmann's that Athanasius and other trinitarian
theologians were exiled because the doctrine of the Trinity undermined
the monotheism that ideologically supported the rule of the one emperor
cannot be accepted without further historical confirmation.[105] Nevertheless, early Christians knew well the relation between conceptions of God
and practice in the social-political context. On the one hand, because
they did not follow the cult of the Roman State, early Christians were
charged with "atheism". On the other hand, after Christianity became a
favored religion, from Eusebius of Caesarea on, Christian theology often
supported the rule of one emperor or one king by relating it to the
universal rule of the one God.[106] It would not be something unheard of
if other theologians grounded their social practice in the trinitarian form
of God. Indeed, there are at least indications of this being done.

Rowan Williams argues that the Cappadocian fathers, for example, saw an unbreakable unity "between theological positions and forms
of Christian life." And as one might expect of the Cappadocians this
unity between theology and practice is expressed in a trinitarian context.
For them, according to Williams, knowledge of God comes "only
through the practice of self-crucifying service, in imitation of Christ."[107]
And, the Hellenistic notion of participation in the divine is modified so
that it is "participation not in what God is, but in what he *does*."[108]
Therefore, "to be restored in the image of God, is consistently to follow
the pattern of God's life as revealed in Jesus."[109] This of course meant a

life characterized by qualities like forgiveness. As God forgives we should too.[110] But it also means a certain form of concrete activity in the social sphere. Basil argues that because Christ was the servant of all, Christians must serve all, whether the righteous or sinners. Williams reminds us of how this worked out concretely in Basil's life with the building of schools, orphanages and hospitals.[111]

This trinitarian notion that one participates in God by participating in what he does in Christ also indicates for the Cappadocians that the Christian is directed to the poor. In his work *The Beatitudes*, Gregory of Nyssa declares, "The man who shares with the poor will have his share in one who became poor for our sake."[112] His exegesis of "Blessed are the poor in Spirit" becomes a critique of wealth that is gained at the expense of the poor and call for a concrete, literal interpretation of the command to sell all that you have and give to the poor.[113] Basil takes this seriously enough to suggest what might be considered a critique of private property, that anything extra you have does not belong to you but to the one who has none. In his "Homily on Luke" Basil states that to keep it makes you a thief:

> When someone steals a man's clothes we call him a thief.
> Should we not give the same name to one who could clothe
> the naked and does not? The bread in your cupboard
> belongs to the hungry man; the coat hanging unused in
> your closet belongs to the man who needs it; the shoes
> rotting in your closet belong to the man who has no shoes;
> the money which you hoard up belongs to the poor.[114]

Because of this principle Basil also condemns usury which he sees as a sign of the "inhumanity" of the "rich". Rather, if you "lend to those from whom ye do not hope to receive" you "lendeth to the Lord."[115]

This is enough to suggest that, at least in the early trinitarian theologies of Basil and Gregory of Nyssa, there is the recognition that theory cannot be separated from praxis. A trinitarian conception of God includes practical activity on behalf of the poor. It is, therefore, not unreasonable to suggest that when Barth and, to a greater extent, Moltmann go much further in uncovering the praxis related to the doctrine of the Trinity, and therefore lay a foundation for apologetics, they are, nevertheless, in line with patristic theology as represented by Basil and Gregory.

If our analysis here is correct, then it is not only trinitarian thinking in Barth and Moltmann that serves an apologetic function. Rather the basis of this function is found in patristic theology as well. In its original formulation the doctrine of the Trinity signified God's concrete involvement with and openness to the world that is made clear in the history of Jesus. Thus it provided a framework in which to respond to questions raised from the world. This means that conceptions of the Trinity that are speculative, esoteric or serve to isolate Christianity from engagement with the world are actually misinterpretations. And precisely these misinterpretations help account for the eclipse of the doctrine of the Trinity in the churches and among theologians who are attempting to relate the Christian faith to the world and who consequently turn elsewhere to find a point of contact to show Christianity's relevance. What a proper understanding of the doctrine of the Trinity demonstrates, however, is that Christianity contains the basis for its relevance to the world within its own identity, the identity of the triune God. A rejection of this proper understanding of the doctrine of the Trinity, therefore, would mean not only a loss of Christian identity but also would be indicative of a theological withdrawal from the world.

The openness for the world that we have seen in the responses of trinitarian theology to protest atheism is suggestive for further work. Can the doctrine of the Trinity serve as the basis of a response to other questions about and critiques of the Christian faith? For instance, can a trinitarian response to Freud be developed that goes beyond those presently available?[116] Or, is it possible that the trinitarian position might provide the basis for a fruitful dialogue with Judaism and Islam?[117] Moreover, it may be that a trinitarian conception of God can be developed which will be able to take more seriously positivistic and other critiques of the Christian faith which are more theoretical in nature.

These challenges undoubtedly would involve new perspectives on and formulations of trinitarian thinking and indicate the need for further reflection on the doctrine of the Trinity itself. One direction that might bring fruitful results is a closer examination of the role of the Third Person. Barth and Moltmann have recovered and developed extensively the doctrine of the Trinity for theology. Nevertheless, following the theological tradition, they have concentrated their attentions on the Second Person, God the Son. Moltmann, as we have seen, has begun also to open up the role of the Spirit. Nevertheless, this remains a perspective mostly unexplored. Could it be that by examining in greater detail the work of the Holy Spirit, who signifies the continuing event character of God and who therefore brings the openness of God for the world to the world, that an even more open, more liberating and more concrete conception of the Trinity could be developed? In any case, however the trinitarian formulation is further unfolded and employed in response to questions asked of the Christian faith, it must be clear that like the being to which it refers the doctrine of the Trinity is open and self-transforming.

NOTES

[1] For an analysis of contemporary apologetics to which I am indebted see Theodore W. Jennings, pp. 29-39.

[2] See Paul M. van Buren, *The Secular Meaning of the Gospel* (New York, 1963).

[3] See Langdon B. Gilkey, "A New Linguistic Madness," in *New Theology No. 2*, p. 40, on this and his wider analysis and critique of van Buren's position (pp. 39-49). See also Langdon B. Gilkey, *Naming the Whirlwind: The Renewal of God Language* (New York, 1969), pp. 124-129.

[4] van Buren, *The Secular Meaning of the Gospel*, p. 84.

[5] *Ibid.*, p. 103.

[6] *Ibid.*, pp. 159ff. See Gilkey, "A New Linguistic Madness," p. 46. Gilkey also makes the witty observation that "only a semanticist with an Anglican background would reject the use of the word 'God' in theological language and then worry about the relation of his thought to Chalcedon!" (*Ibid.*, p. 49).

[7] van Buren, *The Secular Meaning of the Gospel*, p. 160.

[8] *Ibid.*, p. 155.

[9] *Ibid.*, p. 132.

[10] On this see Gilkey, *Naming the Whirlwind*, p. 127.

[11] I am indebted to Jennings, pp. 33f, for this insight.

[12] Gilkey, "A New Linguistic Madness," pp. 48f.

[13] *Ibid.*, p. 46.

[14] Ogden, *The Reality of God*, p. 14.

[15] See Lonnie D. Kliever, *The Shattered Spectrum: A Survey of Contemporary Theology* (Atlanta, 1981), p. 39, for this quotation and critique.

[16] Ogden, *The Reality of God*, p. 14. Van Buren, in response to criticism and further reflection on how language means, in later writings does recover the word "God" for Christian faith and theology, not as referring to some object but as the linguistic expression of the human

experience of wonder and awe. See Paul M. van Buren, *The Edges of Language* (New York, 1972), particularly pp. 115-50.

[17] van Buren, *The Secular Meaning of the Gospel*, p. 17.

[18] Macquarrie, *Thinking About God*, p. 94.

[19] *Ibid.*, p. 90.

[20] Ogden, *The Reality of God*, p. 16. See also Gordon D. Kaufman "On the Meaning of 'God'" in *New Theology No. 4*, ed. Martin E. Marty and Dean G. Peerman (New York, 1967), pp. 70-73 and Langdon Gilkey, "Dissolution and Reconstruction in Theology" in *Frontline Theology*, ed. Dean Peerman (Richmond, 1967), pp. 29-33, for similar positions.

[21] Ogden, *The Reality of God*, p. 19.

[22] *Ibid.*

[23] See Macquarrie, *Thinking About God*, p. 106, where he talks about reconstructing theism. Likewise, Ogden, *The Reality of God*, pp. 44ff, titles a section of his argument "Toward a New Theism."

[24] See Kaufman, "On the Meaning of God," p. 73, n. 6:

> "It should be observed that the present paper is concerned with the question of the *meaning* rather than the *truth* of statements containing the word 'God.' No attempt will be made here to prove either that God does or does not exist . . . ."

See also Gilkey, *Naming the Whirlwind*, pp. 232, 415.

[25] Gilkey, "Dissolution and Reconstruction in Theology," p. 33. See Macquarrie, *Thinking About God*, p. 88, for his agreement with Gilkey and where he claims that "the problem of God . . . remains at the top of the theological agenda." Also see Ogden, *The Reality of God*, p. x, where he asserts that "the reality of God 'is' the *sole* theme of all valid Christian theology even as it is the one essential point to all authentic Christian faith and witness."

[26] Gilkey, "Dissolution and Reconstruction in Theology," p. 33.

[27] See *Ibid.*, pp. 33f; also Gilkey, *Naming the Whirlwind*, pp. 232ff; Ogden, *The Reality of God*, p. 20; and Kaufman, pp. 73ff.

[28] Kaufman, "On the Meaning of God," p. 74.

[29] *Ibid.*, p. 75. In the text we will deal with Kaufman, Ogden and Macquarrie. For Gilkey's position on this issue see *Naming the Whirlwind*, p. 250, where he asserts that secularism raises "questions with which secular symbols cannot fruitfully deal, questions which only religious discourse and religious symbols and myths can thematize . . . ."

[30] Kaufman, "On the Meaning of God," p. 77.

[31] Ogden, *The Reality of God*, p. 31.

[32] *Ibid.*, p. 30.

[33] *Ibid.*

[34] *Ibid.*

[35] Macquarrie, *Thinking About God,* p. 91.

[36] *Ibid.*, p. 93.

[37] *Ibid.*, p. 92.

[38] *Ibid.*, pp. 91f.

[39] *Ibid.*, p. 92.

[40] Ogden, *The Reality of God,* pp. 30f.

[41] Macquarrie, *Thinking About God,* p. 93. See Kaufman, "On the Meaning of God," p. 76, for his discussion of this and Gilkey, *Naming the Whirlwind,* pp. 250ff.

[42] Macquarrie, *Thinking About God,* pp. 90f.

[43] Ogden, *The Reality of God,* p. 31. The parenthetic phrase appears in Ogden.

[44] *Ibid.*, p. 21. The parenthesis is inserted by me but includes Ogden's words from the same page.

[45] *Ibid.*, p. 36.

[46] *Ibid.*, pp. 36f.

[47] See Gilkey, *Naming the Whirlwind,* pp. 250-260, for an understanding similar to that of Ogden.

[48] See John Macquarrie, *Principles of Christian Theology* (New York, 1966), p. 42. Also see Jennings, pp. 31f, on this.

[49] *Ibid.*, p. 110.

[50] See, for instance, Schubert M. Ogden, *Christ Without Myth* (New York, 1961).

[51] Ogden's move away from existentialist philosophy reflects his growing interest in the doctrine of God. [See Schubert M. Ogden, "The Understanding of Theology in Ott and Bultmann," in *The Later Heidegger and Theology,* ed. J.M. Robinson and J.B. Cobb, Jr. (New York, 1963), p. 159.] He believes that Bultmann's "restrictively existentialist" theology means that " . . . Bultmann cannot speak of God directly, but only indirectly by speaking of man and his possibilities of existential self-understanding" (p. 158). According to Ogden process thought gives theology access to god-language. On this see also C.J. Curtis, *Contemporary Protestant Thought* (New York, 1970), p. 73.

[52] Ogden, *The Reality of God,* p. 59.

[53] I am indebted to Jennings, pp. 31ff, for some of the following points in this paragraph.

[54] Robert McAfee Brown, *The Spirit of Protestantism* (New York, 1965), p. 76, makes a similar criticism of Bultmann: "His [Bultmann's] attempt is a creative one, although it is open to question

whether Heidegger is any more intelligible to 'modern man' than St.
Paul . . . ."

⁵⁵ For example see Langdon Gilkey, "God," in *Christian Theology*,
ed. Peter C. Hodgson and Robert H. King (Philadelphia, 1982), pp.
67-70.

⁵⁶ See for instance Schubert M. Ogden, *Faith and Freedom:
Toward a Theology of Liberation* (Nashville, 1979); also Delwin Brown,
To Set at Liberty: Christian Faith and Human Freedom (Maryknoll,
New York, 1981).

⁵⁷ Ogden, *The Reality of God*, p. 31.

⁵⁸ See Ogden, *Faith and Freedom: Toward a Theology of
Liberation*.

⁵⁹ *Ibid.*, pp. 76-77:

> "Because everything that is anything at all must in part
> determine itself, it to that extent has a power of its
> own . . . . Consequently all that could be coherently meant
> by 'omnipotence' is all the power that any one thing could
> be conceived to have, consistently with there being other
> things having lesser powers . . . ."

⁶⁰ *Ibid.*, p. 80.

⁶¹ *Ibid.*, pp. 84-85.

⁶² *Ibid.*, p. 89.

⁶³ *Ibid.*, p. 89-90.

⁶⁴ *Ibid.*, pp. 74-75.

⁶⁵ *Ibid.*, p. 79

⁶⁶ See for instance *Ibid.*, p. 92.

⁶⁷ *Ibid.*, p. 94.

⁶⁸ See Ogden, *The Reality of God*, pp. 5, 26; Macquarrie, *Thinking
About God*, pp. 234ff.

⁶⁹ See *CD* I/1, 217ff; also Karl Barth and Emil Brunner, *Natural
Theology: Comprising "Nature and Grace" by Professor Dr. Emil Brunner
and the Reply "No!" by Dr. Karl Barth*, ed. John Baillie, trans. Peter
Fraenkel (London, 1946); also Smart, pp. 192ff.

⁷⁰ This discussion will be restricted to the earliest manifestation of
the trinitarian debate — the relation of the Son to the Father.

⁷¹ See Gilkey, "God", pp. 67-70. The doctrine of the Trinity does
not appear in the index of Gilkey's *Naming the Whirlwind*, or Gilkey's
Reaping the Whirlwind (New York, 1976).

⁷² *Ibid.*, p. 67.

⁷³ *Ibid.*, p. 68.

⁷⁴ *Ibid.*

[75] *Ibid.*

[76] See Bernard Lonergan, *The Way to Nicea*, trans. Conn O'Donovan (Philadelphia, 1976), p. 130.

[77] See *Ibid.*, p. 135.

[78] Quoted in J. N. D. Kelly, *Early Christian Doctrine* (New York, 1960), p. 245.

[79] *Ibid.*, p. 243. See also Gonzalez I, 298, 300.

[80] Kelly, p. 233. See also p. 243, where Kelly quotes Athanasius: "the Word could never have divinized us if He were merely divine by participation and were not Himself the essential Godhead, the Father's veritable image." See also Athanasius *Against the Arians* 2.70; also Gonzalez, I, 297-298, 304, 306; also Rowan Williams, *Christian Spirituality* (Atlanta, 1980), p. 49.

[81] See Gonzalez, p. 306.

[82] Williams, p. 49. Charles Norris Cochrane, *Christianity and Classical Culture* (New York, 1944), p. 236, makes a similar point: "Stripped of the somewhat formidable phraseology of contemporary thinking, this [the Nicene formulation] amounts to a denial that there existed any such hiatus as the pagans had supposed between being and becoming, God and nature." On this discussion of the relationship of the absolute conception of God to the patristic church's formulation of the doctrine of the Trinity, see Wolfhart Pannenberg, *Jesus-God and Man*, trans. Lewis L. Wilkins and Duane A. Priebe (2nd ed.; Philadelphia, 1977), pp. 164-165. Pannenberg places the development of the trinitarian formulation in the context of Logos Christology, which brought the philosophical conception of God into the center of Christian theology. Thus the Logos doctrine supported Arius. "The Nicene dogma," Pannenberg writes, "which established the identity of the divinity of the Son with that of the Father meant a breakthrough out of the conceptual structure of Logos Christology" (p. 164). This also meant a move from the God of philosophy to the Biblical God (p. 165).

[83] See Lonergan, p. 133.

[84] See Williams, pp. 47f; also Gonzalez, I, 270f, 298.

[85] See Gonzalez, I, 207; also Williams, p. 48.

[86] See Williams, p. 50; also Lonergan, p. 130.

[87] Gonzalez, I, 307.

[88] Williams, p. 50.

[89] Athanasius *Incarnation of the Word* 54. See also, for instance, Gregory of Nyssa *The Great Catechism* XXV.

[90] On the concept of "deification" in Athanasius, see Kelly, pp. 381ff, and Williams, p. 49. Both of these commentators suggest that deification "did not mean sharing in the divine 'substance'" but was

participation in the triune life of God. See, for instance, Athanasius *Against the Arians* 2. 59.

⁹¹ Jennings, p. 14, writes,

> "In the modern era characterized by debates about theism and atheism it is difficult to remember that the distinctive character of Christianity's understanding of God is not the development of theism — or "monotheism." The initial problem for Christian theology was not to distinguish Christianity from sheer unbelief but from superstition. In this struggle the opponents did not believe that there was no God, but were all too sure that there was at least one and possibly several."

⁹² On this see Lonergan, pp. 133ff; also Kelly, especially pp. 231ff. Jennings, p. 14, concludes,

> "The distinctive character of Christianity then lay not in its assertion of the reality of the divine (more than granted by hellenistic religions) nor the absolute unity of God as the first principle (already asserted in the philosophical schools) nor the existence and power of a single and personal God (something maintained in Judaism). In the context of these competing perspectives Christianity was compelled to articulate its own position with respect to God. This it did in the language and conceptuality of the time but in such a way as to distinguish itself from these competing perspectives. This was done was by way of a doctrine of the Trinity."

⁹³ See Aloys Grillmeier, *Christ in the Christian Tradition*, trans. J.S. Bowden (New York, 1965), p. 176. Also see Gonzalez, I, 270ff, 297f.

⁹⁴ Kelly, p. 227.

⁹⁵ See *Ibid.*, pp. 231-233.

⁹⁶ Quoted in Williams, p. 18.

⁹⁷ See Chapter IV, n. 89.

⁹⁸ See Williams, p. 48.

⁹⁹ See Athanasius *Against the Arians* 2. 69. 3. 33. Also Williams, p. 49.

¹⁰⁰ Athanasius *Easter Letter* 13. 6.

¹⁰¹ Athanasius *Incarnation of the Word* 7.

¹⁰² *Ibid.*, para. 9:

> ". . . while it was impossible for the Word to suffer death, being immortal, and Son of the Father; to this end He takes

> to Himself a body capable of death, that it, by partaking of
> the Word Who is above all, might be worthy to die in the
> stead of all."

See also Williams, p. 49.

[103] On this see Gonzalez, I, 309.

[104] Athanasius *Against the Arians* 3. 31-32.

[105] See Moltmann, *CG*, p. 326. Athanasius was exiled several times
by various emperors and these exiles were due to his defense of the
trinitarian position. But it is hard to defend the position that the
emperors perceived the political danger in the trinitarian formulation
itself, even though it was Arians like Eusebius of Nicomedia — who of
course stressed an absolute monotheism — who were able to turn the
emperors against Athanasius and other defenders of the Nicene faith. It
should be remembered that Arius himself and other Arians also suffered
exiles. Furthermore, it should also be noted that above all the emperors
were interested in maintaining peace and order. On the one hand, Arians
like Eusebius, by retreating from the more rigorous statements of their
position, were able to present themselves to the emperor as moderates,
willing to compromise and not stir up unnecessary trouble. On the other
hand, in much of the empire the Nicene *homoousia* was not popular,
even among non-Arians, because it left little defense against Sabellian-
ism. Therefore, it can be argued that it was often politically expedient for
the emperor to side with the Arians and banish uncompromising, trou-
ble-making trinitarians, even without perceiving the political danger to
monarchy inherent in the doctrine of the Trinity. On these complex
issues see Gonzalez, I, 273-298. Moltmann's position receives some
support from Cochrane, pp. 257ff.

[106] On both these points, see Moltmann, *CG*, pp. 322, 325.

[107] Williams, p. 52.

[108] *Ibid.*, p. 53.

[109] *Ibid.*, p. 62.

[110] *Ibid.*, p. 54.

[111] See *Ibid.*, p. 100.

[112] Quoted in *Ibid.*, p. 53.

[113] *Ibid.*, p. 54. Basil also criticizes wealth. See Homily VI, Homily
VII and Second Homily on Psalm XIV.

[114] Quoted in Jose Miranda, *Marx and the Bible*, trans. John
Eagleson (New York, 1974), p. 16.

[115] Basil Second Homily on Psalm XIV.

[116] On a response to Freud, see MacIntyre and Ricoeur, pp. 59-98.

[117] On a Jewish-Christian dialogue that includes a trinitarian perspective, see Pinchas Lapide and Jürgen Moltmann, *Jewish Monotheism and Christian Trinitarian Doctrine*, trans. Leonard Swidler (Philadelphia, 1979).

SELECTED BIBLIOGRAPHY

Primary Sources and Reference Material: Theological

Aquinas, Thomas. *Summa Theologica.* 2 Volumes. Translated by Fathers of the English Dominican Province and Revised by Daniel J. Sullivan. New York: Encyclopaedia Britannica, Inc., 1952. (Great Books of the Western World, Vols. XIX-XX.)

Barth, Karl. *Against the Stream: Shorter Post-War Writings 1946-52.* Edited by R. Gregor Smith. Translated by E. M. Delacour and S. Godman. London: SCM Press, 1954.

_____. *Anselm: Fides Quaerens Intellectum. Anselm's Proof of the Existence of God in the Context of his Theologicol Scheme.* Translated by Ian W. Robertson. London: SCM Press, 1960.

_____. *The Christian Life.* Translated by Geoffrey W. Bromiley. Grand Rapids: William B. Eerdmans Publishing Company, 1981.

_____. *The Church and the Political Problem of Our Day.* New York: Charles Scribner's Sons, 1939.

_____. *Church Dogmatics: A Selection.* Translated and edited by G. W. Bromiley. New York: Harper and Row, Harper Torchbooks, 1961.

_____. *Church Dogmatics,* I-IV. Volume I/1 translated by G. T. Thomson. Volumes I/2-IV/4 translated by G. W. Bromiley. Edinburgh: T. & T. Clark, 1936-1962.

_____. *Community, State, and Church.* Introduction by Will Herberg. Gloucester, Mass.: Peter Smith, 1968.

_____. *Credo.* New York: Charles Scribner's Sons, 1962.

_____. *Dogmatics in Outline.* Translated by G. T. Thomson. New York: Philosophical Library, 1949.

_____. *The Epistle to the Romans.* Translated by Edwin C. Hoskyns from the sixth German edition. London: Oxford University Press, 1922.

_____. *Final Testimonies.* Edited by Eberhard Busch. Translated by Geoffrey W. Bromiley. Grand Rapids: Wm. B. Eerdmans Publishing Company, 1977.

_____. *The German Church Conflict.* Translated by P.T.A. Parker. Richmond: John Knox Press, 1965.

_____. *How I Changed My Mind.* Introduction and epilogue by John D. Godsey. Richmond: John Knox Press, 1966.

_____, and Hamel, Johannes. *How to Serve God in a Marxist Land.* Introductory essay by Robert McAfee Brown. New York: Association Press, 1959.

_____. *The Humanity of God.* Translated by John Newton Thomas and others. Atlanta: John Knox Press, 1974.

_____. *The Knowledge of God and the Service of God According to theTeaching of the Reformation.* Translated by J.L.M. Haire and Ian Henderson. London: Hodder and Stoughton, 1960.

_____. *Letters 1961-1968.* Edited by Geoffrey W. Bromiley, Jürgen Fangmeier, and Hinrich Stoevesandt. Translated by Geoffrey W. Bromiley. Grand Rapids: William B. Eerdman's Publishing Company, 1981.

_____, and Brunner, Emil. *Natural Theology: Comprising "Nature and Grace"by Professor Dr. Emil Brunner and the Reply "No!" by Dr. Karl Barth.* Edited by John Baillie. Translated by Peter Fraenkel. London: Centennary Press, 1946.

_____. *Protestant Thought: From Rousseau to Ritschl.* Translated by Brian Cozens. New York: Harper and Brothers, 1959.

_____. *The Resurrection of the Dead.* Translated by H.J. Stenning. New York: Fleming H. Revell Company, 1933.

_____. *Revolutionary Theology in the Making: Barth-Thurneysen Correspondence, 1914-1925.* Translated by James D. Smart. Richmond: John Knox Press, 1964.

_____. *Theological Existence Today!* Translated by R. Birch Hoyle. Lexington: American Theological Library Association, 1962.

_____. *Theology and Church.* Translated by Louise Pettibone Smith. New York: Harper & Row, 1962.

_____. *The Word of God and the Word of Man.* Translated by Douglas Horton. New York: Harper and Brothers Publishers, 1957.

Calvin, John. Institutes of the Christian Religion. 2 Volumes. Edited by John T. McNeill. Translated by Ford Lewis Battles. Philadelphia: The Westminster Press, 1960. (The Library of Christian Classics. Vols. XX-XXI.)

Fairweather, A.M., editor and translator. *Nature and Grace — Selections from the Summa Theologica.* Philadelphia: The Westminster Press, 1954. (The Library of Christian Classics. Vol. XI.)

Gilkey, Langdon. *Naming the Whirlwind: The Renewal of God Language*. New York: Bobbs-Merrill, 1969.

_____. *Reaping the Whirlwind: A Christian Interpretation of History*. New York: Seabury Press, 1976.

Godsey, John D. editor. *Karl Barth's Table Talk*. Richmond: John Knox Press, 1963.

Herzog, Frederick. "Politische Theologie und die Christliche Hoffung" in *Diskussion zur politischen Theologie*. München: Chr. Kaiser Verlag, 1969.

Kaufman, Gordon D. *God the Problem*. Cambridge, Mass.: Harvard University Press, 1972.

Macquarrie, John. *Principles of Christian Theology*. New York: Charles Scribner's Sons, 1966.

_____. *Thinking About God*. New York: Harper and Row, 1975.

Moltmann, Jürgen. *The Church in the Power of the Spirit*. Translated by Margaret Kohl. New York: Harper & Row, 1977.

_____. *The Crucified God*. Translated by R. A. Wilson and John Bowden. New York: Harper & Row, 1973.

_____. *The Experiment Hope*. Edited and translated by M. Douglas Meeks. Philadelphia: Fortress Press, 1975.

_____. *Experiences of God*. Philadelphia: Fortress Press, 1980.

_____. *The Future of Creation*. Translated by Margaret Kohl. Philadelphia: Fortress Press, 1979.

_____. *The Gospel of Liberation*. Translated by H. Wayne Pipkin. Waco: Word Books, 1973.

_____; Cox, Harvey; Harvey, Van A.; Gilkey, Langdon; and Macquarrie, John. *The Future of Hope: Theology as Eschatology*. Edited by Frederick Herzog. New York: Herder and Herder, 1970.

_____. *Hope and Planning*. Translated by Margaret Clarkson. London: SCM Press Ltd., 1971.

_____, and Lapide, Pinchas. *Jewish Monotheism and Christian Trinitarian Doctrine*. Translated by Leonard Swindler. Philadelphia: Fortress Press, 1981.

_____. "Liberation in the Light of Hope." Translated by M. Douglas Meeks. *The Ecumenical Review*, XXVI, No. 3 (July, 1974), 411-429.

_____. *Man*. Translated by John Sturdy. Philadelphia: Fortress Press, 1974.

_____. "On Latin American Liberation Theology: An Open Letter to Jose Miquez Bonino." Translated by M. Douglas Meeks. *Christianity and Crisis* (March 29, 1976), 57-63.

_____. *The Passion for Life.* Translated by Douglas Meeks. Philadelphia: Fortress Press, 1978.

_____, and others. *Religion and Political Society.* Edited and translated by The Institute of Christian Thought. New York: Harper and Row, 1974.

_____. *Religion, Revolution and the Future.* Translated by Douglas Meeks. New York: Charles Scribner's Sons, 1969.

_____. *Theology of Hope.* Translated by James W. Leitch. New York: Harper and Row, 1967.

_____. "The Trinitarian History of God." *Theology,* LXXVIII (December, 1975), 632-646.

_____. *The Trinity and the Kingdom.* Translated by Margaret Kohl. New York: Harper and Row, 1981.

Niebuhr, Reinhold. *Applied Christianity.* New York: Meredian, 1959.

Ogden, Shubert M. *Christ Without Myth.* New York: Harper, 1961.

_____. *The Reality of God.* New York: Harper & Row, 1966.

_____. *Faith and Freedom: Toward a Theology of Liberation.* Nashville: Abingdon, 1979.

Pauck, Wilhelm, editor. *Melanchthon and Bucer.* Philadelphia: The Westminster Press, 1969. (The Library of Christian Classics. Vol. XIX.)

Rahner, Karl. *Theological Investigations,* IV & IX. Translated by Graham Harrison. New York: Herder & Herder, 1972.

_____. *The Trinity.* Translated by Joseph Donceel. New York: Herder and Herder, 1970.

Robinson, James M., editor. *The Beginnings of Dialectical Theology.* Part I translated by Keith R. Crim. Part II translated by Louis De Grazia and Keith R. Crim. Richmond: John Knox Press, 1968.

Schaff, Philip and Wace, Henry, editors. *A Select Library of Nicene and Post-Nicene Fathers of the Christian Church.* Second Series. Volumes IV, V, VII, VIII. New York: Charles Scribner's Sons, 1893-1907.

Schleiermacher, Friedrich. *The Christian Faith.* Edited by H.R. Mackintosh and J.J. Stewart. Philadelphia: Fortress Press, 1976.

_____. *On Religion: Speeches to its Cultured Despisers.* Translated by John Oman. New York: Harper and Row, 1958.

van Buren, Paul M. *The Edges of Language.* New York: Macmillan Co., 1972.

_____. *The Secular Meaning of the Gospel.* New York: MacMillan Co., 1963.

Primary Sources and Reference Material: Critiques of Religion

Adorno, Theodor W. *Negative Dialectics.* Translated by E. B. Ashton. New York: Seabury Press, 1973.

Bloch, Ernst. *Philosophy of the Future.* Translated by John Cumming. New York: Herder & Herder, 1970.

_____. *Atheism in Christianity: The Religion of the Exodus and the Kingdom.* Translated by J.T. Swann. New York: Herder and Herder, 1972.

Camus, Albert. *The Myth of Sisyphus and Other Essays.* Translated by Justin O'Brien. New York: Vintage Books, 1955.

_____. *The Plague.* Translated by Stuart Gilbert. New York: The Modern Library, 1948.

_____. *The Rebel.* Translated by Anthony Bower. New York: Vintage Books, 1956.

_____. *The Stranger.* Translated by Stuart Gilbert. New York: Vintage Books, 1946.

Dostoevsky, Fydor. *The Brothers Karamazov.* Translated by Constance Garnett. New York: The American Library, 1957.

Feuer, Lewis S., editor. *Marx and Engels: Basic Writings on Politics and Philosophy.* New York: Doubleday and Co., Inc., 1959.

Feuerbach, Ludwig. *The Essence of Christianity.* Translated by George Eliot. New York: Harper Torchbooks, 1957.

_____. *The Essence of Faith According to Luther.* Translated by Melvin Cherno. New York: Harper & Row, 1967.

_____. *The Essence of Religion.* Translated by Alexander Loos. New York: Asa Butts & Co., 1873.

_____. *Lectures on the Essence of Religion.* Translated by Ralph Manheim. New York: Harper & Row, Publishers, 1967.

_____. *Principles of the Philosophy of the Future.* Translated by Manfred Vogel. Indianapolis: The Bobbs-Merril Company, Inc., 1966.

_____. *Sämtliche Werke.* Volumes I-X edited by Wilhelm Bolin and Friedrich Jodl; Volumes XI-XIII edited by Hans-Martin Sass. Stuttgart-Bad Cannstatt: Frommann Verlag, 1959-1964.

Fromm, Erich. *Marx's Concept of Man.* New York: Frederick Ungar, 1966.

Garaudy, Roger. *The Alternative Future.* Translated by Leonard Mayhew. New York: Simon and Schuster, 1974.

_____. *From Anathema to Dialogue: A Marxist Challenge to the Christian Churches.* Translated by Luke O'Neill. New York: Herder and Herder, 1966.

_____. *Marxism in the Twentieth Century.* Translated by Rene Hague. New York: Charles Scribner's Sons, 1970.

Habermas, Jürgen. *Theory and Practice.* Translated by John Viertel. Boston: Beacon Press, 1973.

Horkheimer, Max. *Critical Theory.* Translated by Matthew E. O'Connell & others. New York: Herder & Herder, 1972.

_____. *Critique of Instrumental Reason.* Translated by Matthew J. O'Connell and others. New York: The Seabury Press, 1974.

_____ and Adorno, Theodor W. *Dialectics of Enlightenment.* Translated by John Cumming. New York: Herder & Herder, 1972.

Machovec, Milan. *A Marxist Looks at Jesus.* Philadelphia: Fortress Press, 1976.

MacIntyre, Alasdair and Ricoeur, Paul. *The Religious Significance of Atheism.* New York: Columbia University Press, 1969.

Miranda, Jose. *Marx and the Bible.* Translated by John Eagleson. New York: Orbis Books, 1974.

Books and Monographs

Anscombe, Elizabeth, and Geach, Peter Thomas, editors and translators. *Descartes: Philsophical Writings.* Indianapolis: Bobbs-Merrill Company, Inc., 1971. (The Library of the Liberal Arts.)

Berkouwer, G.C. *A Half Century of Theology.* Translated by Lewis B. Smedes. Grand Rapids: William B. Eerdmans, 1977.

_____. *The Triumph of Grace in the Theology of Karl Barth.* Grand Rapids: William B. Eerdmans Publishing Co., 1956.

Bloesch, Donald G. *Jesus Is Victor! Karl Barth's Doctrine of Salvation.* Nashville: Abingdon Press, 1976.

Bonhoeffer, Dietrich. *Letters and Papers from Prison.* Edited by Eberhard Bethge. Translated by Reginald H. Fuller. New York: The MacMillan Company, 1953.

Braaten, Carl E. and Jenson, Robert W. *The Futurist Option.* New York: Newman Press, 1970.

Brightman, Edgar Sheffield. *A Philosophy of Religion.* New York: Prentice-Hall, Inc., 1940.

Bromiley, Geoffrey W. *Historical Theology: An Introduction.* Grand Rapids: William B. Eerdmans, 1978.

Bronowski, J. and Mazlish, Bruce. *The Western Intellectual Tradition.* New York: Harper and Row, 1960.

Brown, Delwin. *To Set at Liberty: Christian Faith and Human Freedom.* Maryknoll, New York: Orbis Books, 1981.

Brown, Robert McAffee. *The Spirit of Protestantism.* New York: Oxford University Press, 1965.

_____. *Theology in a New Key.* Philadelphia: Westminster Press, 1978.

Busch, Eberhard. *Karl Barth.* Translated by John Bowden. Philadelphia: Fortress Press, 1976.

Cochrane, Charles Norris. *Christianity and Classical Culture.* New York: Oxford University Press, 1944.

Cone, James H. *A Black Theology of Liberation.* New York: Seabury Press, 1970.

_____. *God of the Oppressed.* New York: Seabury Press, 1975.

Copleston, F.C. *Aquinas.* Baltimore: Penquin Books, 1955.

Curtis, C.J. *Contemporary Protestant Thought.* New York: The Bruce Publishing Company, 1970.

Ellul, Jacques. *Hope in Time of Abandonment.* Translated by C. Edward Hopkin. New York: The Seabury Press, 1973.

Forell, George W., editor. *Christian Social Teachings.* Garden City: Anchor Books, Doubleday and Company, 1966.

Frei, Hans W. *The Doctrine of Revelation in the Thought of Karl Barth, 1909 to 1922: The Nature of Barth's Break with Liberalism.* Ph. D. dissertation, Yale University, 1956.

Gardavsky, Vitezslav. *God Is Not Yet Dead.* Translated by Vivienne Menkes. Baltimore: Penguin Books, 1973.

Gay, Peter. *The Enlightenment: An Interpretation.* 2 Volumes. New York: Alfred A. Knopf, 1969.

Gilson, Etienne. *God and Philosophy.* New Haven: Yale University Press, 1941.

_____. *Reason and Revelation in the Middle Ages.* New York: Charles Scribner's Sons, 1938.

Gonzalez, Justo L. *A History of Christian Thought.* 3 volumes. Nashville: Abingdon Press, 1970-1975.

Grillmeier, Aloys. *Christ in Christian Tradition.* Translated by J. S. Bowden. New York: Sheed and Ward, 1965.

Gunton, Colin E. *Becoming and Being: The Doctrine of God in Charles Hartshorne and Karl Barth.* Oxford: Oxford University Press, 1978.

Hartshorne, Charles and Reese, William L., editors. *Philosophers Speak of God.* Chicago: University of Chicago Press, 1953.

Hodgson, Leonard. *The Doctrine of the Trinity*. New York: Charles Scribner's Sons, 1944.

Hodgson, Peter C. and King, Robert H., editors. *Christian Theology*. Philadelphia: Fortress Press, 1982.

Hume, David. *The Natural History of Religion*. Edited by A. Wayne Colver. Oxford: Clarendon Press, 1976.

Hunsinger, George, editor and translator. *Karl Barth and Radical Politics*. Philadelphia: Westminster, 1976.

Jennings, Theodore W. Jr. *Beyond Theism: A Grammar of God-Language*. New York: Oxford University Press, 1985.

Jenson, Robert W. *Alpha and Omega: A Study in the Theology of Karl Barth*. New York: Thomas Nelson & Sons, 1963.

_____. *The Knowledge of Things Hoped For*. New York: Oxford University Press, 1969.

Jüngel, Eberhard. *The Doctrine of the Trinity: God's Being Is in Becoming*. Translated by Scottish Academic Press. Grand Rapids: William B. Eerdmans, 1976.

Kant, Immanuel. *Critique of Practical Reason*. Translated by T. M. Greene and H. H. Hudson. New York: Harper and Brothers, 1960.

_____. *Prolegomena to Any Future Metaphysics*. Edited by Lewis White Beck. Indianapolis: The Bobbs-Merrill Company, Inc., 1950. (The Library of Liberal Arts.)

_____. *Religion Within the Limits of Reason Alone*. Translated by T. M. Greene and H. H. Hudson. New York: Harper and Brothers, 1960.

Kelly, J. N. D. *Early Christian Doctrine*. New York: Harper and Row, 1960.

Kliever, Lonnie D. *The Shattered Spectrum: A Survey of Contemporary Theology*. Atlanta: John Knox Press, 1981.

Küng, Hans. *Does God Exist?* Translated by Edward Quinn. New York: Doubleday, 1980.

Lehmann, Paul. *Ethics in a Christian Context*. New York: Harper & Row, 1963.

Lepp, Ignace. *Atheism in Our Time*. Translated by Bernard Murchland. New York: The MacMillan Company, 1963.

Lichtheim, George. *From Marx to Hegel*. New York: Herder & Herder, 1971.

Locke, John. *An Essay Concerning Human Understanding*. Edited by A. D. Woozley. New York: New American Library, 1964.

Lonergan, Bernard. *The Way to Nicea*. Translated by Conn O'Donovan. Philadelphia: Westminster Press, 1976.

Marquardt, Friedrick-Wilhelm. *Theologie und Sozialismus: Das Beispiel Karl Barths*. München: Chr. Kaiser Verlag, 1972.

Marty, Martin E. and Peerman, Dean G., editors. *New Theology*, Volumes 2, 4, 5 and 6. New York and London: The Macmillan Company, 1965-1969.

Meeks, M. Douglas. *Origins of the Theology of Hope*. Philadelphia: Fortress Press, 1974.

Metz, Johannes B., editor. *New Questions on God*. New York: Herder and Herder, 1972. (*Concilium*, Volume LXXVI.)

Morse, Christopher. *The Logic of Promise in Moltmann's Theology*. Philadelphia: Fortress Press, 1979.

Niebuhr, Richard R. *Schleiermacher on Christ and Religion*. New York: Charles Scribner's Sons, 1964.

Norris, Russell Bradner. *God, Marx, and the Future: Dialogue with Roger Garaudy*. Philadelphia: Fortress Press, 1974.

Nüdling, Gregor. *Ludwig Feuerbach's Religionsphilosophie*. 2nd edition; original edition 1936. Paderborn: Ferdinand Schoningh Verlag, 1961.

Oestreicher, Paul, editor. *The Christian Marxist Dialogue*. London: The MacMillan Company, 1969.

Ogletree, Thomas W., editor. *Openings for Marxist-Chirstian Dialogue*. Nashville: Abingdon Press, 1969.

O'Neill, John, editor. *On Critical Theory*. New York: Seabury Press, 1976.

Ott, Heinrich. *God*. Translated by Iain and Ute Nicol. Richmond: John Knox Press, 1971.

Pannenberg, Wolfhart. *Basic Questions in Theology*, II. Translated by George H. Kehm. Philadelphia: Fortress Press, 1971.

_____. *Jesus - God and Man*. 2nd ed., translated by Lewis L. Wilkins and Duane A. Priebe. Philadelphia: The Westminster Press, 1977.

_____. *Theology and the Kingdom of God*. Edited by Richard John Neuhaus. Philadelphia: The Westminster Press, 1969.

Peerman, Dean, editor. *Frontline Theology*. Richmond: John Knox Press, 1967.

Peterson, Erik. "Monotheismus als politisches Problem" in *Theologische-traktate*. München: Chr. Kaiser Verlag, 1951.

Ramsey, Paul, editor. *Faith and Ethics: The Theology of H. Richard Niebuhr.* New York: Harper and Row, 1965.

Richardson, Cyril C. *The Doctrine of the Trinity.* New York and Nashville: Abingdon Press, 1958.

Ritschl, Albrecht. *The Christian Doctrine of Justification and Reconciliation, III.* Translated by H.R. MacKintosh and A.B. Macaulay. Edinburgh: T. and T. Clark, 1900; Clifton, N.J.: New Jersey Reference Book Publishers, 1966.

Robinson, J.M. and Cobb, J.B., Jr., editors. *The Later Heidegger and Theology.* New York: Harper and Row, 1963.

Rumscheidt, Martin, editor. *Footnotes to a Theology — The Karl Barth Colloquium of 1972.* Canada: S.R. Suplements, 1974.

Sawyer, Edward Hill. *Secularization and the Problem of God in Ludwig Feuerbach's Philosophy of Religion.* Th.D. dissertation, Graduate Theological Union, 1970.

Schilling, S. Paul. *God in an Age of Atheism.* Nashville: Abingdon, 1969.

Smart, James D. *The Divided Mind of Modern Theology.* Philadelphia: Westminster Press, 1967.

Sykes, S. W., editor. *Karl Barth: Studies of his Theological Method.* Oxford: Clarendon Press, 1979.

von Balthasar, Hans Urs. *The Theology of Karl Barth.* Translated by John Drury. New York: Holt, Rinehart and Winston, 1971.

van Leeuwen, Arend Th. *Critique of Heaven.* New York: Charles Scribner's Sons, 1972.

Welch, Claude. *In This Name.* New York: Charles Scribner's Sons, 1952.

———. *Protestant Thought in the Nineteenth Century.* New Haven: Yale University Press, 1972.

West, Charles. *Communism and the Theologians.* New York: S.C.M. Press, 1958.

Whitehead, Alfred North. *Process and Reality.* New York: The MacMillan Co., 1929.

Williams, Rowan. *Christian Spirituality: A Theological History from the New Testament to Luther and St. John of the Cross.* Atlanta: John Knox Press, 1980.

Zahrnt, Heinz. *The Question of God: Protestant Theology in the Twentieth Century.* Translated by R. A. Wilson. New York: Harcourt Brace Jovanovich, Inc., 1969.

Periodical Literature

Almond, Philip C. "Karl Barth and Anthropocentric Theology." *Scottish Journal of Theology*, XXXI, No. 3 (1978), 435-447.

Attfield, D. G. "Can God Be Crucified? A Discussion of J. Moltmann." *Scottish Journal of Theology*, XXX (1977), 47-57.

Bauckham, Richard. "Moltmann's Eschatology of the Cross." *Scottish Journal of Theology*, XXX, No. 4 (1977), 301-311.

Bettis, Joseph. "Political Theology and Social Ethics: The Socialist Humanism of Karl Barth." *Scottish Journal of Theology*, XXVII, No. 3 (August, 1974), 287-305.

————. "Theology and Politics: Karl Barth and Reinhold Niebuhr on Social Ethics After Liberalism." *Religion in Life*, XLVIII (September, 1979), 53-62.

Braaten, Carl E. "A Trinitarian Theology of the Cross." *The Journal of Religion*, LVI, No. 1 (January 1, 1976), 113-121.

Butler, Gerald A. "Karl Barth and Political Theology." *Scottish Journal of Theology*, XXVII, No. 4 (November, 1974), 441-458.

Carr, Anne. "Review of *The Church in the Power of the Spirit*." *Journal of Religion*, LVIII (April, 1978), 213.

Chapman, G. Clark, Jr. "Jürgen Moltmann: The Theologian as Friendly Critic of Marxism." Paper presented at meeting of American Academy of Religion, November 17, 1979.

————. "Moltmann's Vision of Man." *Anglican Theological Review*, LVI, No. 3 (July, 1974), 310-330.

Deschner, John. "Karl Barth as Political Activist." *Union Seminary Quarterly Review*, XXVIII, No. 1 (Fall, 1972), 56.

Dumas, Andre. "Review of *The Church in the Power of the Spirit*." *Ecumenical Review*, XXX (January, 1978), 305.

Glasse, John. "Barth on Feuerbach." *Harvard Theolgical Review*, LVII, No. 2 (April, 1964), 69-96.

Gunton, Colin. "Karl Barth and the Development of Christian Doctrine." *Scottish Journal of Theology*, XXV, No. 2 (May, 1972), 171-180.

Hendry, George S. "The Freedom of God in the Theology of Karl Barth." *Scottish Journal of Theology*, XXXI, No. 3 (1978), 229-244.

Hood, R. E. "Karl Barth's Christological Basis for the State and Political Praxis." *Scottish Journal of Theology*, XXXIII (1980), 223-231.

Hunsinger, George. "The Crucified God and the Political Theology of Violence: A Critical Survey of Jürgen Moltmann's Recent Thought: I." *Heythrop Journal*, XXIV (1973), 266-279.

———. "The Crucified God and The Political Theology of Violence: A Critical Survey of Jürgen Moltmann's Recent Thought: II." *Heythrop Journal*, XXIV (1973), 379-395.

Irish, Jerry A. "Moltmann's Theology of Contradiction." *Theology Today*, XXXII (April, 1975), 21-31.

Jenson, Robert W. "Response." *Union Seminary Quarterly Review*, XXVIII, No. 1 (Fall, 1972), 31-34.

Klinck, Dennis R. "Towards a Trinitarian Politics." *Studies in Religion* (Winter, 1979), 57-66.

Lehmann, Paul L. "Karl Barth, Theologian of Permanent Revolution." *Union Seminary Quarterly Review*, XXVIII (1972-1973), 67-81.

Lochman, Jan Milic. "The Trinity and Human Life." *Theology*, LXXXVIII (April, 1975), 172-191.

McWilliams, Warren. "The Passion of God and Moltmann's Christology." *Encounter*, XL (Fall, 1979), 313-26.

Meeks, M. Douglas. "A Handbook for the Church." *Interpretation*, XXXIII, No. 3 (July, 1979), 301-304.

Migliore, Daniel. "Review." *Theology Today*, XXXII (April, 1975), 98-106.

Miller, Crawford. "Divine Transcendence Over Time and Christian Hope." *Reformed Theological Review*, XXXII (January-April, 1973), 10-18.

Neuhaus, John Richard. "Moltmann vs. Monotheism." *Dialog*, XX (Summer, 1981), 239-243.

Niebuhr, Reinhold. "Barth's East German Letter." *Christian Century*, LXXVI, No. 6 (February 11, 1959), 168.

———. "The Quality of Our Lives." *Christian Century* (May 11, 1960), 571.

———. "Toward New Intra-Christian Endeavors." *Christian Century*, LXXXVI (December 31, 1969), 1662-67.

Pannenberg, Von Wolfhart. "Die Subjektivität Gottes und die Trinitatslehre." *Kerygma and Dogma*, XXIII (January- March, 1977), 25-40.

Parker, Thomas D. "The Political Meaning of the Doctrine of the Trinity: Some Theses." *The Journal of Religion*, LX (April, 1980), 165-184.

Perkins, Davis. "The Problem of Suffering: Atheistic Protest and Trinitarian Response." *St Luke's Journal of Theology*, XXIII, No. 1 (December, 1979), 14-32.

Scott, David A. "Ethics on a Trinitarian Basis: Moltmann's *The Crucified God*." *Anglican Theological Review*, LX (April, 1978), 166-179.

Simcox, Carroll E. "The Forsaken God." *Christian Century*, XCII (March 19, 1975), 290-291.

Smith, John E. "The Significance of Karl Barth's Thought for the Relation Between Philosophy and Theology." *Union Seminary Quarterly Review*, XXVIII, No. 1 (Fall, 1972), 15-30.

Sturm, Richard E., editor. *Union Seminary Quarterly Review: Karl Barth Colloquim*, XXVIII, No. 1 (Fall, 1972).

Zimany, Roland. "The Meaning of the Crucifixion and the Resurrection in Moltmann's *The Crucified God*." *The Modern Churchman*, XXI, No. 1 (Winter, 1977), 6-10.

_____. "Views and Counterviews: Moltmann's *The Crucified God*." *Dialog*, XVI (Winter, 1977), 49-56.